澜沧江—湄公河
农业合作发展报告 2019

Report on the Development of Lancang-Mekong
Agricultural Cooperation

农业农村部对外经济合作中心
云南省农业科学院国际农业研究所 主编

中国农业出版社
北京

图书在版编目（CIP）数据

澜沧江—湄公河农业合作发展报告 . 2019 / 农业农村部对外经济合作中心，云南省农业科学院国际农业研究所主编 . —北京：中国农业出版社，2021.3
ISBN 978-7-109-27903-2

Ⅰ.①澜… Ⅱ.①农… ②云 Ⅲ.①澜沧江—流域—农业合作—国际合作—区域经济合作—研究报告—2019②湄公河—流域—农业合作—国际合作—区域经济合作—研究报告—2019 Ⅳ.①F333

中国版本图书馆 CIP 数据核字（2021）第 022879 号

澜沧江—湄公河农业合作发展报告 2019
LANCANG JIANG—MEIGONG HE NONGYE HEZUO FAZHAN BAOGAO 2019

中国农业出版社出版
地址：北京市朝阳区麦子店街 18 号楼
邮编：100125
责任编辑：孙鸣凤
版式设计：王　晨　责任校对：吴丽婷
印刷：北京中兴印刷有限公司
版次：2021 年 3 月第 1 版
印次：2021 年 3 月北京第 1 次印刷
发行：新华书店北京发行所
开本：700mm×1000mm　1/16
印张：22.75
字数：450 千字
定价：128.00 元

澜沧江—湄公河农业合作发展报告 2019

Report on the Development of Lancang-Mekong
Agricultural Cooperation

编委会

主　　任：隋鹏飞　张陆彪

副 主 任：吴昌学　李洪涛

委　　员：徐玉波　杨　光　祝自冬　姜　晔　肖　毅
　　　　　欧毅霞　黎民英　王辉武

主　　编：李洪涛　李　露

副 主 编：祝自冬　姜　晔　刘振环

编译成员：张　芸　张　斌　刘志颐　茹　蕾　刘　兰
　　　　　祁梦超　李忻蔚　芮艳兰　徐　璐　郭　文
　　　　　莫　楠　张应青　胡新梅　刘庆生　韦庆芳
　　　　　陈继群　刘　怡　张红亮　薛晶洁　唐丽霞
　　　　　张一珂

英文校稿：颜仕梁

前言 PREFACE ///////////

2016 年 3 月，澜沧江—湄公河合作（"澜湄合作"）首次领导人会议召开，澜湄合作机制正式建立。农业是澜湄合作五大优先领域之一，2017 年澜湄合作农业联合工作组建立以来，澜湄农业合作在机制完善、战略对接、规划研究、科技交流、项目实施、经贸合作等方面取得了良好成效，为促进澜湄流域经济发展带建设做出了积极贡献。

澜湄农业合作中心是澜湄合作机制下继水资源合作中心、全球湄公河研究中心、环境合作中心之后成立的又一中心，设在中国农业农村部对外经济合作中心，是推动澜湄农业合作的协调、服务和支持机构。为做好澜湄农业合作的成果归集与宣传工作，澜湄农业合作中心自 2019 年起开始组织编制《澜湄农业合作发展报告》（以下简称《报告》），定期梳理澜湄农业合作的进展、成效和经验做法，供澜湄六国农业部门及相关机构交流参考。

2019 年《报告》由农业农村部对外经济合作中心与云南省农业科学院国际农业研究所共同编制，从多视角系统梳理了近三年澜湄农业合作的进展与成效，包括总报告、专题篇和区域篇。总报告总体梳理分析了澜湄农业合作的现状、形势与发展前景，专题篇从行动计划、科技合作、项目实施、乡村振兴等角度对澜湄农业合作进行了分类分析，区域篇对柬埔寨、老挝、缅甸、泰国、越南 5 个湄公河国家及中国云南、广西、海南 3 个重点省区开展澜湄农业合作的情况进行了梳理概括。

在编制《报告》过程中，得到了来自农业农村部国际合作司、云南省农业农村厅、广西壮族自治区农业农村厅、海南省农业农村厅的指导与支持，同时也得到了湄公河五国农业部门的支持与帮助，在此表示诚挚的感谢。疏漏和不足之处，恳请各位读者提出宝贵意见。我们将不断提高报告编制水平，努力将《报告》打造成为澜湄农业合作领域的权威知识产品。

编委会

2020 年 12 月

目 录 CONTENTS ///////////////////

前言

Ⅰ 总 报 告

1 澜湄农业合作进展与前景 ················· 3

1.1 澜湄农业合作的现状与最新进展 ········· 3

1.2 澜湄农业合作面临的机遇与挑战 ········· 6

1.3 澜湄农业合作的工作重点与发展前景 ········· 8

Ⅱ 专 题 篇

2 澜湄农业合作中心职责定位与工作进展 ················· 13

2.1 成立背景 ················· 13

2.2 职责定位 ················· 13

2.3 工作进展 ················· 14

3 澜湄农业合作三年行动计划（2020—2022） ················· 16

3.1 编制背景 ················· 16

3.2 发展目标 ················· 17

3.3 基本原则 ················· 17

3.4 重点领域与任务 ················· 17

1

3.5 组织实施 ·· 21

4 澜湄区域农业科技交流合作进展与成效 ··················· 23

4.1 背景 ·· 23

4.2 澜湄合作农业科技交流平台机制的建立 ··················· 24

4.3 澜湄区域农业科技交流合作成效 ·························· 25

5 澜湄合作专项基金中方农业项目实施进展与成效 ············ 28

5.1 完善澜湄农业合作机制，夯实合作基础 ··················· 28

5.2 开展境外试验示范，打造产业合作关键支撑 ··············· 29

5.3 搭建信息与技术平台，完善农业支持服务体系 ············· 30

5.4 开展联合研究与行动，共建创新绿色澜湄 ················· 31

5.5 开展能力建设合作，构建人才培育支撑系统 ··············· 32

6 澜湄合作共促区域乡村振兴的实践探索 ··················· 34

6.1 搭建交流平台，共享乡村振兴经验 ······················ 34

6.2 开展减贫示范合作，促进乡村全面可持续发展 ············· 35

6.3 建基础设施补民生短板，推动乡村建设步伐 ··············· 39

6.4 抓技术推广促产业兴旺，助力乡村脱贫致富 ··············· 42

Ⅲ 区域篇

7 中国云南省农业发展与澜湄农业合作进展 ················· 47

7.1 农业发展概况 ·· 47

7.2 澜湄农业合作情况 ·· 49

7.3 下一步合作展望 ·· 52

8 中国广西壮族自治区农业发展与澜湄农业合作进展 ··········· 55

8.1 农业发展概况 ·· 55

   8.2 农业国际合作情况 ·· 56

   8.3 澜湄农业合作情况 ·· 57

   8.4 下一步合作展望 ·· 61

9 中国海南省农业发展与澜湄农业合作进展 ············· 63

   9.1 农业发展概况 ·· 63

   9.2 农业国际合作情况 ·· 64

   9.3 澜湄农业合作情况 ·· 66

   9.4 下一步合作展望 ·· 69

10 柬埔寨农业发展与澜湄农业合作进展 ··············· 71

   10.1 农业发展概况 ·· 71

   10.2 农业投资政策 ·· 76

   10.3 澜湄农业合作进展与成效 ···························· 78

11 老挝农业发展与澜湄农业合作进展 ··············· 85

   11.1 农业发展概况 ·· 85

   11.2 农业投资政策 ·· 89

   11.3 澜湄农业合作进展与成效 ···························· 92

12 缅甸农业发展与澜湄农业合作进展 ··············· 98

   12.1 农业发展概况 ·· 98

   12.2 农业投资政策 ·· 102

   12.3 澜湄农业合作进展与成效 ···························· 105

13 泰国农业发展与澜湄合作进展 ··············· 108

   13.1 农业发展概况 ·· 108

   13.2 农业投资政策 ·· 114

   13.3 澜湄农业合作进展与成效 ···························· 117

14 越南农业发展与澜湄农业合作进展 ···························· 121

14.1 农业发展概况 ··· 121

14.2 农业投资政策 ··· 125

14.3 澜湄农业合作进展与成效 ································· 128

I

总 报 告

1 | 澜湄农业合作进展与前景

2016 年 3 月，澜沧江—湄公河（以下简称"澜湄"）合作首次领导人会议在中国海南省举行，澜湄合作机制正式建立。农业是澜湄合作的五大优先领域之一，澜湄农业合作基础好、潜力大、成效显著。同时，随着国际形势的发展变化，澜湄农业合作也面临着新的机遇与挑战，六国应携手在机制完善、规划研究、战略对接、科技交流、投资贸易等领域加强合作，共同实施重点项目，推动次区域农业合作不断深化，助力澜湄流域经济发展带建设。

1.1 澜湄农业合作的现状与最新进展

1.1.1 构建澜湄农业合作机制及体系初显成效

（1）成立澜湄合作农业联合工作组，共商农业合作计划。2017 年 9 月 11 日，澜湄合作农业联合工作组第一次会议在中国广西壮族自治区召开，会议讨论了澜湄合作农业联合工作组概念文件，澜湄农业合作机制正式启动。2019 年 6 月 12—13 日，澜湄合作农业联合工作组第二次会议在柬埔寨暹粒召开，柬中两国代表团团长联合担任会议主席。会上，中国提出了成立澜湄合作农业科技交流协作组、共建澜湄农业技术推广与信息交流平台、共同将澜湄农业合作中心建设成为区域性支持服务机构，编制澜湄农业合作三年行动计划等倡议，得到各国与会代表支持。

（2）设立澜湄农业合作中心，服务区域农业合作。为落实澜湄合作第二次领导人会议"设立澜湄农业合作中心"的共识，中国农业农村部于2019 年 1 月底在农业农村部对外经济合作中心设立澜湄农业合作中心，围绕"一带一路"倡议和澜湄合作机制，聚焦重点领域，打造澜湄次区域农业技术交流、联合研究及投资贸易合作平台，促进该地区农业与粮食领域的经验分享、立场协调与务实合作。在 2019 年 6 月召开的澜湄合作农业联合工作组第二次会议上，中方向与会代表介绍了澜湄农业合作中心成立的背景、工作职责、思路和计划，提出将该中心打造成为澜湄合作农业联合工作组的常设执行机构，打造区域性支持服务机构的目标愿景，得到全体与会代表的支持。

(3) 建立澜湄合作农业科技交流协作组和水生态合作工作小组，完善澜湄农业合作的支持体系。为落实 2019 年 6 月澜湄合作农业联合工作组第二次会议六国达成的合作共识，响应《澜湄合作五年行动计划（2018—2022)》中"扩大农业科技领域的交流与合作，支持科研机构加强信息分享交流和人员互访"的提议，在原有大湄公河次区域农业科技交流合作组的基础上，中国云南省农业科学院于 2019 年 8 月牵头成立了覆盖范围更广、合作内容更丰富的澜湄合作农业科技交流协作组。下一步，协作组将积极扩大成员单位范围，联合澜湄国家更多农业科研和教育机构，在种植、畜牧和渔业等更广泛的领域开展科技交流与合作。为完善澜湄流域水生生物保护合作机制，促进水产健康养殖能力建设合作，建立水资源生态养护合作平台，中国农业农村部长江流域渔政监督管理办公室牵头发起的澜湄流域水生态合作工作小组即将成立。

(4) 举办澜湄合作村长论坛，促进基层组织交流。2017 年 4 月，澜沧江—湄公河农业合作暨中柬老缅泰村长论坛在中国云南省勐腊县举办，围绕"加强乡村合作，造福基层农民"，为澜湄国家村长提供村寨合作、乡村建设、农业发展的交流平台，促进各国乡村总结发展经验、分享合作成果、挖掘合作潜力。第二届澜沧江—湄公河合作村长论坛于 2018 年 4 月在云南省芒市举办，澜湄六国围绕共同推进乡村振兴主题进行经验分享与交流讨论。论坛发出《澜湄村社合作芒市倡议》，展览展示对接活动促成现场签署 8 份合作协议，签约金额约 1.2 亿元。

1.1.2 开展澜湄农业合作规划研究取得初步进展

(1) 正式通过《澜沧江—湄公河农业合作三年行动计划（2020—2022)》。《澜沧江—湄公河合作五年行动计划（2018—2022)》中提出，

"加强政策协调，确保粮食、营养安全和食品安全，创造投资机会，加强农业可持续发展合作"。为加强澜湄各国农业战略对接，务实有序推进澜湄农业合作，澜湄农业合作中心牵头起草了《澜沧江—湄公河农业合作三年行动计划（2020—2022）》，于2019年6月提交澜湄合作农业联合工作组第二次会议讨论，各国代表充分肯定编制该计划的意义，并在会上和会后反馈了对计划的意见建议，该计划已于2020年初正式通过。

（2）编制《澜沧江—湄公河农业合作发展报告》。 为及时跟踪各领域、国别、地方省区澜湄农业合作的进展、成效和经验，澜湄农业合作中心在云南省农业科学院等机构及专家的支持下，于2019年9月首次启动《澜沧江—湄公河农业合作发展报告》编制工作，定期编写年度报告，供澜湄合作农业联合工作组、有关政府部门和科研机构交流参考。

（3）开展澜湄重点产业和国别农业合作研究。 为推进澜湄各国优势产业合作，澜湄农业合作中心着手与有关科研机构及企业建立伙伴关系，加强稻米、天然橡胶、食糖、棕榈、水果等澜湄国家特色农业产业研究，以及澜湄各国农业发展现状、产业特点、投资政策与环境等信息收集与研究，为推动澜湄农业合作战略对接、项目设计与实施、企业开展经贸合作提供基础支撑。

1.1.3 拓展农业贸易与投资合作成效明显

（1）农产品贸易规模不断扩大。 近年来，中国与湄公河五国农产品贸易规模不断扩大，进口增速高于出口增速。2018年，中国与湄公河五国农产品贸易总额189.18亿美元，占中国农产品贸易总额的8.7%，比2017年增长15.8%，比2002年中国—东盟自贸区建立之初增长近10倍。其中，农产品进口金额96.52亿美元，比2017年增长19.1%；出口金额92.66亿美元，比2017年增长12.5%。

（2）农业对外投资蓄势增长。 湄公河国家是中国农业对外投资的重要区域，截至2018年底，中国在湄公河五国农业投资存量31.6亿美元，占中国对东盟农业投资存量的62.7%，占中国对外农业投资存量总额的16%。中国在湄公河五国投资建设企业280余家，占中国境外投资企业总数的近 30%。投资环节从海外直接种植发展到加工、仓储、物流等产业链各个环节，产业涉及粮食（水稻）、经济作物（橡胶、棕榈、木薯、甘蔗）等多种农产品。

（3）共建农业产业园区，搭建对外经贸合作平台。中国认真落实《澜沧江—湄公河合作五年行动计划（2018—2022）》中"共建农业园区"的倡议，与柬埔寨、老挝等国家共同建设了一批农业产业园区，开展稻米、天然橡胶、热带水果等优势农产品品种培育、技术示范、生产加工、贸易物流等全产业链合作，推动澜湄国家优势农产品生产标准体系建设，形成产业、资金、技术集聚效应，为拓展澜湄国家农产品贸易、农业投资合作搭建平台。

1.1.4 实施农业技术交流项目进展顺利

（1）澜湄农业技术交流成效显著。利用大湄公河次区域农业科技交流合作组、境外农作物优良品种试验站、农业科技示范基地、联合实验室等多种平台，澜湄各国围绕共同关心的农业技术问题，开展联合研究与合作，培育适合当地种植品种并进行示范推广，在动植物疫病联防联控、联合研究、人员培训等方面开展一系列合作。

（2）澜湄农业合作项目实施顺利。中国充分利用澜湄合作专项基金、亚洲区域合作专项资金等渠道，调动各方资源，落实澜湄合作领导人会议重要倡议，打造合作亮点和样板项目，提升澜湄国家农业科技水平和综合生产能力。2017—2018 年，中国农业农村部组织申报并实施澜湄基金项目 15 个，预算资金总额 2 698 万元。通过开展境外试验示范与技术合作、能力建设、联合研究与行动等，促进农业合作交流成效初显。

1.2 澜湄农业合作面临的机遇与挑战

1.2.1 机遇分析

（1）"一带一路"倡议助推各国农业发展战略对接。澜湄国家山水相连、地缘相近、人文相亲，是"一带一路"中国—中南半岛经济走廊、孟中印缅经济走廊的重要组成部分。2017 年 5 月，中国农业部等四部委联合发布了《共同推进"一带一路"建设农业合作的愿景与行动》，明确了合作目标、原则、思路及重点，规划了行动步骤。其中，明确提出"强化澜沧江—湄公河合作等现有涉农多边机制"及"共同编制双边农业投资合作规划，增强对最不发达国家农业投资"等行动要求。"一带一路"倡议为促进澜湄国家战略对接，开展优势互补、互利共赢的农业合作提供了重大历史性机遇。

（2）澜湄国家农业国际合作需求强烈。澜湄各国都把农业作为基础产业，发展农业、解决粮食安全问题一直是重中之重。各国在农业资源、技术、产业结构等方面具有很强的互补性，彼此合作诉求强烈。湄公河国家对于改善农业基础设施、发展现代化农业，扩大农产品出口、吸引外资、开展农业国际合作的需求强烈。中国高度重视农业的基础地位和作用，相继对促进农业发展和农业对外开放做出了重大战略部署，2016 年国务院办公厅出台了关于促进农业对外合作的若干意见，为开展农业国际合作、澜湄农业合作提供了保障。2018 年中国开始实施乡村振兴战略，亟须拓展农业发展空间，与周边国家尽快构建形成资源禀赋互补、技术优势互补、产品流向互补、产业格局互补的互利共赢局面。

（3）东亚一体化进程提供良好地区环境。当前东亚地区一体化进程稳步进展，区域全面经济伙伴关系协定正式签署。中日韩自贸区谈判全面提速，商定在 RCEP 基础上，打造"RCEP＋"的自贸协定，并大力推进三国在第四方的合作。中国与东盟关系不断取得新发展，共同发布《中国—东盟战略伙伴关系 2030 年愿景》，中国—东盟自贸区升级议定书全面生效，产品原产地规则修订版正式实施，中国与东盟关系实现了从量的积累到质的飞跃，为推动东亚地区繁荣稳定发展做出重要贡献。澜湄合作作为中国—东盟合作的新纽带，六国均是 RCEP 成员国，也是中日韩三方、四方合作的重点区域，新时期平稳向好的东亚地区形势为澜湄农业合作提供了良好的宏观环境。

1.2.2 挑战分析

（1）全球贸易保护主义、单边主义势力抬头。当前，国际形势正在发生深刻复杂变化，自全球金融危机以来，主要经济体复苏乏力，世界经济运行甚至出现衰退风险，给包括澜湄次区域在内的世界各国带来新的严峻挑战。同时，全球保护主义愈演愈烈，多边规则和国际秩序受到冲击，进一步恶化了农业国际合作的外部环境。面对诸多复杂、不确定因素以及世界经济下行压力，中国和湄公河国家应共同维护以联合国为核心的国际体系和以世贸组织为核心的多边贸易体制，共同维护各领域合作的宝贵成果和次区域合作不断深化的大好局面，造福地区国家和人民。

(2) 气候变化、自然灾害及国际因素加剧次区域合作脆弱性。当前全球气候变化加剧，极端天气频繁出现，直接威胁澜湄次区域的粮食安全和社会经济的可持续发展。澜湄地区自然灾害频繁发生，灾害损失和强度时有加剧，澜沧江—湄公河流经区域的洪涝灾害或干旱、上下游的水资源分配、生态与环境问题等，都会给澜湄地区的农业生产与农业合作带来直接的影响。此外，作为世界大米、天然橡胶的重要生产供应基地，澜湄地区的农业生产与国际合作还受到世界市场供求关系、宏观政策、汇率变动等影响。

(3) 农业基础设施建设相对滞后。推动澜湄农业合作，需要各国良好的基础设施建设作为有力支撑。澜湄地区水、电、交通、通信等基础设施相对落后，农田水利设施建设投资较少，靠天吃饭现象较为普遍，农用工业发展落后，制约了农业合作项目的顺利开展，也增加了外商投资的难度。

1.3 澜湄农业合作的工作重点与发展前景

1.3.1 建立完善澜湄农业合作机制及体系

完善政府间合作机制，在农业联合工作组基础上，逐步拓展建立澜湄农业合作高官会、部长会机制。充分发挥澜湄农业合作中心作为农业联合工作组常设执行机构的协调服务作用，以目前中国成立的澜湄农业合作中心为核心，推动成立澜湄农业合作国际中心。发挥澜湄合作农业科技交流协作组在次区域农业科技交流中的引领作用，逐步建立澜湄植物病虫害防控合作机制、动物疫病防控合作机制，推动建设澜湄流域水生态合作工作小组、澜湄合作农业产业发展协作组,不断完善澜湄农业合作机制及体系。

1.3.2 深入开展澜湄农业合作规划研究

跟踪分析澜湄国家农业发展环境、重点产业国际投资动态及农业合作需求,推动成立澜湄农业合作研究所,加强澜湄国家农业研究机构交流合作,开展联合研究,建立澜湄各国农业产业研究、规划、技术专家储备库,逐步形成澜湄国家农业合作研究支持体系。定期梳理总结澜湄农业合作的进展和成果,编制澜湄农业合作发展年度报告。在《澜沧江—湄公河农业合作三年行动计划(2018—2022)》基础上,细化研究农业合作重点项目和政策建议,完善澜湄农业合作顶层设计,推动务实合作。

1.3.3 不断深化次区域各层面农业交流合作

发挥澜湄农业合作中心作为次区域协调支持机构职能,推动各层面农业合作交流不断深入,加强横向、纵向战略对接。一方面,加强澜湄各国间农业合作战略对接与横向交流合作,共同谋划推动次区域农业科技、经贸、跨境疫病防控等领域合作。另一方面,加强各国部、省(区市)、县等各级农业部门以及政府、企业、研究机构等农业合作相关部门间纵向战略对接,加强规划解读与政策宣介,使各部门与国家战略做好衔接,找到对接点、共赢点,促进协同联动。

1.3.4 逐步优化澜湄国家农产品贸易合作

在建设澜湄次区域一体化和命运共同体意识更加深入的背景下,澜湄国家的农产品贸易面临良好的发展机遇。逐步发挥政府作用和服务功能,合理引导农产品贸易产品结构优化升级,转变"粗放型"模式,提升层次,延伸价值链,提高农产品市场竞争力。适度缩小农产品贸易国别差异,挖掘各国资源潜力和互补性优势,优化利益分配和国别结构。加强和完善农产品贸易设施建设,深化农产品检验检疫监管合作,提高农产品贸易便利化程度。

1.3.5 提升澜湄国家农业投资合作层次

随着近年农业投资合作总体增长的发展趋势，澜湄国家农业投资合作将不断拓展、提升层次。投资领域和方式更加多样，由传统的粮食、天然橡胶、木薯、甘蔗、热带水果种植向品种研发、加工、物流拓展，加强重点农产品质量安全与生产标准合作。支持和推动澜湄国家农业合作园区建设，打造澜湄农业投资合作平台，吸引产业链相关的国内外企业入园，形成产业集聚效应，共享资源、互利共赢，提升园区产品竞争力，带动当地相关产业发展与农民就业。

1.3.6 逐步聚焦和树立重点项目品牌

结合澜湄各国发展需求，以澜湄合作专项基金项目实施为重点，逐步聚焦，重点在澜湄农业技术推广与信息交流、农业技术试验示范与推广、能力建设、农业园区建设、农产品质量与安全合作等领域加强项目合作，整合资源，打造合作亮点和品牌，由点及线、以线带面，形成集群效应，提高澜湄次区域农业生产和产品竞争力，服务澜湄流域经济发展带建设。

（农业农村部对外经济合作中心　姜晔、祝自冬）

II

专题篇

2 | 澜湄农业合作中心 职责定位与工作进展

2.1 成立背景

2018年1月，在澜湄合作第二次领导人会议上，中国建议共同设立澜湄农业合作中心，得到澜湄各国的认可。2019年1月底，中国农业农村部正式设立澜湄农业合作中心（以下简称"中心"），围绕"一带一路"倡议和澜湄合作机制，聚焦重点领域，打造澜湄次区域农业技术交流、联合研究及投资贸易合作平台，促进该地区农业与粮食领域的经验分享、立场协调与务实合作，助力澜湄流域经济发展带建设。

2.2 职责定位

在中国农业农村部设立澜湄农业合作中心是落实澜湄合作第二次领导人会议上有关建议的初步举措，未来将以现有中心为基础，逐步将澜湄农业合作中心升级为六国共建、共管的协调和服务机构，成为澜湄合作农业联合工作组的常设执行机构，推动澜湄农业合作快速、可持续发展。中心主要职责包括：

（1）加强澜湄各国农业合作战略对接、研究交流与成果宣传。 跟踪分析澜湄国家农业发展环境、重点产业国际投资动态及农业合作需求，研究提出面向次区域农业合作的规划、政策和项目建议，组织编制次区域农业研究报告。

（2）做好澜湄农业合作机制维护工作。 保障澜湄农业合作机制正常运转并逐步提升。作为澜湄合作农业联合工作组的常设执行机构，实施相关工作计划和已签订的相关农业合作协议协定、谅解备忘录等合作事项。做好发展伙伴关系与工作网络建设工作，广织澜湄朋友圈。

（3）协助组织开展澜湄合作农业项目的立项、论证、实施与管理等工作。以澜湄基金项目为重点，协助开展澜湄区域农业投资合作、技术合作、联合研究等项目的立项、论证、实施与管理等工作。推进重大农业合作项目实施，促进次区域农业农村发展。

2.3 工作进展

自成立以来，中心讨论拟订了机构职责、目标思路和工作计划，与湄公河国家农业部门，中国有关部委、重点省区地方政府、科研机构和企业等广泛对接，听取意见建议。发展伙伴关系，逐步建立澜湄农业合作工作网络，宣传澜湄农业合作中心新形象。一年来，中心以建成区域性支持服务机构为目标，重点围绕促机制、夯基础和强手段等方面任务开展工作，取得预期成效。

（1）推动澜湄农业合作机制完善和体系建设。支持柬埔寨农林渔业部成功在柬埔寨召开澜湄合作农业联合工作组第二次会议，会上与各国代表研究讨论了澜湄农业合作中心的发展定位，提出编制澜湄农业合作三年行动计划以及建设澜湄农业科技交流协作组、澜湄农技推广与信息交流平台等倡议，得到各国的高度关注与认可。推动成立澜湄合作农业科技交流协作组、澜湄流域水生态合作工作小组，作为澜湄农业合作窗口单位日益发挥规划、协调、落实和宣传等农业联合工作组常设执行机构职能。

（2）组织开展澜湄农业合作规划研究与顶层设计。起草《澜湄农业合作三年行动计划（2020—2022）》并提交澜湄合作农业联合工作组第二次会议审议，该计划拟作为澜湄合作第五次外长会和第三次领导人会议成果文件。组织编制《澜湄农业合作发展报告（2019）》，供澜湄合作各国农业工作组、有关部门和科研机构交流参考。赴中国有关省区调研澜湄农业合作开展的经验做法，共同谋划合作思路。

（3）协助管理与实施澜湄农业合作重点项目。协助开展澜湄合作专项基金中国农业项目管理工作。实施澜湄基金支持的澜湄农业技术推广与信息交流平台建设项目，利用信息化手段，建立和完善澜湄国家农业公共信息分享、农技推广服务体系（手机 App）。跟踪了解澜湄区域农业合作项目实施进展，建立澜湄农业合作项目库、专家库。

（4）积极开展对外宣传，建立合作网络。与澜湄国家农业部门政府、科研机构、企业等开展交流合作、建立合作关系，组织设计澜湄中心标识，编制澜湄农业合作宣传片，对外展示澜湄农业合作中心新形象。

（农业农村部对外经济合作中心　祝自冬、杨光、姜晔）

3 | 澜湄农业合作三年行动计划 (2020—2022)[①]

3.1 编制背景

农业对于改善民生、促进澜沧江—湄公河（下称"澜湄"）六国经济社会可持续发展发挥着重要作用。

澜湄合作机制首次领导人会议确定农业合作是澜湄合作优先领域之一，并明确了澜湄农业合作的发展方向。2017年9月，澜湄合作农业联合工作组第一次会议在中国广西召开，澜湄农业合作的工作机制正式成立。农业联合工作组概念文件明确工作组的职责包括讨论确定澜湄农业合作的重点领域、合作方式，制定农业合作计划。

2018年1月，澜湄合作第二次领导人会议发布了《澜沧江—湄公河合作五年行动计划（2018—2022）》，进一步明确了农业合作的重点领域及总体要求。

为促进未来几年澜湄六国农业务实合作，依据澜湄合作领导人会议通过的《三亚宣言》《金边宣言》《澜沧江—湄公河合作五年行动计划（2018—2022）》，以及农业联合工作组的有关文件，结合各国的农业发展战略、发展规划和发展需求，编制本行动计划。

本行动计划包含澜湄农业合作的发展目标、基本原则、重点领域与任务、实施机制等，旨在有效促进《共同推进"一带一路"建设农业合作愿景与行动》《东盟2025：携手前行》等涵盖澜湄区域的农业合作战略计划

---

① 柬埔寨、中国、老挝、缅甸、泰国、越南六国农业部门于2020年1月正式通过。

的落实，推动澜湄流域经济发展带建设。

3.2　发展目标

　　本行动计划致力促进成员国之间开展更加紧密的农业交流与合作，推进农业资源保护与利用，提高本区域粮食安全与营养水平，促进自然资源可持续利用，保障食品安全，提升农业国际竞争力和促进农产品出口，加快物流基础设施建设，促进农产品贸易便利化，推动落实联合国 2030 年可持续发展议程涉农目标，实现乡村振兴和共同发展。

3.3　基本原则

　　本行动计划遵循澜湄合作首次领导人会议发布的《三亚宣言》中确立的原则。行动计划的实施将建立在协商一致、平等相待、相互协商和协调、自愿参与、共建、共享的基础上，尊重《联合国宪章》和国际法，符合各成员国国内法律法规和规章制度。
　　本行动计划秉持开放包容的理念，推动与现有湄公河次区域机制的农业合作相互补充、协调发展，并加强与澜湄合作机制框架下减贫、环境等其他领域的交流与合作。

3.4　重点领域与任务

3.4.1　农业政策对话

　　政策沟通是成员国开展务实有效农业合作的前提和保障。为此，在尊重各国国情和农业发展阶段的基础上，成员国将积极完善政策对话平台，加强协商协作、交流互鉴，促进发挥各自的特点和优势，推动缩小农业发展差距。
　　主要的合作方向包括但不限于以下内容：
　　（1）完善澜湄农业合作机制框架
　　——定期召开澜湄合作农业联合工作组会议；根据需要，在工作组内设立专门的工作小组，如澜湄农作物灾害监控工作小组、澜湄林业合作工作小组、澜湄畜牧兽医合作工作小组、澜湄流域渔业和水生态合作工作小组、澜湄热带农业产业提升工作小组、澜湄农业农村人力资源开发合作工作小组等。

——定期举办澜湄合作村长论坛。

——适时举办澜湄合作农业部长会议。

——逐步将澜湄农业合作中心升级成次区域合作中心，为六国提供支持服务。

（2）鼓励多层次、多主体参与

——通过双边互访，保持成员国政府官员的经常性接触，保证政策信息沟通顺畅，同时促进各国农业发展战略的对接与耦合。

——加强多边平台交流合作，逐步开展并不断丰富与全球涉农机构、国际及区域金融组织、非政府组织的对话，围绕政策交流、技术转移和投资促进有序推进。

——支持成员国地方农业部门之间建立和完善对话机制，推动政策交流和经验分享常态化，并做好合作项目对接。

——加强农业合作智库网络建设，探讨定期举办科技论坛，推动相关领域的专家、学者开展研讨交流；研究定期发布《澜湄农业合作发展报告》。

3.4.2 提升农业产业发展水平

农业生产的水平直接影响粮食安全。为此，成员国将加强农业生产合作，从数量、质量、生态三个方面保障澜湄区域粮食安全，促进农业可持续发展。

主要的合作方向包括但不限于以下内容：

（1）强化农业科技交流合作

——支持涉农高校和科研院所加强合作，围绕共同关心的问题，开展联合研究、技术研发，并提出合作建议；促进农业人才互访交流；加大高等学历教育联合培养工作力度。

——通过共建联合实验室、网络实验室、技术试验示范基地、技术促进中心和科技示范园区等，在种质资源、农作物耕作栽培管理、农作物灾害防控、动物疫病防控、农机装备、农业信息化、农业资源环境、适应和减缓气候变化、热带作物产业价值链延伸方面开展合作，推动高效、安全、低碳、循环、智能技术的集成创新与示范应用。

——研究成立澜湄农业合作科技协作组。

（2）完善农业支持服务体系

——加强农技推广经验交流，分享良好实践做法，推动完善农技推广服务体系。

——建立澜湄农业数据库，建设农业技术推广与市场信息系统交流平台。

——深化跨境动植物疫病联防联控合作，促进疫病疫情信息共享，提高疫病疫情监测预警与联防联控能力，加强实验室能力建设，推动动物移动可追溯体系建设，联合开展动物及动物产品跨境移动管理，促进家畜及畜产品贸易安全和便利化。

——开展水资源生态养护合作，推动建立澜湄流域生态养护交流合作机制，共建野生鱼类增殖救护中心，以加强鱼类多样性、鱼类数量和鱼群巡游等信息共享，促进在水产养殖能力建设等方面的渔业合作。

——加强林业资源养护与利用，促进澜湄国家森林生态系统的综合管理。

（3）保障农产品质量安全

——加强经验分享，推动健全从农田到餐桌的农产品质量和食品安全监管机制，开展农产品全程可追溯合作，提高检验检测能力，促进农产品推广。

——加强种子种苗、植物品种保护、种养植管理、农产品质量分级、农产品保鲜及采后减损、农业投入品、农产品地理标志等的标准化合作，促进标准的制定、对接、互鉴、互认。

（4）推动中小型农产品加工企业发展

——制定规章和政策，支持和鼓励新建的和现有的中小型农产品加工企业和年轻企业家发展。

——加快能力建设，提供技术支持，以推动中小型农产品加工企业符合良好农业规范（GAP）、食品良好卫生规范（GHP）、药品生产质量管理规范（GMP）、危害分析和关键控制点（HACCP）等的要求和标准。

——建设农产品加工示范区，以推广技术、分享经验。

——促进产品开发、食品科学、技术创新等方面的研究。

3.4.3 农产品贸易与农业私营部门投资合作

在充分发挥各国农业发展优势的基础上，成员国将进一步扩大域内农产品贸易合作，加强农业全产业链投资合作，同时携手开拓世界市场，提升本地区农业竞争力。

主要的合作方向包括但不限于以下内容：

（1）农产品贸易合作

——加强农产品仓储、加工、供应链、物流等基础设施建设，深化进出境农产品检验检疫监管合作，提高农产品贸易便利化水平。

——推动发展农产品跨境电子商务，研究建立澜湄农产品跨境电商平台。

——提高农产品生产者和加工者的品牌、标签和包装意识，增加农产品附加值，加大农产品品牌建设和宣传力度，提高农产品的市场竞争力和出口竞争力。

——充分利用博览会、展览会等展销平台，加强农产品推介。

——推动建立澜湄国家农产品投资贸易数据合作平台，促进农产品投资贸易信息交流。

——加强质量监督体系建设，通过澜湄国家间的边境贸易分享农业投入品信息。

（2）农业私营部门投资合作

——鼓励成员国政府优化营商环境，吸引外国直接投资参与农业产业化发展。

——鼓励成员国私营部门积极参与生产、加工、储运、流通等环节价值链建设，开展优势互补、互利共赢的双向投资合作。

——共建农业产业合作园区，积极引导社会民间力量参与园区建设和运营。

——推动建立澜湄合作农业产业协作组，促进企业、行业协会之间发展伙伴关系，不断延长产业链发展，带动小农参与市场，促进订单农业模式在澜湄国家的推广应用。

3.4.4　能力建设与知识分享

成员国将持续推进澜湄区域农业信息沟通、知识传播、技术转移和人力资源开发。

主要的合作方向包括但不限于以下内容：

——通过互派技术专家、举办培训班和研修班、实地考察等方式，加强对农民、技术员、官员等各层次人员的能力建设。

——加强共建农业培训基地、人才培训中心和农业技术转移中心，支持共享次区域现有的培训资源。

——分享农村减贫和乡村发展经验，支持农业农村全面发展。

——支持开展农业文化遗产保护能力建设，分享农业文化遗产发掘和保护经验，促进成员国农耕文化交流互鉴。

3.4.5　与其他领域的协作

在澜湄合作框架下，农业合作与互联互通、产能、经贸、减贫、水资源、林业、环保、海关和质检等多个领域的合作息息相关。为此，成员国将积极探索与相关领域开展协作的机会。

主要的合作方向包括但不限于以下内容：

——共同促进农业基础设施建设、农产品贸易和农业投资发展。

——联合开展与农业相关的标准信息交换，加强标准信息资源共享；推动完善标准体系，促进标准联通。

——联合申请和实施涉农国际合作项目。

3.5　组织实施

3.5.1　机构安排

本行动计划经澜湄合作农业联合工作组审议通过后即生效。经成员国一致同意，可对行动计划进行必要的修改、补充。

澜湄合作农业联合工作组牵头组织实施本行动计划，包括但不限于与实施行动计划有关的设计、建议、联络、沟通、协调、监测和报告等。通过澜湄合作高官会，农业联合工作组每年向澜湄合作外长会报告本行动计划的落实进展。根据需要，农业联合工作组可以提出并组织召开澜湄合作农业部长会议。农业部长会议将评估行动计划的实施情况，并为其未来发展指明方向。

各国的农业工作组组长负责：提出落实行动计划的项目和活动；本国项目和活动的总体协调、执行与监督；向本国的农业部长报告进展情况，争取支持和接受指导；与本国的澜湄合作秘书处/协调机构保持联系，加强沟通；定期向农业联合工作组反馈进展情况。

澜湄农业合作中心作为澜湄农业合作的协调服务机构，在与农业联合工作组加强协调的基础上，为本行动计划的实施提供支持。

各国将结合合作项目和活动的需求，邀请相关领域的专家、学者对实施行动计划提供技术、知识和智力支撑。

3.5.2 资金支持

坚持政府引导、多方参与的模式，鼓励成员国政府提供资金支持，同时积极争取其他渠道的资金。支持行动计划实施的资金来源包括但不限于：

——成员国政府提供的资金和资源；

——中国政府设立的澜湄合作专项基金；

——国际和地区合作机构提供的资金和资源；

——来自域外国家的资金和资源；

——企业、个人等私营部门的资金和资源。

3.5.3 合作伙伴

鼓励和支持各利益相关者积极参与，建立和发展广泛的合作伙伴关系网络，探索以适当的形式开展合作，推动实现本行动计划的目标。

这些合作伙伴包括但不限于：成员国的政府机构、科研单位、金融部门、企业、民间组织、社会团体，域外国家的政府机构和私营部门，以及国际涉农机构、全球及区域金融组织、非政府组织等。

4 澜湄区域农业科技交流合作进展与成效

4.1 背景

现代科技在农业领域的广泛应用，极大地促进了农业生产力水平提升，农业科技越来越成为现代农业发展的主动力。随着世界多极化、经济全球化和区域化进程的加快，世界农业的关联度不断提高，各国日益关注和重视农业科技合作以提升本国农业竞争力。澜湄次区域多数国家农业资源丰富，但开发利用程度较低，通过开展农业科技合作，引进符合高产、优质、高效、生态、安全等要求的先进适用技术、装备，应对气候变化，满足粮食安全、减少贫困、保护环境，实现本国农业升级和可持续发展是澜湄国家的迫切要求。

相对而言，中国比邻湄公河国家的云南、广西、海南等省（自治区）依托中国内地，在肉类产品、水果、蔬菜及其加工品等方面有出口竞争优势；而其依托湄公河国家，在大米、椰子、椰干、菠萝罐头、胡椒、香草、天然橡胶、椰子油和棕榈仁油、热带水果等方面有极强的进口竞争优势。更主要的是，中国的云南、广西、海南等地与湄公河国家农业发展共同面对小规模手工农业、发展水平低、农民贫困、农村欠发展、生态环境和生物多样性亟须保护等挑战。中国云南、广西、海南的农业科学技术与湄公河大多数国家相比，既有共性，也有互补性，在很多方面还有先进性。多年来，中国云南、广西、海南等地通过加大考察、访问和各类科技培训的力度，推进双边和多边实质性合作与交流，不断地向湄公河五国推出技术、产品和人才，取得了引人注目的成绩。但是，在澜湄区域国家农

23

业及农业科技合作取得重要进展的同时，澜湄国家也必须面对越来越多的共性问题，挑战在不断出现，过去以国家之间双边合作为主的合作交流，已不能满足可持续发展的需求，尤其是在农业科技合作交流方面，各国对建立区域的、多边的农业科技合作平台和机制的需求十分迫切。

4.2 澜湄合作农业科技交流平台机制的建立

为顺应区域农业经济发展和澜湄国家农业科技合作的迫切需求，2008年3月，云南省农业科学院在多年与湄公河五国交流合作的基础上，经云南省人民政府批准，在中国农业部、云南省科技厅和佩罗基金等支持下，与云南省科技厅等单位在昆明共同召开了大湄公河次区域农业科技交流合作发展研讨会。在会上，由云南省农业科学院主导，联合柬埔寨农业科学院、老挝农林科学院、缅甸农林牧渔科学院、泰国农业合作部农业司和越南农业科学院成立了大湄公河次区域农业科技交流合作组（以下简称"合作组"），并发表《联合宣言》。经过10年的运行和发展，至今合作组已逐步成为具备试验、示范、交流、培训等功能的区域合作平台，长效机制逐渐完善，在推进澜湄区域农业及农业科技的协调发展，实践"同饮一江水，命运紧相连"亚洲命运共同体建设中，合作组在域内外的影响力逐渐扩大，成为澜湄区域农业科技交流合作的主要平台和机制。

2019年6月，在柬埔寨召开的澜湄合作农业联合工作组第二次会议上，柬埔寨、中国、老挝、缅甸、泰国、越南一致同意在原有大湄公河次区域农业科技交流合作组的基础上，建立覆盖范围更广、合作内容更丰富的澜湄合作农业科技交流协作组（以下简称"协作组"）。

2019年8月，澜湄合作农业科技交流协作组在中国云南昭通宣布成立，来自东南亚、南亚的13个国家农业科研单位以及中国农业农村部、中国农业科学院和18家中国省级农业科学院代表共同见证了协作组成立，协作组成员单位共同讨论并通过了协作组工作章程。

协作组遵循共建、共管、共享的原则，重点围绕澜湄农业合作相关行动计划开展工作，积极扩大成员单位范围，联合澜湄区域更多农业科研和教育机构，在种植、畜牧和渔业等更广泛的领域开展科技交流与合作，配合澜湄农业合作中心构建澜湄国家农业合作支持体系，打造澜湄农业科技交流与联合研究平台，逐步建立跨境植物病虫害、动物疫病联防联控机制和渔业生态养护合作机制，推动落实联合国 2030 年可持续发展议程涉农目标，促进澜湄流域经济发展带建设。

4.3　澜湄区域农业科技交流合作成效

多年来，中国各省区特别是云南、广西、海南都与湄公河五国开展了卓有成效的农业科技交流与合作，相关内容在本报告区域篇进行了详细的介绍，本部分仅对过去十多年来大湄公河次区域农业科技交流合作组所取得的成效作简要总结，同时，间接说明建立澜湄区域农业科技交流协作机制和平台的必要性、已有的基础和发展前景。

大湄公河次区域农业科技交流合作组由理事会、秘书处和专业工作组组成。理事会负责制订政策，通过工作计划、经费预算、工作报告等，理事会主席由各国轮流担任；秘书处执行理事会决议，负责处理合作组日常工作，为相关合作项目和活动进行组织、协调等，秘书处常设在中国昆明，协调员和常任秘书由中方人员担任；专业工作组由各国研究及开发人员组成，在理事会的领导下，根据合作内容要求开展工作。2008—2019年，合作组在各国共同选择并一致同意的情况下，先后组成了陆稻、大豆、甘蔗、马铃薯、植物保护和农业经济 6 个工作组。

4.3.1　主要粮经作物科技合作初显成效

十多年来，在大湄公河次区域农业科技交流合作组平台上，各工作组共同交换和筛选试验相关作物栽培品种 543 份，初步选育出适宜各国品种（组合）124 个。其中陆稻 1 个品种在越南通过审定，另外，陆稻 2 个、大豆 2 个、甘蔗 1 个品种有望在缅甸、越南、柬埔寨通过审定或大面积推广。适宜品种中，平均增产陆稻 31.1%，大豆 11.1%，甘蔗 33.3%，马铃薯 10.5%；最高增产陆稻达到 146.8%，大豆达 105.3%，甘蔗达 49%。云南省农业科学院选育的杂交水稻、陆稻、杂交小麦、大麦、玉米、大豆、甘蔗、马铃薯、花卉、蔬菜等粮经作物品种已被东南亚国家引进并示范推广，示范推广面积累计超过 200 万亩[①]。这为澜湄国家山区农户粮食安全、减贫增收作出了贡献，也为中国进口大豆来源国多元化打下了科技基础。

4.3.2 联合研究支撑跨境植物疫病联防联控合作机制建设

2011 年以来，大湄公河次区域农业科技交流合作组植物保护工作组对水稻、蔬菜、水果和其他经济作物的病、虫、草害开展了联合调研，充分掌握了澜湄区域主要病虫草害发生、危害与防控情况。尤其是针对澜湄区域国家水稻主产区的水稻病虫草害开展了联合调查、样品采集以及菌种资源的分离保存工作，为进一步深入研究稻瘟病菌与寄主的协同进化、稻瘟病菌的演化与远距离传播、病原菌的起源、白背飞虱种群遗传多样性及其可能的迁飞路径、入侵杂草在澜湄区域的灾变特点与成因等奠定了坚实的基础，这些研究结果极大地促进了澜湄区域水稻主产区主要病虫草害联合监控预警及防治工作。2019 年 8 月，植物保护工作组针对草地贪夜蛾近年在东南亚大部分国家发生日益严重的态势，开展了联合监测、预警与防控技术合作研究，以期掌握草地贪夜蛾种群发生特征及规律，共享研究成果与经验，提高区域防控水平。

4.3.3 科技交流助推人力资源能力提升

十多年来，云南省农业科学院先后选派 9 名青年科技人员分别到柬埔寨农业科学院、缅甸农林牧渔科学院、泰国农业合作部农业司、越南农业科学院等开展学习与合作研究工作。1 名缅甸科技人员、8 名缅甸杰出青年科学家先后获资助到云南省农业科学院分别开展博士后工作及 1 年的学习与合作研究。各国交流科技人员能力得到了提升，也拓展了合作领域和空间，为今后合作研究奠定了坚实基础。

其间，云南省农业科学院先后组织召开了 10 届大湄公河次区域农业科技交流合作组理事会，50 多次研讨会 500 多场学术报告，来自大湄公河次区域各国农业科学家约 770 人次出席研讨会、参加培训班和互访交流，各国农户、科技人员、相关管理人员约 7 000 人次参加了互访交流、

---

① 亩为非法定计量单位，15 亩＝1 公顷。下同。——编者注

培训、现场观摩等。通过多年持续参与大湄公河次区域农业科技交流合作，一大批来自云南省农业科学院、柬埔寨农业科学院、缅甸农业灌溉部农业研究司、泰国农业合作部农业司以及越南农业科学院的科技人员及管理人员的能力得到了提升。

4.3.4 产学研结合促进农业经贸合作

在推动农业科技合作的同时，云南省农业科学院注重与企业合作，以市场为导向，牵头成立了由涉农企业、科研院所等42家单位组成的，跨行业产学研相结合的云南农业"走出去"产业技术创新战略联盟。十年来，云南省农业科学院选育的杂交水稻、杂交玉米、陆稻、大豆、甘蔗、马铃薯等适宜新品种在次区域各国累计推广超过15万公顷，出口马铃薯种薯8 000多吨。

合作组分别以山区粮食安全、农业生产市场化、农业生产结构调整等为主题召开4届学术交流会议，提出通过农业示范园区、科技交流、农业技术推广、农产品贸易等打造农业生产的利益共同体，建设"跨境农业经济带"。

4.3.5 充分发挥交流平台作用，提升国际影响力

多年来，合作组为17个国家和国际组织、19个中国省、自治区、直辖市（包括广东、广西、海南、福建、四川、重庆、贵州、新疆、浙江、江苏等）的科研单位以及中国农业科学院、中国热带农业科学院、40多家企业搭建了与湄公河五国商洽合作的平台，国内外影响日益扩大。

2008年亚洲开发银行（Asian Development Bank，ADB）同意吸纳合作组成为其大湄公河次区域经济合作农业工作组合作伙伴。国际农业发展基金（International Fund for Agriculture Development，IFAD）在合作组成立时便派代表列席会议，并把云南省农业科学院列为其在澜湄国家技术合作的依托单位。国际生物多样性中心（Bioversity International）与云南省农业科学院签署协议，利用合作组共同针对东南亚国家开展工作。国际水稻研究所（International Rice Research Institute，IRRI）与云南省农业科学院一道积极推动在云南筹建有害生物综合防治实验室。

（云南省农业科学院国际农业研究所　李露）

5 | 澜湄合作专项基金中方农业项目实施进展与成效

2017—2018 年，中国农业农村部组织实施澜湄合作专项基金项目 15 个，预算资金总额 2 698 万元。项目形式以技术合作为主，包括研讨交流、试验示范、能力建设等，其中机制平台类项目 5 个、技术合作项目 4 个、人员培训项目 3 个、联合研究与行动项目 2 个，媒体项目 1 个。项目实施对完善澜湄农业合作机制，落实澜湄合作领导人会议重要倡议，强化技术支撑，输出中国农业技术、设备、人才，分享中国农业发展经验，宣传澜湄农业合作进展与成果，推动澜湄流域经济发展带建设发挥了积极作用。

5.1 完善澜湄农业合作机制，夯实合作基础

（1）**召开澜湄合作村长论坛，搭建了澜湄区域农业农村合作的新平台。**中国农业农村部与云南省政府连续两年在云南召开澜湄合作村长论坛，论坛发出了《澜湄村社合作芒市倡议》，倡议成立"澜湄村社发展联盟"，促成 19 家单位的合作对接，现场签署 8 份合作协议，中国发展产业兴村、三产融合强村、电子商务富村、生态保护美村、收益共享富民，促进乡村全面振兴的经验做法引发与会代表强烈兴趣与合作愿望，为今后不断推进澜湄农业、农村、农民全方位合作开好了头。

（2）**召开澜湄农业合作联合工作组会议，建立了澜湄农业合作的伙伴关系网络。**中国农业农村部积极落实工作组首次会议成果，促成各国就概念文件达成一致。各国明确了工作组的负责人和联络员，确定了联系机制，就农业发展政策、申报实施澜湄合作专项基金项目等事宜进行密

切联系。从政企产研四个角度，与主管部门、业务部门、外交渠道、科研机构等建立了良好的合作关系，组建专家团队，为后续合作打下基础。

(3) 开展澜湄农业合作研究。 编制了《澜沧江—湄公河农业合作三年行动计划（2020—2022）》，明确了澜湄农业合作的方向与重点，得到澜湄六国农业部门认可，并在 2020 年初正式通过。围绕天然橡胶、香蕉等特色产业以及重点国别开展专题研究，形成研究报告。

5.2 开展境外试验示范，打造产业合作关键支撑

由中国广西壮族自治区农业农村厅组织实施的湄公河水稻绿色增产技术试验示范项目，围绕绿色高效理念，突出引领示范功能，加强技术的引进、试验，优化组装为适合当地实际的新技术，在保护当地生态环境的前提下实现了增产增收，为推动当地水稻提质增效提供了有效的技术支撑，也为水稻科研育种提供了科学依据。项目共从中国引进水稻品种 44 个，筛选出适合当地的优良品种 15 个；建立水稻绿色增产技术试验示范基地 8 655 亩，根据当地实际情况引入中国较为成熟的育秧、栽培、水肥管理和病虫害绿色防控等技术，辐射带动面积超过 4.5 万亩，帮助当地水稻单产提高 25% 以上，每亩平均增收达 200 元；围绕发展稻虾、稻鱼、稻鸭等 6 种稻田综合种养模式，开展绿色水稻综合种养技术试验示范和推广。经测算，稻鸭模式每亩增加经济收益 220 元，稻鱼模式每亩增加经济收益 413 元，稻田套养罗氏沼虾项目每亩增产 3 000 元。示范基地成为当地农技人员和农户参观、培训的重要平台。

中国海南省在中—柬热带生态农业合作示范区的基础上开展了澜湄热带农业产业合作示范区建设项目，以中国热带农业科学院等单位为支撑，以"走出去"企业为主体，共同建设热带农业产业合作示范区。支持中资企业在柬埔寨建设椰子产业合作示范基地 1 000 亩，其中椰子种质资源苗圃 50 亩；邀请柬埔寨、老挝、缅甸、泰国、越南五国人员共计 15 人到海南培训 20 天；邀请中国热带农业科学院专家赴柬埔寨皇家农业大学和产业园区内现场举办培训班。

5.3 搭建信息与技术平台，完善农业支持服务体系

澜湄农技推广与信息交流平台建设项目采用国内最新的移动互联技术，整合各方农业科技资源、市场信息，构建澜湄农业技术推广与农业信息共享的农业综合服务平台（手机 App），将中国先进的农业实用技术和农业信息服务模式转移输出，创新湄公河国家农业信息服务手段，增强澜湄区域农业政策交流、信息共享与成果转化。平台中英、柬英版本应用程序框架已开发完毕，进入试运营阶段。平台拟实现两大功能：一是信息发布，澜湄国家农业部门、科研单位和涉农企业可发布农业政策、技术、农情、市场行情和公共信息等，指导农业生产、加工、仓储和销售；二是农技服务，聘请专家针对农户和基层农技人员提出的问题予以在线解答。

澜湄流域农作物病虫害绿色防控合作平台建设项目针对流域内绿色防控的技术需求，围绕政策支撑、绿色防控发展模式、有关绿色防控学术与管理政策开展研讨、交流与培训。由中国农业科学院植物保护研究所联合湄公河五国相关植物保护研究及管理机构，共同组建农作物绿色防控联合平台，即农作物病虫害绿色防控合作实验室，总部设在北京（中国农业科学院植物保护研究所）。平台的创建对提升次区域跨境病虫害联合监测预警与联防联控能力，提升次区域农业综合生产能力和粮食安全保障水平具有重要意义，对促进农产品贸易、助力澜湄流域经济发展带建设具有深远意义。

东南亚智慧农业监控平台建设项目搭建覆盖老挝、柬埔寨等国家的"互联网＋农业"智慧农业信息交流和数据库平台。该平台建设利用土地和确定适宜的种植制度的农业气候分析，统计重要农业活动的气象资料，对虫病情报和土地状况进行气候预测与环境监测，能够为农业生产提供及时准确的一手环境资料，提高对农业生产的实时精准监控，对促进澜湄流域农业生产具有积极作用。

澜湄国家农业科研机构合作平台建设项目依托中国热带农业科学院举办的第二届"一带一路"热带农业科技合作论坛等平台，邀请泰国梅州大学、泰国农业大学、泰国农业合作部农业司、柬埔寨经济、社会和文化委

员会、柬埔寨劳工与职业培训部、柬埔寨农林渔业部等湄公河国家高等院校和科研机构相关负责人来华访问，并签署《中国热带农业科学院与泰国梅州大学谅解备忘录》等 3 份合作协议，与泰国农业合作部农业司等 7 家机构建立起联系渠道。

5.4 开展联合研究与行动，共建创新绿色澜湄

中国农业农村部长江流域渔政监督管理办公室（以下简称"长江办"）联合老挝、柬埔寨、泰国等湄公河国家多次开展联合执法和增殖放流活动。其中，中老联合放流丝尾鳠 12 万尾、大鳞四须鲃 6.5 万尾，胡子鲶 20 万尾，并连续五年累计赠送老挝南塔省用于增殖放流的鱼苗 61.4 万尾，其中鲤鱼 56 万尾、丝尾鳠 4.4 万尾、大鳞四须鲃 1 万尾；中泰联合放流当地土著鱼种银鲫 50 万尾、罗氏沼虾 100 万尾；中柬联合放流 700 多千克亲本和 100 多万尾（只）珍稀濒危土著鱼类、龟类和蛙类等水生生物成体和苗种到吴哥窟护城河，对澜湄流域渔业资源快速养护、维护生态系统稳定发挥了积极作用。2019 年中老举行联合执法暨增殖放流活动，现场收缴、销毁电鱼机 60 套、地笼 36 个、渔网 110 张和电拖网、迷魂阵等非法捕鱼工具，两国执法人员乘渔政执法船在澜沧江上开展了渔政联合巡航执法，保障了增殖放流的效果。此外，还组织开展了水生生物保护宣传活动，通过标志标牌、宣传材料、报纸、电视媒体等宣传渠道，向参与项目实施国家的群众宣传联合增殖放流开展情况及重要意义，提高活动影响力，提升公众生态保护意识。印制项目背景材料、技术手册、项目成果展板，多渠道向澜湄国家有关部门及联合国粮食及农业组织等国际组织宣传联合增殖放流项目实施内容、效果和成果等。2018 年 11 月长江生物资源保护论坛邀请了澜湄国家渔业主管部门参加，各国代表高度肯定中国在澜湄流域水生生物保护方面取得的成果，达成了加强在澜湄流域水生生物保护的合作共识。2019 年 5 月长江办就《澜湄流域渔业和水生态合作工作小组筹建方案（中国建议草案）》向湄公河国家征求意见，拟择机召开组织筹备会议，建立澜湄流域水生态养护交流合作机制。2019 年组织柬埔寨湄公河湄公江豚科学考察 2 次，估算柬埔寨湄公河段湄公江豚种群数

量约 80 头。

澜湄流域种植橡胶对生物多样性的影响联合研究项目开展了澜沧江（中国云南植胶区）—湄公河区域（越南、柬埔寨、老挝、泰国和缅甸）橡胶林植物多样性的调查工作，获取了大量橡胶野外观测数据，掌握了澜湄区域橡胶林物种组成特征与多样性、区域分布等，加强了与国际热带农业中心亚洲分中心、越南国家农业大学等橡胶生产研究机构的合作，提出了开展橡胶科技联合攻关、解决关键技术，建设环境友好型生态胶园的建议。截至 2018 年底，该项目共计完成了 247 个橡胶林群落样方的野外调查，同时对橡胶园的管理模式、割胶制度及胶乳产量也从多方面进行了调研，对推动天然橡胶产业健康发展具有重要意义。

5.5 开展能力建设合作，构建人才培育支撑系统

中国热带农业科学院等 4 家单位实施了澜沧江—湄公河流域国家热带农业人才培育工程、跨境动物疫病防控技术交流与合作、沼气技术培训班、澜湄国家农药风险管理研修班 4 个培训项目，在华举办涉外培训班 10 个，参训 185 人次；派出专家团组 20 余个，开展技术交流与现场培训，培训当地农户和技术人员 2 500 人次。

热带农业人才培育工程项目建设澜湄农业人才培训专家库（目前在库专家 163 人）、培训实践基地库（在库基地 9 个）和 13 个配套精品培训课程，在华举办热带农业有害生物疫情监测、预警、综合防治等培训班 6 期，培训湄公河五国政府官员、农技人员、科研人员总计 124 名，在泰国畜牧发展厅反刍动物饲养标准研究与发展中心、泰国梅州大学动物科技学院举办了 2 期畜牧领域培训，培训技术人员 67 名。围绕培训工作核心，以学员回访为抓手，稳步推动科学研究与科技合作，并与柬埔寨劳工与职业培训部和湄公学院、孔敬大学、梅州大学、清迈大学等泰国单位签订合作协议或达成合作意向，撰写《澜湄区域国家农业可持续发展项目建议报告》《澜湄区域国家技术人才需求分析报告》，为澜湄流域国家热带农业人才培育工程建设提供支撑。

跨境动物疫病防控技术交流与合作项目通过"请进来"培训，教授活

牛口蹄疫带毒检测技术，提升了澜湄国家兽医实验室对口蹄疫诊断监测能力；通过专家"走出去"培训，开展了跨境动物疫病诊断技术培训，提高了老挝活牛口蹄疫带毒检测能力和技术水平，加深了与中—缅—泰实验室间的紧密联系，为澜湄区域跨境动物疫病联防联控、畜产品安全贸易提供了技术支撑。

沼气技术培训班完成了对湄公河国家学员的技术交流、成果示范、企业推介、经验分享，鼓励学员申报合作项目，提交了《关于中越禽畜废弃物处理及沼气技术合作平台建设的建议》等合作意向。受柬埔寨学员邀请，赴柬埔寨举办联合国工业发展组织支持的商业化沼气技术培训班 2 期，受邀投标了联合国工业发展组织发起的柬埔寨老挝生物质能能力建设项目 1 个。

澜湄国家农药风险管理研修班旨在进一步加强澜湄各国在农药风险管理方面的经验交流，从而提高区域农药风险管理能力，落实第二届"一带一路"高峰论坛成果清单，推动农业标准国际互认。培训分为北京阶段、广西阶段、云南阶段共 3 个阶段先后进行，28 名参训学员围绕生物多样性与病虫害防治、植物病害生物防治、中国农药管理政策与环境风险控制等进行理论交流和实践学习，并赴云南富民、斗南、呈贡、宜良、安宁以及广西遂宁等地参观农药厂，在花卉、水果、农作物等病虫害防治示范基地进行现场教学，为加强与澜湄次区域农药领域的交流、推动农药产业的国际贸易合作提供了的契机。

（农业农村部对外经济合作中心　张芸；

农业农村部国际合作司　徐玉波）

6 | 澜湄合作共促区域 乡村振兴的实践探索

澜湄合作是中国与湄公河五国共同发起和建设的新型次区域合作平台，旨在深化六国睦邻友好合作，构建澜湄国家命运共同体，为推进南南合作、落实联合国 2030 年可持续发展议程做出新贡献。2018 年 1 月中国政府颁布了《关于实施乡村振兴战略的意见》，明确了"乡村振兴"的战略目标和路径，坚持农业农村优先发展，按照"产业兴旺、生态宜居、乡风文明、治理有效、生活富裕"的总要求，有序推进乡村振兴建设。如今乡村振兴已经不仅仅在中国实践，也推广到其他国家。澜湄流域拥有大量丰富的农业生产资源，农业人口众多，农业是澜湄国家的基础产业，乡村建设是各国重点关注的领域。基于这一共同基础，中国将乡村振兴理念融入澜湄合作框架中，通过开展乡村振兴领域合作，在交流平台搭建、农业技术推广、民生领域建设、能力培训、减贫示范等方面积极探索合作，促进六国乡村振兴发展。

6.1 搭建交流平台，共享乡村振兴经验

为促进区域乡村振兴，各国通过建立多层次的交流平台，促进农村基层组织交流，分享发展经验，挖掘合作潜力。

6.1.1 召开澜湄合作村长论坛，促进村社交流

为加强澜湄国家村长间交流合作，助推区域农村发展，造福基层农民，中国倡议召开澜湄合作村长论坛，并纳入《澜湄合作五年行动计划（2018—2022）》。2017 年 4 月，澜沧江—湄公河农业合作暨中柬老缅泰村

长论坛在中国云南省西双版纳傣族自治州勐腊县召开，来自中柬老缅泰五国近百名村长、企业代表和相关政府部门官员参加此次论坛，论坛期间，国内外共 11 家村寨和企业签署了 8 份合作协议，涉及蔬菜种植、咖啡生产加工、水稻高产示范、农业技术服务、休闲农业等领域。

2018 年 4 月，第二届澜沧江—湄公河合作村长论坛在中国云南省德宏傣族景颇族自治州芒市举办，来自澜湄各国农业部、省、村（合作社）代表近 200 人参加论坛，论坛围绕"合作、创新、共赢，共同推进乡村振兴"的主题，通过主题报告、交流讨论、双边会谈、展览展示、企业村（寨）对接、实地参观等形式，共同分享了农村发展经验。论坛发出《澜湄村社合作芒市倡议》，倡导村社企交流合作、推行绿色生产方式、提高农产品质量、加强标准认可和培训、重视农业产业链和价值链发展，成为村社合作的方向标。中国村社发展促进会倡议成立"澜湄村社发展联盟"，展览展示对接活动促成现场签署 8 份合作协议，签约金额约 1.2 亿元。

6.1.2 建立科技交流合作机制，促进技术升级与产业发展

中国云南省农业科学院先后牵头成立大湄公河次区域农业科技交流合作组、云南农业"走出去"产业技术创新战略联盟、中国—南亚农业科技交流合作组、南亚东南亚农业科技创新联盟等一系列合作机制与平台，促进各方农业技术交流，帮助东道国选育适宜品种并进行示范推广，促进农业增产、农民增收。2019 年 8 月，澜湄合作农业科技交流协作组正式成立，将搭建次区域各国种植、畜牧、渔业等多领域农业技术交流平台，针对次区域重点病虫害、动物疫病、水生态养护等方面加强合作，推动农业技术升级与产业发展。

6.2 开展减贫示范合作，促进乡村全面可持续发展

贫困问题一直是澜湄地区关注的重要民生问题，也是政府迫切需要解决的问题。近年来，为促进中国与东亚国家共享减贫理念和经验，不断深化中国和周边国家减贫交流合作，双方建立了一系列机制化合作平台，包括国家减贫与发展高层论坛、中国—东盟社会发展与减贫论坛等。中国国

务院扶贫办牵头成立了澜湄合作减贫工作组，组织实施了东亚减贫示范合作技术援助项目，开展了东盟减贫论坛、减贫研修班、东盟村官交流等多种形式的澜湄减贫合作活动。中国国际扶贫中心也举办了多期减贫发展培训班，招收大量澜湄国家学员。2016年至今，共有来自越老柬缅泰五国的95名官员来华参加研修，面向基层村官的"东盟＋3村官交流项目"已连续举办了7届。

2014年中国提议实施"东亚减贫合作倡议"，提供1亿元人民币开展乡村减贫推进计划，建立东亚减贫合作示范点。按照项目设计，云南省国际扶贫与发展中心、广西外资扶贫项目管理中心和四川省扶贫和移民局项目中心分别承担缅甸、老挝和柬埔寨的减贫示范合作技术援助项目。东亚减贫示范合作技术援助项目已在缅甸、老挝和柬埔寨6个项目村落地，主要援助内容包括改善村内基础设施和公共服务设施，开展产业发展项目和能力建设活动等。减贫示范项目的实施切实改善了当地村民的生产生活条件，增强了村庄的发展活力。

6.2.1 中国援助缅甸埃羌达村和敏彬村减贫示范合作项目案例

农业是缅甸的支柱产业，缅甸政府一直致力改善人民生活水平，为农村发展和农村贫困人口脱贫付出了巨大努力，但很多村庄依然处于贫困状态之中。缅甸约有70%的人口居住在农村，农村贫困人口约占全国人口的23%。2017年11月，中缅签署中国援助缅甸减贫示范合作项目实施协议。2018年2月，项目正式启动，在内比都达贡镇埃羌达村和莱韦镇敏彬村建设道路、供水、学校、卫生所等基础设施，惠及1481户7820位村民。

埃羌达村是一个由4个村庄搬迁成立的移民村，共有村民483户2274人，农田缺乏、用水紧张，没有农业灌溉水利设施。村里大部分房屋十分破旧，由木板或者竹子编织的材料建成；全村仅170户通电，占总户数的35%，电力需求较大。按每人每天生活支出1.25美元的国际贫困线标准计算，埃羌达贫困户占全村总户数的2/3，贫困发生率在65%以上，贫困面大、贫困程度深，是缅甸中部有代表性的贫困村。雨季埃羌达村的道路十分湿滑，雨水和泥土掺杂变成泥泞土路，且排水沟排水不畅；

村内供水依靠一口 25 英尺①深的机井，水质较差，有苦涩味；一些农户还自己修建较大水池从屋顶接雨水存储，用来日常使用甚至饮用。饮用水安全得不到保障，严重制约村民生产生活。

项目组在实地调研后决定在三年的时间内采取先易后难的全方位减贫措施：先启动以基础设施为主的建设活动，包括道路、饮水工程。考虑到村庄所在区域降水较多，在修缮村内所有道路的同时整修道路两侧的排水沟、涵洞等，开发一口 600 英尺深的水井，并建设提水泵站从地下取水，新建清水池、铺设管网到每家每户，解决农户取水困难问题。扶贫项目配备变压器、输电线，解决全村居民用电问题，并在房屋集中区、重点路段、学校、寺庙等地点实现公共照明，在户户通水的同时，实现家家通电。在基础设施建成后，开展社区环境治理以及提供专业培训等项目，帮扶村庄发展种植、养殖等产业。种植业方面，引进高品质和丰产、稳产的粮食作物和经济作物良种，提高产量。畜牧业方面，建立村级畜牧繁殖与疫病防控示范户，引进优质种公猪，为畜牧饲养户提供肉质好、生长快的牲畜幼崽；帮助进行畜圈修建，对 100 户养殖户修建标准化圈舍，推广牲畜的家庭人工饲料喂养，增加副业收入。此外，开展 150 户农户庭院经济示范，实现多重创收。结合埃羌达村有家庭手工织布的传统，帮助村民成立纺织合作社发展手工业。

敏彬村有 1 000 多户农户，村内道路条件较差，路面崎岖不平，非常颠簸。和埃羌达村一样，综合村庄交通不便、饮水条件差的现实情况，专家组制定了三年期方案，第一年集中打井、修村内道路，第二年主要建设村民活动中心和通电，第三年主要修建防洪堤和学校。项目还将可持续发展和环境保护作为实施目标，设立垃圾处理公共服务项目，增强农户环保意识。2019 年 4 月，中国组织两个示范村 40 多位村民代表赴仰光南部地区教丹镇区垃圾处理示范村 Kan Pyung 和 Wae Gyi 考察交流。通过实地考察和交流学习活动，让村民对环境整治活动有了更加直观的感受，增强了环保意识；提升了项目各级管理人员组织能力，对推动中缅项目环境改善及垃圾处理项目活动有所启发和借鉴。

---

① 英尺为非法定计量单位，1 英尺＝0.304 8 米。下同。——编者注

6.2.2　中国援助柬埔寨斯瓦安普乡减贫示范合作项目案例

2017 年 12 月 21 日，中国援助柬埔寨减贫示范合作项目启动仪式在柬埔寨干丹省斯瓦安普乡举行，项目计划用 3 年的时间在柬埔寨干丹省莫穆坎普区斯瓦安普乡谢提尔普洛斯村和斯瓦安普村两个项目示范村合作，使 886 户 3 900 多人直接获益。项目因地制宜、因贫施策，以治理致贫因素和发展需求为导向，开展社区减贫活动。项目建设涵盖基础设施、产业发展、技术培训等内容：开展农村道路、供水等基础设施建设，改善当地安全饮水等生产生活条件；建立农村卫生室、学习中心等公共服务设施，满足当地群众基本需求；扶持村民发展种植、养殖等产业，派遣专家对村民进行技术培训等工作。以政府主导、群众参与的实施方式，改善社区生产生活条件，增强社区自我发展能力，探索农户增收途径，为东亚国家减贫、改善民生提供示范。

项目已经建成一栋总面积为 400 米^2 的社区活动中心，用作斯瓦安普乡乡村干部的日常办公场所，以及整个斯瓦安普乡社区的广大民众活动场所，特别是作为会议、培训或开展其他活动的场所。活动中心底层有 2 间办公室，1 间物料间，1 间会议室，2 间休息室，2 间卫生间；一楼设有 1 间厨房，2 间卫生间，1 间餐厅，能同时容纳 100 人就餐。2019 年 9 月 5 日，农村饮用水工程也在斯瓦安普乡正式开工，此次开工建设的农村饮用水工程，包括新建水源工程、净水工程（水厂）、输水和配水管网工程（含入户管网及水表）及其附属工程建设等，将解决斯瓦安普乡 2 村 800 户 3 840 人的饮用水问题。在技术培训方面，已经开展乡村项目执行人员培训和项目村村民劳务技能培训各 1 次，从各方面提升村庄发展能力。针对贫困群体，目前已改建 100 户贫困户厕所；完成 82 户贫困户电力接入；为村民发放 500 个灶台和 1 000 个省柴灶。与此同时，还帮助一户贫困户开办了小商铺，平均每月可实现 60～120 美元的收入。斯瓦安普乡减贫示范合作项目还在建设中，已取得一定的阶段性成果，得到了当地政府和村民的肯定。

6.2.3　经验启示

中国在缅甸、柬埔寨的减贫示范合作项目，通过基础设施完善和发展能力培养两个角度开展合作，软硬结合，更好地实现乡村减贫目标，促进可持续发展。一方面，根据实地情况帮助当地完善基础设施建设，为后期的经济发展提供有力的基础保障；另一方面，立足于培养发展能力和实现可持续发展的目标，设立多领域的交流合作项目，搭建众多培训平台，拓展人才培养渠道，全方面提升人才素质，为各国乡村建设培养人才，提升乡村的自我发展能力，改善社区的生产生活条件。

同时，中国将"精准扶贫"和"整村推进"的扶贫理念带入湄公河国家。项目从可行性研究到最终实施计划都将贫困村和村民的实际情况和需求纳入进来，中国调研组在项目实施过程中进村入户、实地勘察，绘制资源图，了解当地生产季节和传统文化。在项目选择上广泛听取群众意见，与当地各级扶贫机构进行座谈，召开群众代表会议，在村干部、各村民小组组长及村民代表的共同参与下，对项目村的基本情况、农户贫困状况进行分析。项目建设过程中引导村级成立实施小组和监督小组，确保建设按时按质完成，项目建成后引导村级制定好后续管理办法。项目实施更注重综合发展，以中国精准扶贫"整村推进"的工作经验为基础，全面考虑当地农户所需，实现内部基础设施、非常重要的民生项目及产业发展项目协同长期可持续发展。

6.3 建基础设施补民生短板，推动乡村建设步伐

民生是涉及范围最广、与农民联系最近的领域，是实现农村发展和区域减贫的关键。完善的基础设施建设是实现农村跨越式发展的前提，然而澜湄流域各国工业发展薄弱，基础设施完善程度不高，参与可持续基础设施建设开发能力有限，尤其在农村地区，基础设施缺口较大，进而制约了发展速度。因此，实现区域乡村振兴需要加快补齐农村民生短板，这在改善农村交通物流设施条件、加强农村水利基础设施网络建设等方面尤为突出。此外，在基础设施建设过程中还需要注重资源保护与节约利用，以民生和可持续为导向，从改变农民生活方式出发，推动乡村建设与发展。

6.3.1 中国援老挝班索村和象龙村减贫项目案例

2017 年中国援老挝减贫示范合作项目确定，将老挝万象市桑通县班

索村和琅勃拉邦市琅勃拉邦县象龙村两个村庄作为示范村庄建设。中国援老项目共 17 个，其中万象市的桑通县班索村 9 个，琅勃拉邦市象龙村 8 个，重点是桥梁、村内道路、入户供水、活动中心、卫生室、学校师生宿舍、太阳能路灯等基础设施和公共设施完善项目。通过项目建设，改善了当地社区生产生活条件，增强了社区自我发展能力，构建社区尤其是贫困人口多样化的增收途径，为东亚国家减贫和改善民生提供示范和样本。

老挝是一个农业国家，农业资源丰富，土壤肥沃，但基础设施状况有待提升，缺少铁路和高速公路，很多地方走的是二级公路。项目所在的两个村庄的森林覆盖率很高，人均土地占有量较高，但缺少灌溉等水利设施，土地开发利用率较低。另外，因资金和技术相对缺乏，无法进行农业深度开发，农业生产"靠天收"，农村产业发展的底子比较薄弱，村民自我改变的动力不足。村民对什么是合作社、如何发展合作社不太了解。为了有效推进减贫工作，中老双方建立了多部门联系制度，从资金、人员等各方面给予支持；同时，广西专家组加强与老挝的合作，多次实地考察项目村和项目点，就项目模式、项目规划、实施方案、机构设置等与老挝达成共识。2016 年 10 月、12 月和 2017 年 5 月，广西先后三次派出专家组赴老挝，与老挝有关人员实地考察项目点，精心确定项目选址，做好项目前期准备工作。中国和老挝双方对项目实行联合管理模式，即广西外资扶贫项目管理中心与老挝国家农村发展与减贫委员会共同合作，分级成立联合项目管理办公室，并在办公室派驻中方专家和技术人员，与老挝共同组织实施和管理项目。在建设过程中，老挝有关部门充分参与，为项目实施提供管理协助、劳务投入、工程建设用地等，这种联合管理有助于项目完成后更好地在当地发挥作用。与此同时，在项目选择上广泛听取群众意见，项目建设过程中引导村级成立实施小组和监督小组，确保按时按质完成，项目建成后引导村级制定好后续管理办法。

饮用水设施问题与生产生活密切相关。琅勃拉邦县象龙村的生活用水主要依靠流经村旁的南康河。由于南康河旱季提水困难且水质达不到饮用水标准，加之象龙村原有的自来水管已经老化无法使用，村民只能省吃俭用购买桶装饮用水。一个家庭每月至少需要 20 桶桶装水满足需求，折合人民币约 200 元，对于困难家庭来说，这是一笔不小的支出。为解决"饮水难"问题，中老减贫合作示范项目组成员和当地政府官员多次实地调研，并和项目村干部群众一起翻山越岭寻找水源，最终在距离村子 5 公里的双山寻找到干净的山泉水。在村民自愿参与的原则下，中国扶贫专家和老挝当地政府合力组织大家投工投劳，开挖、回填水沟 4 000 米，铺设水管 13 000 米，投入 5 000 多个工日，从双山引来符合饮用标准的山泉水，让当地农户告别买桶装水过日子的历史。饮用水问题的解决不仅促进了农村基础设施的建设，还改善了农户的生计环境，为接下来减贫任务的开展提供条件。

因地制宜、因贫施策，村民们最迫切需要什么，中国就援助什么。与象龙村相比，班索村发展面临的主要问题是交通设施建设。作为村庄交通要道的木质班索大桥，至今已经使用了十多年，破损严重，成为危桥，桥下是深约 20 米的河流，存在着极大的安全隐患。为消除安全隐患，项目组把班索村原有木板破损的危桥建设成为安全的班索大桥，将村里的居住区和耕作区连接起来，方便农户生产生活。基础设施不断完善后，如何提高生计条件成为下一个关注领域。班索村共有村民 2 000 余人、3 438 公顷土地，自然禀赋优良。但由于缺少资金和技术，农业基础设施落后，家家户户每年种植水田面积较小，只满足基本的生活需求，生产效率低且撂荒土地较多。针对当地粗放式的水稻种植现状，中国通过加强水利灌溉基础设施建设，加大技术培训，以合作社的形式，由能人带动，致力提高水稻单产，增加当地农民收入。

在完善基础设施的基础上，项目还包含两个村的技术培训、产业发展和交流合作。2018 年上半年，中老减贫示范合作项目已完成农户种植养殖、旅游培训等共 155 人次，项目管理人员培训 35 人次，老挝能人来华培训 10 人次；扶持 70 户中低收入家庭开展种植养殖活动①。基于象龙村旅游风景区基础，根据当地居民的需求，项目规划方案增加了微型加工业的扶持，以帮助他们发展家庭手工业，利用旅游资源带动特色手工艺品及周边产品销售。此外，中老双方还设立了"友好村"交流活动。自中老减贫示范合作项目开展以来，龙胜—琅勃拉邦"友好村"活动已经举办了两

---

① 韦继川，2018. 广西实施东亚减贫示范合作技术援助老挝项目见闻 [N]. 广西日报，05 - 30.

届。2019 年老挝"友好"项目琅勃拉邦县代表、村长代表、贫困户家庭代表共 12 人来到中国广西，通过座谈会、实地走访村干部、致富带头人、贫困农户，学习广西龙胜各族自治县脱贫攻坚的经验和做法。

6.3.2 经验启示

基础设施建设是当前澜湄减贫合作项目实施的重要领域，项目更加关注与受援国当地人民密切相关的民生工程。项目实施不仅仅改善了当地的物质条件，还注重提高当地村民的主体意识和责任感，培养和提升村民的管理能力，将中国的参与式扶贫、产业扶贫等扶贫经验和模式带到当地，发挥村民主人翁意识，使村民参与项目设计、规划、实施、监督和检查各环节中，激发村民的积极性和主动性。项目充分利用当地发展资源与优势产业，结合当地的发展诉求与瓶颈问题，完善产业发展最需要的基础设施。在打好发展基础的同时，培养本土人才和技术力量，逐步让村民走上自力更生、独立发展的道路。

6.4 抓技术推广促产业兴旺，助力乡村脱贫致富

澜湄流域自然条件优越、土地肥沃，劳动力成本相对低廉，农业资源禀赋优良，是亚洲乃至全球最具发展潜力的地区之一，也是世界粮食、糖料作物、热带经济作物主产区。湄公河五国是传统农业国家，农业是经济支柱产业，发展潜力巨大，但是苦于没有技术支持和指导，潜力并没有得到应有的发挥。技术示范项目可以帮助农民更好地种植农作物，提升作物品质，在获得农业经济效益的同时实现收入增加。中国凭借地缘和技术优势，致力湄公河国家农业技术示范与推广，针对当地情况，开展各领域合作，帮助建立现代农业产业体系、生产体系、经营体系，通过发展壮大乡村产业，激发各国农村活力，实现脱贫致富。

6.4.1 中国援老挝金花村有机蔬菜种植区项目案例

2013 年，中国广西农业职业技术学院承担起在老挝金花村建设中国—老挝合作农作物优良品种试验站的重要任务。2015 年，中国国际扶

贫中心和广西外资扶贫项目管理中心委托广西农业职业技术学院,依托该院在老挝金花村承建的中国—老挝合作农作物优良品种试验站,开展中老合作社区减贫示范项目建设。2019 年又在金花村启动了中国—老挝减贫合作社区示范项目有机蔬菜种植区,通过与企业合作,在金花村成功开展了大棚有机蔬菜种植示范,大幅提高当地农民的收入。

金花村位于湄公河支流南俄河边,一到雨季,水流四溢,农地经常被淹。村民缺乏农业设施和技术,靠一年一季的水稻种植为生。中国专家在经过详细的实地调研后发现,万象市及周边蔬菜市场供不应求,金花村又有种植蔬菜的天然优势,可以作为未来发展的方向。2016 年,在村内建成 5 栋蔬菜大棚,交给 10 家农户进行示范,专家技术人员现场教授实用先进的种植技术,农户通过专业翻译转述学习,大有收获。项目还开展灌溉设备建设,提供种植技术指导,联系蔬菜经销商,制定大棚租赁管理机制,帮助村庄建设蔬菜基地。

2013—2018 年,试验站试种了 160 多个农作物品种,从中筛选出适合老挝种植推广的农作物优良品种 48 个,其中果树 11 个、瓜菜 31 个、水稻 2 个、玉米 2 个、花生 1 个、牧草 1 个,示范推广农作物面积 2 833 公顷,培训农业技术人员超过 1 000 人次。2013 年底,在广西率先研发南方无土栽培反季节哈密瓜技术取得成功的专家,应邀到金花村负责指导哈密瓜种植,在短短 3 个多月时间内就将哈密瓜试种成功,使得试验站成为老挝唯一的哈密瓜种植基地。随后通过举办技术培训班的方式,将哈密瓜种植技术传授给老挝农业技术人员和种植户。除了哈密瓜,中国专家还在当地推广水稻、玉米、火龙果种植等实用先进的农业技术。同时,试验站还接纳老挝高校 230 名毕业生实习并提供培训指导,推荐 7 名老挝农业技术员到中国公费留学。如今,试验站已成为老挝农业技术推广的重要平台,使金花村从默默无闻的小村庄发展成了小有名气的蔬菜基地①。

6.4.2 其他技术交流与产业合作项目案例

2018 年澜湄合作专项基金支持贵州山地特色农业技术助推澜湄区域

---

① 简文湘,2019. 志同而气和,相交更相亲:"走东盟万里,看丝路画卷"之老挝篇 [N]. 广西日报,09 - 10.

减贫示范，研究重点包括贵州特色辣椒品种、珍稀食用菌、红心猕猴桃、金钗石斛在澜湄流域的示范栽培，以及中国西南地区特色农业技术在澜湄流域推广的经济效益评估。2014 年起，中国广西在湄公河流域设立了中国（广西）—东盟农作物优良品种试验站项目，为相关国家引进农作物试验试种 300 多个，筛选适合当地种植的品种和提纯复壮品种共 30 个，累计示范推广面积超过 6 万亩。此外，澜湄国家跨境动物疫病防控技术交流与合作项目、澜湄联合增殖放流项目等，都对深化次区域技术交流合作、促进乡村产业发展、提升农民收入起到重要推动作用。

为促进农村产品销售流通，还开展跨境电子商务相关培训，推动电子商务与农村发展相联结。2016 年 6 月，大湄公河次区域（GMS）跨境电子商务合作平台企业联盟在云南昆明成立，各国企业可以在平台上注册企业电子商务网站，开展 B2B 及 B2C 电子商务。2019 年 3 月，湄公学院举办了澜湄国家农村电子商务发展区域模块化培训，通过各种单元课程，把最新的农村电商发展知识与技能教授给各国参与者，助力当地农村电子商务发展。

6.4.3 经验启示

为促进澜湄区域技术合作和产业发展，技术示范项目关注产业链前后端，侧重生产和销售两个环节，推动技术和产品升级发展。一方面，充分发挥澜湄区域各国的农业资源优势，针对农业技术短板，进行精准合作。中国云南、广西、贵州等边境省区农业技术适用性较高，可实现技术推广和应用效果在澜湄区域最大化。同时，结合当地农业生产条件，研发出适合当地生长的高品质农产品类型，帮助培养当地农产品品牌，为实现可持续发展提供条件。另一方面，为促进产品升级、流通，将合作拓展至产品销售环节，通过村企对接和电子商务平台建设，为农产品销售开辟了新的途径，多角度促进产业发展与振兴。

（中国农业大学人文与发展学院　唐丽霞、张一珂）

III

区域篇

7 中国云南省农业发展与澜湄农业合作进展

7.1 农业发展概况

7.1.1 总体发展情况及特点

在中国农业农村部的大力支持下，近年，云南省大力推进农业现代化，全力推进乡村振兴战略实施，加快推进农业绿色发展，稳步推进农业农村改革，乡村振兴实现良好开局，农业农村现代化迈出坚实步伐，全省农业农村实现了高质量跨越式发展。

（1）农民收入迈上新台阶。 全省农村常住居民人均可支配收入保持持续较快增长，2018 年首次突破万元大关，达到 10 768 元，同比增长 9.2%，增速高于全国农村居民人均可支配收入 0.4 个百分点。

（2）农业生产能力再上新水平。 2018 年全省农林牧渔业增加值达 2 552.78 亿元，同比增长 6.3%，居全国第 2 位。粮食播种面积 6 261.9 万亩，产量 1 861 万吨，综合生产能力实现连续 3 年稳步提高。划定水稻、小麦粮食生产功能区和重要农产品生产保护区 964 万亩，完成高标准农田建设 243.9 万亩。主要农产品供给稳定，农产品加工产值与农业总产值之比提高到 1.11∶1。农产品出口额 38.75 亿美元，连续多年稳居西部第一，继续保持全省第一大类出口商品地位。

（3）农村发展呈现新面貌。 全省 65 个县（市）域完成乡村建设规划。启动实施农村人居环境整治，农村生活垃圾收集处理率达 88.37%，农村生活污水处理率达 26%，新（改）建冲水公厕 1 870 座，新增无害化卫生户厕 45.92 万座，卫生户厕普及率达到 72.92%。

（4）产业扶贫迈出新步伐。新型经营主体带贫扶贫帮贫路子更加明晰，贫困户"绑"专业合作社、专业合作社"绑"龙头企业的"双绑"机制更加完善。全省与贫困户建立利益联结机制的新型经营主体达 3.3 万个，覆盖 612 万人，占贫困人口的 89.3%，产业覆盖面不断扩大，带贫益贫能力明显提升。

（5）绿色发展引领新格局。"绿色食品牌"打造点燃高原特色现代农业绿色发展新引擎，茶叶等 8 个优势产业农业产值、综合产值分别增长 10.7%、15.5%，实现量效齐增。首次开展十大名茶、十大名花、十大名果、十大名菜等绿色食品"十大名品"评选，深受广大群众欢迎，评选出的绿色食品"10 强企业""20 佳创新企业"，树立了一批云南农业企业标杆，在全国反响强烈。新认证绿色食品 428 个、有机农产品 665 个。全省主要农作物绿色防控覆盖率达 31%，化肥、农药使用量双双实现负增长。畜禽养殖禁养区划定等任务全面完成，畜禽粪污综合利用率达 76%，比全国高 6 个百分点。

（6）安全保障实现新提升。全省动物防疫整村推进乡镇覆盖率达 95.5%，高致病性禽流感、口蹄疫、小反刍兽疫免疫密度均达到 100%，马传染性贫血防控工作通过农业农村部达标考核和达标验收。农产品合格率保持在 96.6%，宾川县、嵩明县、麒麟区等 7 个县（区）通过第二批国家农产品质量安全县创建考核。

（7）农村改革孕育新动能。扎实推进涉农领域专项改革，圆满完成 13 项农业农村改革任务。完成承包土地确权面积 10 973.1 万亩，确权承包方 887.2 万个，颁发证书 855.9 万本、颁证率达 96.5%。农村集体产权制度改革、农村集体资产股份权能改革试点加快推进，农垦农场办社会职能改革在全国 35 个垦区中排名第 9，农业综合行政执法体制改革设计初具雏形，"放管服"改革不断深化。

7.1.2　主要经验做法

（1）明确发展思路。坚持以习近平新时代中国特色社会主义思想为指导，以全面建成小康社会为总体目标，以创新、协调、绿色、开放、共享的新发展理念为引领，大力推进农业农村现代化，全力推进乡村振兴战略实施，加快推进农业绿色发展，稳步推进农业农村改革，构建农业全方位对外开放格局。

（2）出台相关政策。 近年，云南省先后出台了《关于加快高原特色农业现代化实现全面小康目标的意见》《云南省人民政府办公厅关于培育壮大农业小巨人的意见》《中共云南省委云南省人民政府关于加快建设我国面向南亚东南亚辐射中心的实施意见》《云南省人民政府关于促进经济持续健康较快发展 22 条措施的意见》《培育绿色食品产业龙头企业鼓励投资办法》《推进云茶产业绿色发展实施意见》《云南省人民政府关于创建"一县一业"示范县加快打造世界一流"绿色食品牌"的指导意见》等政策性文件，聚焦 8 大优势特色产业，明确了"大产业、新平台、新主体"的发展思路，打造世界一流"绿色食品牌"，扩大和深化农业对外开放。

（3）落实相关措施。 坚持农业农村优先发展总方针，以实现农业农村现代化为总目标，以实施乡村振兴战略为总抓手，以农业供给侧结构性改革为主线，推进农业农村改革发展，加快建设面向南亚东南亚辐射中心，务实推进农业对外合作。

7.2 澜湄农业合作情况

7.2.1 合作进展及成效

（1）以顶层设计为核心，统筹农业对外合作。 首次澜湄合作国家领导人会议召开以来，云南省先后印发了关于促进农业对外合作的实施意见，编制了农业对外合作规划，明确了云南农业对外合作的指导思想、基本原则、目标任务和政策措施，并建立了云南农业对外合作联席会议机制，为云南农业参与澜湄农业合作提供了方向性、指导性、决策性依据。

（2）以机制建设为纽带，推进互利互信。 省、州市层面分别与相关澜湄国家签署了一系列合作协议，达成了共同开展农业综合开发的诸多共识，建立了大湄公河次区域农业科技交流合作组，成立了东南亚保护性农业协作网，有力地促进了云南与澜湄国家农业合作朝着健康、高效、可持续方向发展。

（3）以企业投资为重点，促进产业合作。 在国家"一带一路"倡议、加强农业供给侧结构性改革和《三亚宣言》的推动下，越来越多的农业企业参与澜湄农业合作。2018 年，云南省进行对外农业投资的企业为 144 家，同比增长 13.39%；在境外投资设立农业企业 164 家，同比增长 19.71%；对外农业累计投资额达 115 221.70 万美元，同比增长 39.14%；新增投资额为 19 269.4 万美元，同比增长 12.10%；对外投资企业资产总额 206 146.82 万美元，同比增长 117.54%。其中，老挝 68 家、缅甸 70 家、泰国 10 家、越南 5 家、柬埔寨 5 家，占全省对外农业投资企业总数的 96% 以上，雇佣外方人员 4.37 万人，雇佣外方人员工资总额为 1.06 亿美元，向东道国交纳税金达 953.93 万美元。

(4) 以境外农业科技示范园区为桥梁，推动技术合作。先后与柬埔寨、老挝、缅甸合作建设了 4 个农业科技示范园，积极开展优良品种种植示范、实用农业综合配套技术推广、农业技术人员培训等工作；边境州（市、县）在积极开展农业技术援助的同时，深入推进农业技术试验示范，不断拓展辐射中心农业效应；农业科研单位通过大湄公河次区域农业科技交流合作组，与周边国家交换试验品种 264 个、推广示范适宜品种 38 个、示范面积逾 10 万亩、培训相关国家的科技人员和农户超过 1 万人次；此外，云南农业职业技术学院挂牌设立的中国—缅甸农业技术培训中心，还为缅甸培训技术人员 72 人次，培训农民 2 000 余人，为提升澜湄国家的农业科技水平做出应有的努力。

(5) 以产销对接为抓手，推进优质农产品共享。一是立足高原丰富多样的资源优势，大力打造云南省"绿色食品牌"，持续建设农产品质量安全示范区，不断开发名特优农产品，截至 2018 年底，先后建成各级农产品质量安全示范区 10 个、总面积 144.56 万亩，其中国家级示范区 1 个（蒙自）、省级示范区 1 个（泸西）；二是瞄准澜湄国家等国内外市场，定期举办农博会、农交会、茶博会及全国"互联网＋"现代农业新技术和新农民创业创新博览会、云南省蔬菜产销对接大会等创新型、专业型、产业型展会等；三是积极组派赴东南亚、西亚、中东、欧洲和港澳台专场推介，全面开拓国内外市场。据统计，2018 年全省农产品出口金额达 38.75 亿美元，其中澜湄国家占 50% 以上，连续多年稳居西部第一，继续保持全省第一大类出口商品地位，产品已远销 110 多个国家和地区，主要出口品种为蔬菜、马铃薯、水果、咖啡、茶叶、动物及制品、花卉等。

（6）**以跨境动植物疫病联防联控为契机，构建安全屏障**。2018 年，一是促成了中老缅跨境动物疫病区域化管理试点项目的实施，累计完成投资 5 亿多元，目前德宏傣族景颇族自治州瑞丽市屠宰厂一体化试点项目已经投产试运行，西双版纳傣族自治州景洪市的屠宰厂一体化试点项目正在有序推进；二是圆满完成了澜沧江—湄公河区域国家跨境动物疫病防控技术交流与合作项目任务，通过疫病监测和传播风险研究，掌握主要跨境动物疫病传播风险，提出了解决的方案和建议，为澜湄国家制定跨境动物疫病防控对策和畜产品贸易政策提供了科学依据；三是与老越缅联合开展了病原学监测 3 500 份，在昆明、普洱、西双版纳、德宏等地举办国际兽医技术培训班 5 期，为老挝、缅甸、越南培训兽医技术人员 210 余人次，培训境外农民、农业企业人员及政府机构人员 250 余人次；四是进一步完成了老挝琅勃拉邦、丰沙里、乌多姆赛等 5 省的灭蝗后续工作。

（7）**以论坛为平台，造福基层农民**。积极落实澜湄合作领导人会议上的倡议，配合中国农业农村部组织召开了 2017 年度和 2018 年度两届澜湄合作村长论坛，参会人员共计 291 人次，发出《澜湄村社合作芒市倡议》，签署村村、村企、企企间的投资合作协议 11 份，村寨和企业与外方共签约金额超过 1.5 亿元，为五国村长提供了村寨合作、乡村建设、农业农村发展的交流合作平台。

7.2.2　经验做法

（1）**建立农业合作机制**。省级层面：云南省省农业农村厅先后与孟加拉国和斯里兰卡等国分别签署农业合作谅解备忘录；省级农业科研部门与柬埔寨、老挝、泰国、越南、缅甸等国签署了农业科技合作协议，成立了大湄公河次区域农业科技交流合作组。州市级层面：分别与邻国达成共建共识。云南省德宏等 8 个边境州市分别与缅甸、老挝、越南相继开展了跨境经济合作区建设；临沧等边境州市人民政府与缅甸政府签署了农业合作备忘录，双方将共同开展农业综合开发。

（2）**建立农业对外合作联席会议制度**。研究分析云南省农业对外合作面临的形势及发展趋势，制定农业对外合作的目标任务、发展战略、工作规划和指导意见，统筹协调省内各相关单位、各部门开展农业对外合作，研究提出农业对外合作政策建议，研究确定并督促落实农业对外合作举措，协调解决合作中遇到的困难和问题。

(3) 构建农业全方位合作格局。充分发挥云南的区位、技术优势，以湄公河国家为重点，完善农业合作机制、实施农业合作项目，引导农业境外投资，促进农产品贸易，推动科技合作，形成以政府为引导、企业为主体、科技为支撑的全方位、宽领域、多层次农业合作格局。

(4) 深化跨境农业合作。主动服务和融入"一带一路"倡议，围绕打造世界一流"绿色食品牌"，着力推进"大产业＋新主体＋新平台"发展模式和"科研＋种养＋加工＋流通"全产业链发展，鼓励省内企业深化与澜湄国家开展种植业、畜牧业、渔业跨境农业合作，实现互利共赢、共同发展。

7.3 下一步合作展望

7.3.1 合作思路

主动服务和融入国家"一带一路"倡议，紧密围绕打造大湄公河次区域经济合作新高地，面向南亚东南亚辐射中心的总体要求，以创新、协调、绿色、开放、共享的新发展理念为引领，以强化农业供给侧结构性改革、提升高原特色农业综合竞争力、拓展发展空间为目标，以培育开放型农业企业和建设开放式市场体系为重点，强化科技支撑和政府引导，促进形成"企业主动、市场拉动、科技带动、防控联动、政府推动"的农业对外合作"五动"局面，将高原特色农业打造成为云南省服务和融入"一带一路"倡议的先导产业，健全机制、优化布局、深化合作，努力推进澜湄农业合作发展进程。

7.3.2 合作目标

力争到 2020 年，云南省高原特色农产品世界知名度显著提升；力争培育一批具有一定销售收入、国际竞争力和技术优势的开放型农业企业；以区域性国际农产品交易中心、物流中心、期货交易市场和农机生产基地为支点的开放式市场体系初步建成；农业对外投资年度规模扩大到 1.5 亿美元以上；多层次的农业科技合作体系进一步完善，云南省优势农业技术加速输出，优势农作物品种在境外较大范围推广；动植物疫病联防联控体系趋于健全；高原特色外向型现代农业产业体系基本形成，农业对外合作规模质量水平迈上新台阶。

到 2022 年，力争支持大型跨国涉农企业开展对外合作，形成大企业带动、中小企业跟进的农业对外开放企业集群，云南省高原特色农业综合竞争力显著提升；力争区域性农产品交易中心、物流中心、期货交易市场和农机生产基地辐射南亚、东南亚和我国西南及长江经济带区域，高原特色农产品开放式市场体系的资源调配能力显著增强；边境动植物疫病联防联控体系全面建成，跨境农业产业经济带初步建成。云南省农业"走出去"发展成为增进我国与周边国家友谊的重要力量。

7.3.3 合作任务

（1）**着力优化布局，明确对外合作总体思路。**布局突出近远结合、各有侧重。"近"要面向周边国家和地区，支持企业以资金和技术为主"走出去"；"远"要瞄准中东、欧洲和北美等国家，以产品为主"走出去"，实现互利共赢。

（2）**着力培育农业合作主体，构建开放型企业梯队。**打造一批综合效益好、带动作用强的农业龙头企业，鼓励省内开放型企业与农业企业"国家队"合作，组建农业"走出去"企业联盟，提升云南农业产业对外开放水平。

（3）**着力构建开放式市场体系，增强区域市场影响力。**构建辐射内外的重要农产品交易中心、物流中心等国际农产品交易枢纽；鼓励云南省内企业在边境建设农产品加工贸易园区；加强区域特色农产品跨境电商平台和营销体系建设。

（4）**着力打造境外产业经济带，培育产业发展动力。**加强动植物种质资源、优势动植物品种和农产品加工仓储流通环节合作，鼓励云南涉农企业在境外合作建立农产品生产、加工和储运基地，推进农资、农机装备对外合作。

（5）着力深化农业科技交流合作，占领产业技术高地。建立多层次的农业科技交流平台，加强对境外农业生产技术人员和农户的培训。加强农业信息科技合作，推进重要环节技术标准对接。

（6）着力加强动植物疫病防控，保障农业公共安全。推进动植物疫病跨境联防联控体系建设及跨境动物疫病防控区域化试点工作，保障区域范围内农业公共安全。

（7）着力加强人才培养，构建农业对外合作人才储备队伍。培养一批懂农业、通外语、善管理的国际化复合型人才队伍，积极参加中国农业农村部举办的专题性特色培训班，提高农业外事外经部门干部的实际工作能力。

（云南省农业农村厅　胡新梅、刘庆生）

8 中国广西壮族自治区农业发展与澜湄农业合作进展

8.1 农业发展概况

广西自然条件优越，温光水热土等资源丰富。近年，广西围绕资源优势和生态特色，培育壮大了一大批区域特色明显、产业集聚度较高、比较效益突出的农业优势产业带和产业群集，主要农产品总产持续增长，在全国位居前列。广西粮食生产连续多年稳定发展，保持在150亿千克左右；糖料蔗、蚕茧总产持续增长，连续多年稳居全国第一，分别占全国总产的60%、50%以上。蔬菜产量达到3 073万吨，是全国最重要的"南菜北运"基地和最大的秋冬菜生产基地。双孢蘑菇产量创全国"三连冠"，红椎菌产量占全国80%以上；是全国木薯种植第一大省（区）和全国第二大中药材产区。园林水果面积2 067万亩，2018年产量达1 790多万吨，实现从多年全国第二到全国第一的飞跃，其中柑橘、柿子、芒果、火龙果、百香果产量持续保持全国第一。茶叶产量、品质持续提升，广西第一早春茶品牌名闻天下，梧州六堡茶通过茶船古道和海上丝绸之路远销东南亚，茉莉花茶产量占全国80%以上、世界60%以上。全区猪牛羊禽肉类总产418.4万吨，水产品产量330万吨，均排名全国前十，对虾、罗非鱼总产量分别居全国第二、第三位。2018年，第一产业增加值3 114.42亿元，比2017年增长5.6%，为2013年以来增速最快的一年；农村居民人均可支配收入12 435元，增速居全国第二位。

8.2 农业国际合作情况

(1) 农业引资引智稳步推进。 广西积极争取政策项目支持，加大农业对外招商引资力度，搭建农业合作平台，直接引进一批农业企业和项目落户广西发展。2018 年，广西新引进境内农业项目 415 个，项目签约金额 621.5 亿元，同比增长 15.7%。积极组织实施国际金融组织贷款项目，截至 2018 年，共实施了 7 个农业外资项目，总投资 28.82 亿元，其中利用外资约 1.77 亿美元。在引进国外资金的同时，广西重视农业引技引智工作，先后实施罗汉果原料供应链的提升、柑橘新品种引进、选育及示范推广等一大批农业引技项目，举办外国专家广西行等农业引智专题活动，有效促进了广西农业产业发展。

(2) 农产品贸易逐步提升。 广西大力支持优势农产品出口基地和出口农产品质量安全示范区建设，通过多种渠道搭建农产品国际贸易平台，推荐企业对外注册，不断增强广西农产品在国际市场上的竞争能力，有效促进了广西农产品出口贸易发展。2018 年，广西农产品进出口总额 75.33 亿美元，其中出口 21.05 亿美元，同比增长 5.11%。广西农产品出口目的地达 130 多个，品种达 500 多种，主要有生猪、蔬菜、水产品、茶叶、水果、种子、中药材、饲料、竹木草制品等，其中养殖罗非鱼产品出口居全国第三位。目前，广西出口食品农产品质量安全示范区达到 20 个，累计实现产值约 36.3 亿美元，出口创汇约 21.6 亿美元。

(3) 农业科技交流日益加深。 广西农业科技国际交流与合作的领域和范围日趋广泛，涵盖了遗传育种、农业生物技术、作物病虫害综合防治、畜禽疫病防治与控制、农业信息技术和农产品加工等多个领域。相继实施了援建埃塞俄比亚农业示范中心、援柬埔寨农业促进中心技术合作、中国（广西）—东盟农作物优良品种试验站、文莱深海网箱养殖等项目，从技术示范和推广入手，吸引广西本土企业进驻合作发展，逐步延伸产后处理、精深加工、物流仓储及贸易等产业链，成效较为明显。与此同时，广西成立了国际糖业科技协会、桂台农业发展与技术交流协会、中国—东盟农业科技创新联盟，通过举办技术研讨会和培训班、建立示范基地和联合实验室、外派专家等方式，积极与有关国家和地区开展农业科技交流与合作。

（4）农业对外投资步伐加快。广西农业对外投资主要集中在"一带一路"沿线国家，重点包括越南、柬埔寨、缅甸、老挝等东盟国家。在备案的 45 个农业境外投资项目中，34 个项目分布在东盟国家，占 75.6%；涵盖种植业、农副产品加工与贸易、畜牧业养殖等领域，其中种植业项目占据半壁江山，其次为农副产品加工与贸易项目，占比 25% 左右。截至 2018 年底，广西"走出去"农业企业 102 家，协议投资金额 31.4 亿美元，投资流量居全国第四位。2018 年"走出去"农业企业新增投资金额居全国第七位。民营企业成为广西农业"走出去"的主要力量，民营企业"走出去"农业投资项目占全部农业对外投资的 97.3%。

8.3　澜湄农业合作情况

8.3.1　合作进展

澜湄合作是澜沧江—湄公河沿岸中国、柬埔寨、泰国、老挝、缅甸、越南六国共同创建的新型次区域合作机制，是"一带一路"倡议和中国—东盟合作的重要组成部分。近年，广西积极发挥自身区位、资源、平台等优势，积极参与澜湄农业交流合作，取得较好成效。

（1）以"两站"（中国广西—东盟农作物优良品种试验站、东盟农作物优良品种广西试验站）**建设为抓手，双边农业科技交流合作不断提升。**2014 年至今，从自治区本级部门预算中共安排 3 600 万元用于在老挝、越南、柬埔寨、缅甸等澜湄国家建设中国（广西）—东盟农作物优良品种试验站项目。目前，位于老挝、越南、柬埔寨 3 个试验站项目已建设完成并通过验收。试验站在东盟国家试种来自中国蔬菜、水稻等农作物新品种 750 多个，筛选出适合当地种植的品种近 150 个，示范展示面积 2.78 万公顷，累计示范推广农作物优良品种面积超过 500 万亩；这些从中国引进的农作物品种，通过配套先进适用技术和管理模式，表现出产量高、品质优、效益好等优点。特别是产量和效益方面，试验站引进试验示范的农作物品种普遍比当地种植品种增产 20%～50%，亩增收 20% 以上。通过试验站平台，培训了当地农业管理、技术人员、农民和农业院校学生共 8 700 多人次。

为实现农业科技双向交流合作，在区内建设 2 个东盟农作物优良品种广西试验站，为东盟国家优良品种进入中国市场提供展示交流平台。同时，成功举办了 2019 年中国（广西）—东盟蔬菜新品种博览会，集中展示 1 000 多个蔬菜品种，其中来自越南、泰国、柬埔寨、缅甸等东盟国家品种 44 个。两站项目的建设引起了各方高度重视和关注，项目所在国领导人、农业农村部和广西壮族自治区领导先后到越南、柬埔寨试验站考察指导并给予了充分肯定。

同时，组织了广西万川种业有限公司、广西恒宝丰农业发展有限公司等企业承担实施澜湄合作专项基金项目——水稻绿色增产技术试验示范项目建设，在柬埔寨、缅甸、老挝、越南开展水稻新品种引进和示范，建立水稻绿色增产技术试验示范基地，优化组装适合当地的水稻绿色增产技术，开展稻田综合种养模式试验，有效促进了双边农业科技合作，效果良好。如柬埔寨项目采用水稻机械穴直播新技术，降低单位面积用种量，提高田间通风透光性能，有效降低病虫危害程度，对比减少 30% 的农药使用量，每亩比原来增产 25.9%、增收节支达 159.5 元；缅甸项目通过集中育苗培育壮秧、直播、抛秧等方式，平均每亩减少 3 个人工；通过田间投入使用振频杀虫灯和黄板，统一病虫害防控管理，减少农药施用量，每亩增产 10.2%、综合增效 210 元。老挝项目组装推广集中育秧、机插秧、水气平衡、"三控"栽培、精准施肥、稻草还田、重大病虫害综合治理等技术，建立标准化水稻生产种植技术标准。经组织专家现场测定，每亩增产 47.4%、增收 120 元。越南项目开展水稻直播栽培试验示范，经越南北江省科学技术厅先进技术应用中心组织技术专家现场检查见证，每亩比原来增产 10.3%、增加经济效益 112 元。

此外，广西还支持高等院校和科研院所发挥技术优势，组织开展高层次农业人才交流，参与百名东盟杰出青年科学家来华入桂工作计划。以中国—东盟农业技术培训中心和中国（广西）—东盟农作物优良品种试验站为平台，广西重点开展面向东盟国家技术和管理人员培训，"十二五"期间共为越南、老挝、柬埔寨、缅甸等国家举办研修和培训班 60 多期，培训人员超过 3 000 人次。

(2) 以"两区"（境外农业合作示范区和境内农业对外开放合作试验

区）建设为重点，双边农业投资合作不断提升。2018 年初，广西启动建设中国（广西）—越南农业合作示范区、中国（广西）—柬埔寨农业合作示范区和凭祥农业对外开放合作试验区的省级"两区"创建试点，搭建了内外联动、双向驱动的农业产业合作平台。其中，凭祥试验区结合跨境劳务合作试点、边贸国检试验区、沿边金融综合改革试验区建设，推动相关政策先行先试，从劳动力供给、贸易通关和投资便利等方面加大对农业对外开放的支持。目前，凭祥农业对外开放合作试验区引进了盐津铺子、增泰农牧业、万川种业等 9 家企业入驻发展，涉外企业 2 家。中国（广西）—柬埔寨农业合作示范区完成投资 1.2 亿元，初步建成集水稻新品种研发、生产加工、养殖于一体的生态循环农业产业园，总产稻谷 1 万多吨、产值超过 200 万美元。通过柬埔寨农业合作示范区平台服务，金边万宝农业国际投资公司、深圳诺普信公司金边分公司、广西水产科学研究院等多家企业和单位已引进入驻园区或签订入园协议，合作开展农业加工、水产科研及技术推广等业务。中国（广西）—越南农业合作示范区引进越南中央种子股份公司入驻园区，合作成立农作物研究中心。同时，与安徽桐城市亚汇印务有限公司达成进驻园区发展意向。通过承担实施中国（广西）—越南农业合作示范区项目，广西万川种业有限公司与越南中央种子股份公司签订了合作协议，与越南中央果菜总公司及谅山、宣光、高平等省种子企业建立了长期合作关系，企业每年向越南出口销售水稻、蔬菜等种子约 2 000 吨，出口额 6 000 多万元，成为国内种子出口东盟国家数量最多的企业，获评为全国首批农业对外合作百强企业。2018 年，广西推动"两区"建设工作获中国农业农村部肯定并作为典型向全国其他省进行推介。

在"两区"平台辐射带动下，广西一批民营企业和科研单位联合抱团"走出去"，增强了农业"走出去"的科技创新能力和抵御"走出去"风险能力。

（3）突出产业安全，跨境合作亮点纷呈。一直以来，广西高度重视边境农业合作。2008 年开始，广西与越南广宁、谅山、高平等省农业与农村发展厅建立了厅长联席会议制度，并已召开 4 次联席会议，共同磋商解决了一些重大合作问题。先后与越南广宁、谅山等边境省植保、兽医分局等部门签署跨境动植物疫病防控合作备忘录，并在备忘录框架下组织实施了中越边境重大动物疫病防控试验站建设技术支持、中国广西—越南广宁植物病虫害防控等项目，向越南边境省份赠送虫情测报灯，援助建设重大动物疫病防控试验站（诊断实验室），积极推动与越南广宁、高平、谅山等边境省开展跨境动植物病虫害防控合作，提升了越南动植物疫病疫情防控监测能力和水平，也为中国做好动植物病虫害监测预警和防控提供了科学依据。

8.3.2　面临的困难和问题

（1）政策及项目扶持持续性不够。与云南省相比，广西在开展澜湄农业合作方面得到国家层面扶持的政策及项目较少，近三年仅于 2017 年获批承担实施澜湄合作专项基金支持水稻绿色增产技术试验示范项目。加上广西经济发展相对滞后，可以安排用于扶持农业对外合作的项目经费偏少，政策支持呈不断下降的趋势，扶持项目和政策缺乏稳定性和持续性。

（2）联合推动澜湄农业合作机制尚未形成。尽管广西已建立农业对外合作厅际联席会议制度，但由于缺乏对各成员单位的考核激励和约束机制，目前尚无法将金融、财税、保险、通关、营商等方面的资源进行整合，各有关部门的政策、项目及平台等资源较为分散，难以形成联动支持的合力。

（3）企业对外合作能力有待提升。广西农业存在产业大而不强、大而不优，小规模高成本分散经营，以及农业科技创新能力不强等问题；农业对外合作参与主体存在层次偏低、国别集中、模式单一、自主性弱等问题。这些问题导致广西农业在国际市场竞争力偏弱，品牌效应尚未凸显，企业借助直接投资在整合全球资源过程中缺乏优势。目前广西"走出去"企业有 97 家，对外合作比较活跃，但多以民营企业为主，规模普遍较小，缺乏风险预警、控制和防范能力。开拓国际市场的能力仍然较弱，缺乏跨国经营管理人才和复合型人才，投资领域大多集中在较为初级的种养环节，仍以依附国内市场为着眼点，制约了企业的发展。

（4）农产品出口贸易层次和水平有待提高。目前广西与澜湄国家农产品贸易仍以边境小额贸易和互市贸易形式为主，多为低层次的"买进卖出"的过境贸易，农产品精深加工和服务等高层次合作较少。与此同时，广西农产品出口对象主要为越南，对外市场过于单一，农产品贸易多元化程度低。

8.4 下一步合作展望

8.4.1 总体思路

广西是中国唯一与东盟国家既有陆地接壤又有海上通道的省份，在中国与东盟、澜湄交流合作中具有重要的战略地位和作用。下一步，广西将从农业科技、双向投资、农产品贸易及能力建设等方面加强与澜湄国家进行务实交流合作。

8.4.2 重点任务

（1）**探索与创新农业合作机制政策。**突出市场需求和企业主体，在国家对外合作战略引导下，创新和完善广西对外合作体制机制，制定出台广西农业对外合作专项工作规划，在澜湄地区布局建设一批重大合作项目及合作平台。积极推动"一带一路"农业合作，探索在中国（广西）自由贸易试验区内开展跨境农业合作相关先试先行政策。

（2）**拓展澜湄市场，助力农产品出口贸易。**实施广西特色农产品出口提升行动，建设一批出口农产品生产基地，继续举办中国—东盟农业国际合作展、中国（广西）—东盟农产品贸易对接会、广西农业"丝路行"等经贸活动，搭建区域农产品贸易合作平台。支持广西农产品出口企业及行业协会开展国际广告促销、产品推介等国际市场营销活动。

（3）**加快"两区"建设，助推农业"走出去""请进来"双向合作。**坚持企业主导、市场化运作的原则，支持企业在澜湄国家建设一批以稻米、果蔬、畜牧业、渔业等为重点产业的境外农业合作示范区，突出示范引领带动作用，带动国内涉农企业抱团走出去。同时，在广西沿边地区布局建设一批农业对外开放合作试验区，引进、借鉴澜湄国家农业先进经验、技术和模式，搭建农业对外合作服务平台，培育一批具有国际竞争力的跨国农业企业集团。

（4）**聚焦产业薄弱环节，加强农业引资引智。**充分发挥广西区位、资源、环境和市场优势，加大农业利用外资力度，推动开展跨国公司暨世界

500强"八桂行"活动，积极承接国际农业援助项目，争取多双边优惠贷款和无偿援助项目，服务广西农业产业升级。针对广西农业发展的薄弱环节和农业生产中急需解决的问题，加大先进产业、品种、技术、人才和管理经验的引进和借鉴，加强农业引智合作，助力广西脱贫攻坚和乡村振兴。

8.4.3 具体项目计划

(1) 澜湄次区域农作物优良品种试验站建设。项目由广西"走出去"企业在澜湄国家开展农作物新品种的引进、筛选、示范和推广，先进生产技术和病虫害联合防控技术的研究和示范，种质资源的收集和利用，人员交流及培训等。

(2) 中国（广西)—东盟国家农业合作示范区建设。实施一批境外农业合作示范区项目，强化示范区基础设施建设、建立境外农业支持服务机制、建设质量安全标准管理体系、引进并展示中国农作物优良品种等。发挥好示范区引领和服务作用，吸引国内外企业抱团进驻园区合作发展，在当地国建立起服务双边农业交流合作的农业产业链。

(3) 举办中国—东盟农业国际合作展、农业国际合作论坛。中国—东盟博览会期间，继续在广西南宁举办中国—东盟农业国际合作展和中国—东盟农业国际合作论坛系列活动。合作展由中国各省（自治区、直辖市）农业企业参展，邀请澜湄国家农业部门组团参加，重点展示推介各国及地区名特农产品，推介多双边合作项目。论坛活动邀请包括澜湄在内的东盟各国和地区官员、专家学者和企业代表围绕农业科技、投资、贸易及人员交流等方面开展互动交流。

(4) 澜湄次区域水稻绿色增产技术试验示范。由中国广西"走出去"企业在澜湄区域国家开展水稻新品种引进与示范、水稻绿色增产技术改良、稻田综合种养模式试验、人员培训与展示推介等。

(5) 组织畜牧养殖标准化生产东盟培训班。利用中国—东盟农业培训中心平台，由广西农业职业技术学院在广西南宁举办一期畜牧养殖标准化生产业务培训班，帮助澜湄区域国家提高畜牧养殖从业者业务工作水平。

（广西壮族自治区农业农村厅　韦庆芳、陈继群）

9 | 中国海南省农业发展
与澜湄农业合作进展

9.1 农业发展概况

农业是海南的基础产业和优势产业。凭借其优越的热带农业自然资源，海南被赋予打造成为"国家热带现代农业基地"的发展使命[①]，同时致力"一中心两区三基地"（即国家热带农业科学中心，琼海农业对外开放合作试验区、农业绿色发展先行区，国家南繁科研育种基地、全球动植物种质资源引进中转基地）建设。

2018 年，海南农林牧渔业总产值 1 535.73 亿元，比 2017 年增长 3.15%。其中，农业产值 729.51 亿元，比 2017 年增长 3.12%；林业产值 110.44 亿元，比 2017 年增长 2.53%；牧业产值 245.32 亿元，比 2017 年增长 0.11%；渔业产值 387.44 亿元，比 2017 年增长 3.94%；农林牧渔专业及辅助性活动产值 63.02 亿元，比 2017 年增长 12.70%。蔬菜园艺类作物，水果、坚果、饮料和香料作物，以及海水产品，这三个类别的产值均超过 300 亿元，分别占农林牧渔业总产值的 19.76%、19.89% 和 22.70%。蔬菜、水果、海产品成为拉动海南农业产值增长的主要力量，体现了海南独特的热带农业气候资源及海洋资源禀赋优势。

截至 2018 年末，海南农业机械总动力 560.30 万千瓦，比 2017 年增长 0.6%；农用拖拉机 8.75 万台，下降 2.0%；农用运输车 3.53 万辆，

---

① 2018 年 4 月 13 日，习近平总书记在庆祝海南建省办经济特区 30 周年大会上发表重要讲话指出："海南是我国唯一的热带省份。要实施乡村振兴战略，发挥热带地区气候优势，做强做优热带特色高效农业，打造国家热带现代农业基地，进一步打响海南热带农产品品牌。"

下降 4.1%。全年化肥施用量（折纯）47.54 万吨，下降 7.4%；农田水利有效灌溉面积 18.50 万公顷，下降 4.6%。

9.2 农业国际合作情况

9.2.1 农产品进出口贸易情况

近年，海南农产品进出口贸易额相对平稳，稳中有降，保持了绝对的农产品贸易顺差。农产品出口方面，2018 年，海南农产品出口总额 33.48 亿美元，比 2017 年减少 6.27%，农产品出口占所有商品出口总额的 11.24%。出口农产品以冻鱼和冻鱼片等海产品为主，其余种类产品，尤其是具有自然资源禀赋优势的海南热带水果、蔬菜等农产品，受限于保鲜技术、运输时效问题，出口额均较小，农产品出口的结构单一。农产品进口方面，农产品进口总额 14.51 亿美元，比 2017 年减少 5.65%，农产品进口占所有商品进口总额的 2.64%，说明海南农产品的自给率较高。进口农产品种类包括冻鱼、水果、粮食等种类，并以鲜、干水果及坚果的进口为主。

9.2.2 农业使用外资情况

海南积极吸引外资，出台了《关于扩大对外开放积极利用外资的实施意见》《外商投资项目核准和备案服务指南》等政策。2018 年 9 月 6 日，美国美安康质量认证中心与海南农业农村厅签约开展农业标准化体系建设、热带水果保鲜技术研发、深加工价值链提升和产销平台对接等领域合作[1]。此外，海南省农业农村厅还以自贸区优惠政策吸引澳大利亚纯鲜美（海南自贸区）农业发展有限公司中国总部在海口落户，落地琼澳热带生态农业合作示范基地项目等 2 个农业项目[2]。

2018 年，海南与外商共签订农、林、牧、渔业投资项目 18 个，占全部行业签订总项目的 10.78%；农、林、牧、渔业合同外资金额 7 141 万

① 王心武，2018. 26 家国际知名企业与海南签署战略合作框架协议 外资企业看好海南 农业和物流多个领域合作加速 [J]. 中国战略新兴产业（37）：65.
② 傅人意，2018. 省农业农村厅深入推进农业供给侧结构性改革 让海南农业更强农村更美农民更富 [N]. 海南日报，12-29.

美元，仅占全部行业合同外资金额的 1.39％；农、林、牧、渔业实际利用外资 558 万美元，仅占全部行业实际利用外资的 0.75％[①]。

9.2.3　农业对外开放重点建设项目

农业农村部 2018 年印发的《农业农村部贯彻落实〈中共中央国务院关于支持海南全面深化改革开放的指导意见〉实施方案》重点支持海南自贸区总体方案涉农事项"一中心两区三基地"建设。海南根据农业农村部印发的《农业对外合作"两区"建设方案的通知》，推动海南农业对外合作"两区"建设，即国家（琼海）农业对外开放合作试验区和中—柬热带生态农业合作示范区建设。

在推进国家（琼海）农业对外开放合作试验区建设方面，海南正在建设全球动植物种质资源引进中转基地和国家南繁科研育种基地，以及种业国际贸易中心和南繁科技城，发展面向"一带一路"国家和地区的种业贸易。同时，海南还将提高口岸便利化程度和检验检疫水平、拓展保税储存等功能，吸引国际知名种业企业以在海南设立区域总部等形式开展种业贸易。

在推进中—柬热带生态农业合作示范区建设方面，以海南顶益绿洲生态农业有限公司为建设主体，按照"一区多园 N 基地"的思路，拟投资 142 亿元，计划用 10 年时间（2017—2026 年），分三期建设。第一期为产业示范园建设期（2017—2020 年），拟投资约 18 亿人民币；第二期为产业园（全产业链）建设期（2021—2024 年），拟投资约 114 亿人民币；第三期为示范区全域农业观光旅游建设期（2025—2026 年），拟投资 10 亿元人民币[②]。

---

① 海南统计年鉴委员会，2019. 海南统计年鉴 2019 ［M］. 北京：中国统计出版社.
② 一区：柬埔寨—中国热带生态农业合作示范区；多园：柬—中香蕉产业示范园、柬—中胡椒产业示范园、柬—中热带水果产业示范园、柬—中橡胶产业示范园、柬—中木薯产业示范园、柬—中畜禽养殖产业示范园、柬—中农业科技示范园、冷链物流园等；N 基地：香蕉种植基地、胡椒种植基地、香水椰子种植基地、腰果种植基地、芒果种植基地、榴莲种植基地、柚子种植基地、种质资源保护繁育基地、肉牛养殖基地、生猪养殖基地、母猪繁育基地、家禽养殖基地、农产品加工基地等。中国国际贸易促进委员会，2020. 柬埔寨—中国热带生态农业合作示范区园区介绍 ［EB/OL］. ［12 - 22］. https://oip.ccpit.org/ent/parks - introduces/47.

9.3 澜湄农业合作情况

9.3.1 主要进展

(1) 参与澜湄农业合作机制共建。澜湄合作首次领导人会议在海南三亚召开，也说明了海南参与澜湄农业合作的必要性。海南利用博鳌亚洲论坛的平台优势，主动参与到澜湄国家命运共同体建设中，开展与澜湄国家的农业技术交流与农业能力建设合作。海南还利用其旅游文化优势，通过加深与澜湄国家互利共赢机制建设，推进国际农业的合作与发展。海南分别于 2016 年、2018 年举办澜湄国家旅游城市（三亚）合作论坛，不仅推动三亚与澜湄国家旅游城市间在沟通机制、旅游项目等方面的务实合作，还探讨以旅游文化带动和促进农业、经贸等领域的共同发展。

(2) 推动中—柬热带生态农业合作示范区建设。海南与澜湄各国有较好的农业合作基础，其中，与柬埔寨的农业合作成效最为显著。早在 2010 年，海南与柬埔寨磅湛省就缔结了友好省关系，双方积极开展农产品贸易、农业项目投资等多领域合作。在中—柬热带生态农业合作示范区被认定为我国首批境外农业对外合作示范区建设试点后，海南以"一区多园 N 基地"的思路分阶段推进中—柬热带生态农业合作示范区建设。据海南省农业农村厅统计，截至 2019 年 9 月末，在柬埔寨桔井省已建成 5 000 亩香蕉核心示范基地、500 亩胡椒核心示范基地、1 000 亩木薯核心示范基地、2 000 亩橡胶核心示范基地、500 亩榴莲核心示范基地、10 000 亩香水椰子核心示范基地。同时，还联合中柬宏泰农业科技发展有限公司建设柬埔寨农产品加工及仓储物流中心，建立柬埔寨农副产品出口一站式服务平台。

(3) 加强澜湄农业科技交流。除农业产业园区建设，海南还加强与澜湄国家的农业科技交流。2017 年 7 月，海南农业农村厅和中国热带农业科学院在柬埔寨首都金边，与柬埔寨皇家农业大学签订三方战略合作协议。根据协议，三方将合作建立热带农业技术培训中心、组培苗中心、有机肥研发生产中心和热带作物研究中心，将共同开展橡胶、木薯、香蕉、胡椒等热带作物科学研究和新品种研发。此次中国（海南）—柬埔寨项目签约仪式上，现场共签订 10 个重大合作项目，其中院校合作项目 3 个、经贸项目 7 个，签约总金额高达 2.5 亿美元。

2018 年 5 月，中国热带农业科学院联合海南农业农村厅主办的 2018 年中国（海南）—柬埔寨热带农业技术培训班在海口市开班，来自柬埔寨农林渔业部、柬埔寨磅湛省农业厅、柬埔寨皇家农业大学及在柬中资农业企业的 23 名学员参加了为期 22 天的集中培训。2018 年 10 月，澜湄国家植物新品种保护国际研讨培训班在海南儋州海南大学举办，来自湄公河五国及中国从事品种保护和品种管理工作的 23 名代表参加培训。2018 年 11 月，柬埔寨农林渔业部官员热带农业经济管理研修班开班仪式在海南大学举行，柬埔寨农林渔业部及下属三所主要农科大学的管理干部参加了以"中—柬农业贸易与政策"为主题的培训。2018 年 11 月，海南农业农村厅联合柬埔寨皇家农业大学在柬埔寨金边举办 2018 年中国（海南）—柬埔寨热带农业技术培训班（第二期），来自柬埔寨农林渔业部、柬埔寨皇家农业大学和在柬中资企业员工等 70 余人参加了培训。通过以上农业技术培训活动，加强了海南与澜湄各国的沟通交流，为进一步推进澜湄农业合作奠定了坚实基础。

9.3.2 成效与经验做法

（1）**借政策大势推进澜湄农业合作**。澜湄合作机制是"一带一路"倡议的重要组成部分。自中国推进"一带一路"倡议以来，海南作为"海上丝绸之路"的重要地位凸显，不断深化与东南亚国家的经济贸易、文化交流等合作与往来。海南借助"一带一路"倡议为澜湄合作提供的重要契机和广阔空间，在原有国际合作基础上积极推进澜湄农业领域的合作，不断拓展与澜湄国家进行农业合作的有效途径。同时，海南还借助经济特区、国际旅游岛及免税购物、低空航权开放等一系列投资优惠政策，吸引海内外投资者，夯实农业等基础产业发展，为开展国际农业合作创造更有利条件。

（2）**借平台之势推进澜湄农业合作**。海南利用博鳌亚洲论坛的区域影响力和主场外交优势，推动湄公河五国高层互访，促进澜湄国家在农业领域的务实合作。同时，海南利用博鳌亚洲论坛的品牌优势，组织策划多场次活动，开展现代农业技术交流、国际农业问题研讨、特色农产品推介、农业文化传播等，丰富了海南与澜湄国家之间的农业交流平台、拓宽了海南与澜湄国家之间的农业合作渠道。

(3) 借产业优势推进澜湄农业合作。海南在国际旅游、热带农业等方面具备良好的产业发展优势。海南通过与柬埔寨暹粒、老挝琅勃拉邦、泰国普吉岛、越南下龙湾等世界知名旅游地开展"一程多站"澜湄城市旅游合作，不仅实现澜湄城市间旅游业的共赢发展，还有效带动当地特色农产品、休闲农业等领域的合作与发展。海南还借助在热带农业生产领域的技术优势，进行技术输出，与柬埔寨合作开展香蕉、胡椒、橡胶、榴莲等热带作物的种植，中—柬热带生态农业合作示范区建设初显成效。

9.3.3 存在的问题

(1) 尚未形成农业全面合作格局。当前，海南与澜湄国家的农业合作更多体现在与柬埔寨、泰国的合作上，对老挝、缅甸、越南的农业合作程度相对较浅，有待进一步深化。近年，海南与柬埔寨的农业合作依托中—柬热带生态农业合作示范区建设逐步加深，取得了较好的成效。海南与泰国的农业合作得益于中泰两国早期制定的"早期收获"计划和"中泰两国蔬菜水果零关税协定"，在蔬菜、水果方面的贸易合作顺利。海南与老挝的农业合作主要体现在天然橡胶产业，与缅甸的农业合作主要体现在热带水果产业，在农业其他领域的项目合作较少。

(2) 合作平台功能与项目布局有待改善。海南现有的澜湄农业合作平台多以开展农业科技培训与合作交流为主，通过平台推动的澜湄农业合作也多为技术援助和示范推广项目，平台功能及合作形式较为单一。在合作项目布局上往往局限于某一作物或某一国家，尚未形成明显的集聚优势与区域合力。在合作项目设计上，缺少充分体现合作方利益诉求并形成双/多方可持续发展的举措，导致部分外商参与积极性不高、合作项目重建轻管、项目运作可持续性不强等问题出现。

(3) 企业"走向湄公河五国"的能力有待提高。当前，海南与湄公河五国的农业投资及项目建设仍以政府推动为主要动力，以市场为导向的民间自发合作行为相对较少。海南涉农企业的"走出去"能力，尤其是境外地缘政治风险识别、东道国法律风险管理、农产品国际市场价格波动应对等方面的能力亟待提高。海南内有关政府部门、农业科研机构对涉农企业"走出去"的支撑和服务能力亟待加强，以协助和促进更多海南企业走向澜湄国家。

9.4　下一步合作展望

9.4.1　总体思路

在未来与澜湄国家的农业合作中，海南应充分发挥"海上丝绸之路"的区位优势、博鳌亚洲论坛的平台优势、热带农业及国际旅游的产业优势，利用好自由贸易试验区和中国特色自由贸易港的建设发展机遇，推进澜湄国家在农业政策交流、农业科技创新、人员培训、热带作物育种与栽培、优良品种示范推广等更多领域的务实合作，进一步提升海南对澜湄农业合作的参与度和重要性。

9.4.2　重点任务

(1) 开拓澜湄农业合作新局面。 抓住自贸区建设机遇，积极吸引外商投资涉农项目，重点引入促进海南农产品深加工和产业结构调整的投资项目，避免盲目建设。有序扩大与湄公河五国的农产品贸易往来，重点发展与澜湄国家互补性强的农产品进出口贸易，避免同质竞争。加快琼海农业对外开放合作试验区、农业绿色发展先行区建设，开拓澜湄农业全方位、宽领域、多层次的务实合作新局面。

(2) 完善农业合作平台体系建设。 平台优势是海南与云南、广西等省（自治区）相比最为突出的优势。充分借助博鳌亚洲论坛品牌、21世纪海上丝绸之路岛屿经济分论坛以及岛屿观光政策论坛等平台，建设立足海南农业发展实际、符合多方农业发展需求、信息及时共享、更加丰富完善的农业合作交流平台体系，不断提升平台功能。

(3) 加强企业"走出去"科技支撑力度。 依托中国热带农业科学院的科研优势，通过对接海南农业龙头企业及澜湄国家有关商会、组织实施有关科技合作课题研究、为企业培养及输送农业科技人才，推进热带农业科技创新合作研究及产业技术的转移转化，为海南企业走出国门、走向澜湄国家提供有力科技支撑。

9.4.3　具体项目计划

（1）**打造南繁种业国际合作交流平台。**依托国家南繁育种基地，将选育的杂交水稻种子和优质常规水稻、蔬菜种子等，在澜湄地区推广种植，加深海南与澜湄国家的农业务实合作。在此基础上，将南繁基地建设成为我国现代种业科技研发与国际现代种业科技交流的重要平台，实现农业资源信息技术交流、成果转化与交易种质等功能。

（2）**搭建国际农业合作外交服务平台。**结合博鳌亚洲论坛建立农业对外交流合作及农业外交平台，结合中非合作农业会议提升海南发展热带农业战略地位，推动海南农业在更大范围、更广领域、更高层次上参与国际合作，提升海南农业国际竞争力，进一步推动海南与澜湄国家开展更加务实高效的农业合作。

（3）**加快推进中—柬热带生态农业合作示范区建设。**目前，中—柬热带生态农业合作示范区建设已初步完成第一期产业示范园的建设，已建成香蕉、胡椒、木薯、橡胶等多个核心示范基地。下一步将探索建立符合柬埔寨当地实际的产业标准，探索构建"生产—加工—销售"全产业链的产业园发展模式，以产业园示范区形成境外产业集聚和带动效应，与柬埔寨共同打造"环境保护＋生态农业"的农业合作开发新模式。

（4）**开展澜湄热带农业产业合作示范区建设。**海南将在澜湄农业合作框架下，依托中—柬热带生态农业合作示范区建设的成功经验，以中国热带农业科学院等单位为技术支撑，以"走出去"企业为建设主体，分阶段、按步骤开展与柬埔寨、老挝、缅甸、泰国、越南的热带农业产业合作示范区建设。同时，与这些国家开展常态化的农业人才交流培训，增进澜湄区域农业主管官员、重要学者、企业家、农户以及新闻媒体之间的交流互信，为开展澜湄热带农业产业合作示范区建设奠定良好舆论基础并提供必要的人才保障。

（海南省农业农村厅　刘怡、张红亮、薛晶洁）

10 柬埔寨农业发展与澜湄农业合作进展

10.1 农业发展概况

10.1.1 资源环境与发展现状

（1）资源环境。柬埔寨位于中南半岛南部，西部与泰国接壤，东北部与老挝交界，南部与泰国相邻。湄公河自北向南贯穿柬埔寨全境，海岸线长约460千米，水产资源丰富。国土面积18.1万千米^2，森林面积9.8万千米^2，森林覆盖率达55.7%，发展种植业和水产养殖业的自然条件优越。全国总农业用地面积5.46万千米^2，占国土面积的30.9%。其中，可耕土地面积3.80万千米^2，永久性农作物用地0.16万千米^2，永久牧场1.50万千米^2。全国总人口1 571.8万，其中农村人口1 260.1万，占全国总人口的80.17%[①]。柬埔寨属于热带季风气候，高温多雨，全年分为雨季（5—10月）和旱季（11月至次年4月）两季。由于柬埔寨传统的农业耕作习惯，农业的种植主要集中在雨季，旱季种植面积约为雨季的十分之一。

柬埔寨的农作物种植以稻米、玉米和木薯为主。水稻是最主要的农作物，也是柬埔寨政府鼓励优先发展的农作物，种植面积占可用耕地面积的77.63%，湄公河、洞里萨河、巴萨河沿岸是主要的稻产区。其次是玉米，主要分布在东高原和金边附近[②]。经济作物有橡胶、蔬菜、腰果、热带水

---

① 东盟秘书处，2018. 东盟统计年鉴 [M]. 东盟秘书处 [2020 - 12 - 22]. www.asean.org.

② 云南省科学学研究所. 云南省农业科学院农业经济与信息研究所，2006. 云南与东盟农业合作研究 [M]. 昆明：云南科技出版社：190.

果、黄豆、芝麻、花生、甘蔗、烟叶和剑麻等。联合国粮食及农业组织公布的柬埔寨 2018 年收获面积排名前十的农作物如表 10-1 所示。

渔业是柬埔寨农业的重要组成部分，约占柬埔寨农业生产总值的四分之一。柬埔寨渔业总产量的 90% 来自洞里萨湖和湄公河沿岸的淡水区域。据联合国粮食及农业组织和柬埔寨渔业部统计，洞里萨湖是中南半岛上最大的湖泊，也是世界上淡水渔业资源最丰富的渔区，总渔获量居全球第四位。海洋渔业在柬埔寨渔业所占比重较小，主要集中在泰国湾东岸。2018 年柬埔寨自然与饲养水产品 91 万吨，其中，淡水水产 53.5 万吨、海洋水产 12.1 万吨、饲养水产 25.4 万吨；全年完成淡水和海洋水产加工 8.4 万吨，出口量 1.4 万吨[①]。

表 10-1　2018 年柬埔寨收获面积前十的农作物及其产量

序号	农作物	收获面积（公顷）	产量（吨）	单产（千克/公顷）
1	水稻	3 071 696	10 892 000	3 545.9
2	木薯	481 679	12 805 875	26 585.9
3	玉米	242 237	1 232 000	5 085.9
4	天然橡胶	226 028	220 100	973.8
5	大豆	105 000	170 000	1 619.0
6	新鲜蔬菜类	103 768	665 497	6 413.3
7	干菜豆	68 448	88 070	1 286.7
8	芝麻籽	40 000	30 000	750.0
9	香蕉	30 699	142 890	4 654.5
10	甘蔗	28 770	640 000	22 245.4

数据来源：http://www.fao.org/faostat/en/#data.

柬埔寨畜牧业在农业中的占比较低，目前仍以小规模生产为主。从畜牧种类看，主要以家禽、牛、猪养殖为主，基本生产情况如表 10-2 所示。

---

① 王向社，2019.2018 年柬埔寨渔政建设成绩斐然 [J]．世界热带农业信息（4）：28.

表 10 - 2　2018 年柬埔寨畜牧业生产基本情况

畜禽名称	养殖数量（头/只）
鸡	13 200 000
鸭	8 897 000
牛	3 483 060
猪	2 107 659
马	30 629

数据来源：http://www.fao.org/faostat/en/#data.

（2）农业发展现状。农业是柬埔寨的传统支柱产业。长期以来，农业在柬埔寨的国民经济中占据主导地位。随着现代化的发展，柬埔寨的工业、服务业快速发展壮大，经济结构正在从以农业为主向以服务业和工业为主转型。虽然农业规模仍在逐年稳步扩大，但增长的速度相对缓慢和滞后。2000—2010 年，柬埔寨农业增加值以年均 6% 左右的速度增长，在 2010 年之后增长明显放缓，2010—2018 年，农业增加值年均增长率不足 1%（图 10 - 1）。与此同时，农业在国民经济中的占比逐年下降。据世界银行统计，柬埔寨农业增加值占 GDP 的比重由 21 世纪初的 36% 波动下降到 2018 年的 22%，而同时期的工业增加值占 GDP 的比重由 22% 上升

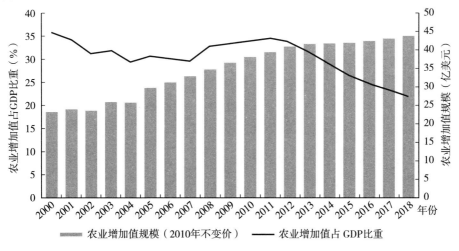

图 10 - 1　2000—2018 年柬埔寨农业增加值变化情况

数据来源：https://data.worldbank.org.cn.

至 32%。在 2018 年农业各领域对 GDP 贡献的构成中，农作物种植业仍占据半壁江山，占比为 58.1%，养殖业占比 11.2%，水产业占比 24%，林业占比 6.7%。

10.1.2 农产品进出口贸易

柬埔寨与世界大多数国家建立了贸易往来关系，农产品贸易规模逐年扩大，从 2013 年的 366 万吨增加到 2017 年的 513 万吨，年均增长 7%[①]。大米是柬埔寨最重要的出口商品，其次是橡胶和木薯，其他主要出口农产品还有玉米、胡椒、热带水果等。据柬埔寨农林渔业部统计，柬埔寨大米的出口量由 2013 年的 37.89 万吨增长至 2017 年的 63.57 万吨。2018 年出口大米 62.62 万吨，其中向中国出口 17.02 万吨，占比 27.17%，连续四年位列第一。前五大出口国还包括法国（8.61 万吨）、马来西亚（4.09 万吨）、加蓬（3.31 万吨）和荷兰（2.67 万吨）[②]。橡胶的出口量由 2013 年的不足 10 万吨增长到 2018 年的 21.75 万吨，主要以天然橡胶干片出口为主。木薯的出口量也有所增长，2018 年出口量约 200 万吨，以干木薯片、鲜木薯、木薯粉出口为主，主要出口到越南、中国、荷兰、捷克、加拿大、意大利和印度等[③]。

据东盟数据库统计，2018 年柬埔寨的农产品十大出口贸易伙伴如表 10-3 所示。柬埔寨对这十个国家的农产品出口金额占其全部农产品出口金额的 79.86%。可见，柬埔寨农产品出口贸易的国别集中度较高，仅对中国的农产品出口就占其全部农产品出口贸易总额的 29.86%。从出口农产品种类看，谷物的出口金额最大，达 4.11 亿美元；糖及糖食的出口金额排名第二，达 8 227.70 万美元；其他出口金额较大的农产品有制粉工业产品、动植物油脂及其分解产品、食用蔬菜及块茎、咖啡、茶及调味香料、食用水果和坚果、粮食粉和糕饼点心、含油的籽、果仁和果实、药用植物、可可及可可制品等。

---

① 根据 2019 澜湄农业农资合作峰会暨经贸洽谈会上柬埔寨农林渔业部农业总局人员发言整理。

② 石登峰，2019. 中国连续四年成为柬埔寨大米最大进口国 [EB/OL]. (01-14) [2020-12-22]. https://finance.sina.com.cn/money/future/agri/2019-01-14/doc-ihqfskcn7046005.shtml.

③ 王向社，2019. 柬埔寨农业概况与近期农业舆情简述 [J]. 世界热带农业信息（9）：8-9.

表 10-3 2018 年柬埔寨十大农产品出口国家及出口金额

序号	出口国家	出口金额（美元）
1	中国	188 713 246
2	越南	97 744 810
3	法国	56 540 056
4	马来西亚	53 356 374
5	加蓬	29 372 328
6	荷兰	25 895 616
7	意大利	15 961 551
8	比利时	13 686 457
9	德国	11 890 607
10	波兰	11 608 400

注：根据 HS 两位编码的货物贸易数据（IMTS），选取 HS01-20 数据整理得出。

数据来源：https://data.aseanstats.org.

2018 年柬埔寨十大进口贸易国家如表 10-4 所示。柬埔寨从这十个国家进口农产品的金额占其农产品进口总额的 75.70%。可见，柬埔寨农产品进口贸易的国别集中度也较高，仅从泰国进口的农产品就占其全部农产品进口贸易总额的 23.22%。从进口产品种类看，谷物、粮食粉、糕饼点心的进口金额最大，达 13 518.35 万美元；麦芽、淀粉、菊粉、麦麸等制粉工业产品的进口金额排名第二，达 7 056.58 万美元；其余进口金额较大的产品有：糖及糖食，乳品、蛋类、天然蜂蜜，动物油脂及其分解物，谷物，肉及其他水生无脊椎动物的制品，活动物，蔬菜、水果、坚果，蔬菜及块茎等。

表 10-4 2018 年柬埔寨十大农产品进口国家及进口金额

序号	进口国家	进口金额（美元）
1	泰国	95 542 207
2	马来西亚	50 658 158
3	越南	43 036 952
4	中国	31 962 039

（续）

序号	进口国家	进口金额（美元）
5	澳大利亚	20 481 895
6	新加坡	18 910 532
7	丹麦	14 706 052
8	美国	12 441 654
9	阿根廷	12 143 931
10	法国	11 514 040

注：根据 HS 两位编码的货物贸易数据（IMTS），选取 HS 01-20 数据整理得出。

数据来源：https://data.aseanstats.org.

10.2　农业投资政策

10.2.1　宏观政策

农业一直被柬埔寨政府列为优先发展的重点领域，受到高度重视。政府通过投资，充分利用国内资源，加强农业生产的深度和多元化，从而促进经济发展、创造就业机会、增加农民收入。同时，政府还鼓励私人投资，为私营领域参与农业开发项目创造良好的环境，优先发展边境地区和偏远农村，发展必需的基础设施，改善人民生活水平，促进当地经济发展。

"四角战略"是柬埔寨经济发展的蓝图规划。2018 年，柬埔寨王国政府颁布实施为期 5 年的第四期"四角战略"发展规划，其政策核心内容是"将柬埔寨贫穷率降至 10% 以下，继续保障国家经济 7% 的年均增长率"。该战略规划强调，一是推进农业生产；二是发展私人经济和增加就业；三是恢复与重建基础设施；四是培训人才与发展人力资源。在"推进农业生产方面"的具体规划包括：提高生产力，保持农业多样化和商业化；促进畜牧业、渔业和水产养殖；进行土地改革及扫雷工作；进行林业改革，促进国家资源的可持续发展。通过上述措施，将农业增长率提高到每年 5% 左右。

10.2.2 相关法律制度

《柬埔寨王国投资法》适用于农业投资。《柬埔寨王国投资法》适用于所有在柬埔寨境内从事投资活动的柬埔寨人和外国人，且投资者不论是自然人还是法人均受到该法律的制约。

柬埔寨与农业生产资料有关的法律、法规有：《柬埔寨王国土地法》《柬埔寨王国森林法》《水资源管理法》《关于水污染管理的行政法规》《化肥与农药管理法》等；与生产经营有关法律、法规主要是《商业管理与商业注册法》《商业合同法》《商业企业法》等；涉农保护制度有《环境保护与资源管理法》《环境影响评估进程实施法令》等。柬埔寨一直实行开放的自由市场经济政策，经济活动高度自由化。欧盟、美国、日本等全球28个国家（地区）给予柬埔寨普惠制待遇（GSP）。柬埔寨的竞争与价格政策较为开放，几乎没有政府垄断，政府不会直接干涉商业货物或是服务价格，不会进行价格管制。

10.2.3 市场准入及农产品贸易制度

（1）农业领域外资管理法律制度及政策体系

外国投资者准入制度：柬埔寨的外资政策相对自由，对外资与内资基本给予同等待遇。强调所有的投资者不分国籍和种族在法律面前一律平等。

农业用土地制度及政策：根据柬埔寨王国宪法，外籍自然人或法人不得拥有柬埔寨王国土地。《柬埔寨王国土地法》适用于农业土地管理，依据该法规定，"允许以特许经营的形式将土地租借给国内外企业或个人从事农业生产。"根据柬埔寨政府关于特许经营用地的第 146 号令规定，特许经营用地（Economic Land Concessions，ELC）指设定一种途径，将国家私有土地通过特许经营权的方式进行授予，用作农业生产或工业化的农业开发，即粮食耕作、工业化种植、畜牧与水产养殖、植物栽培、农业加工业及相关设施等上述某几个或所有产业。特许经营用地可以不同方式批准给本国和外国企业或个人，但要求：最大面积不超过 10 000 公顷；被批准用地只能为国家私有用地；最长期限为 99 年。

涉农领域投资制度及政策：柬埔寨政府一直十分鼓励外国资本对农业及农业加工业发展的直接投资，并给予免征全部或部分关税和赋税投资优惠。

外汇管理制度及政策：根据 1993 年通过的柬埔寨《外汇法》，柬埔寨不实行外汇管制，汇率由市场调节，美元可自由流通。在柬埔寨，无论是汇款还是转账，只需要通过已注册的金融机构即可。柬埔寨大部分交易是以美元计算，汇款仅需支付预扣税。外国投资人可以向境外汇出外汇，用以清偿与投资活动有关的债务以及返还投资收益、剩余资产收益等。

涉农劳动法律制度与政策：《柬埔寨王国投资法》规定雇佣劳动力的自由原则是投资者在柬埔寨王国有权按照《柬埔寨王国劳工法》和《柬埔寨王国移民法》的有关规定，自由选择和雇佣柬埔寨籍或外籍员工。

(2) 农资、农产品贸易制度。柬埔寨与贸易相关的法律法规主要包括《进出口商品关税管理法》《关于颁发服装原产地证明、商业发票和出口许可证的法令》《关于实施货物装运前验货检查工作的管理条例》《加入世界贸易组织法》《关于风险管理的次法令》《关于成立海关与税收署风险管理办公室的规定》和《有关商业公司从事贸易活动的法令》等。

柬埔寨对外贸易发展实行普惠制。在多数情况下，柬埔寨进口货物不需要许可证，但部分产品需要获得相关政府部门特别出口授权或许可后方可出口。柬埔寨政府明令禁止红木的贸易与流通。除天然橡胶、宝石、半成品或成品木材、海产品、沙石 5 类产品，一般出口货物不需缴纳关税。货物在进入柬埔寨时均应缴纳进口税，投资法或其他特殊法规规定享受免税待遇的除外。进口关税主要由四种汇率组成，即 7％、15％、35％ 和 50％。在东盟自由贸易协定的共同有效关税体制下，从东盟其他成员国进口、满足原产地规则规定的产品可享受较低的关税税率。

10.3 澜湄农业合作进展与成效

10.3.1 主要进展

(1) 参与澜湄机制共建及交流活动。2018 年 1 月 10 日，澜湄合作第二次领导人会议在柬埔寨首都金边举行，柬埔寨和中国是共同主席国。2018 年 1 月 11 日，中国国务院总理李克强在金边同柬埔寨首相洪森举行会谈，会后发布了《中华人民共和国政府和柬埔寨王国政府联合公报》（以下简称"公报"）。公报称中国将加强与柬埔寨在农业等重点领域的合作，"大力推进农业合作，共同编制柬埔寨现代农业发展规划，建设农业合作示范园和农产品深加工园区，促进柬埔寨农产品加工、仓储和物流业发展，延伸农业产业链。"中柬双方领导人见证签署了《关于合作编制柬埔寨现代农业发展规划的谅解备忘录》《关于水稻研究合作的谅解备忘录》《关于在柬埔寨建设珍贵树种繁育中心的协议》等 19 份合作文件。

（2）澜湄合作专项基金项目执行情况①。澜湄合作专项基金柬埔寨首批 16 个项目于 2017 年 12 月签署，其中涉农项目 3 个，总预算 150 万美元。目前，首批的 3 个涉农项目正在按计划有序推进，进展情况和阶段性成果如下：

促进制定有效的区域战略，打击湄公河国家非法、未报告和未登记的捕捞活动，以实现湄公河区域可持续渔业管理，预算 50 万美元。目前，已完成《关于澜湄流域当前非法、未报告和未登记捕捞渔业问题、差距和最佳做法评估报告》的第二次修改稿；"打击澜湄流域非法、未报告和未登记捕鱼的有效区域策略"的第二次草案修改；起草独立选举委员会的材料，以提高对违法捕鱼问题的认识和对有效区域战略实践的能力建设；为澜湄流域战略和行动计划制定实施建议。

东南亚森林恢复和促进可持续森林利用，预算 50 万美元。2018 年 7 月，柬埔寨农林渔业部与暹粒林业局举行会议，交付项目设备和巡逻装备，并与泰国和越南举行了首次技术会议。2018 年 12 月，柬埔寨派出一批林业局官员访问泰国，重点考察了让克拉丁森林种植园和树种来源地区、拉永植物园和林业，以及以非木材林产品为基础的恩帕社区林业的有效经验；建立了 2 个苗圃示范地以培育多种本地树种，同时建立了田间试验小区系统（FTPS）以比较本地速生树种的田间表现，试验施肥处理对田间性状的影响，评估植树造林的效果、野生动物栖息地和食物链的恢复

---

① 根据 2019 年澜沧江—湄公河合作农业联合工作组第二次会议柬埔寨代表的报告整理。

以及野生动物种子扩散的安全性。

通过可持续土地管理解决土地退化和改善当地民生，预算50万美元。已采取系列防治土地退化的措施，如合理利用水资源等，目前项目正在平稳推进中，进展顺利。

澜湄合作专项基金柬埔寨第二批19个项目于2019年2月签署，其中涉农项目2个，总预算67万美元。分别是：澜湄国家可持续森林管理能力建设，预算50万美元；渔业社区共同管理—澜湄流域国家能力建设与经验共享，预算17万美元。目前，项目正在组织规划阶段，将很快开展实施工作。

澜湄合作专项基金执行过程中面临一些挑战。主要体现在：农业生产方面，生产力和产品质量相对低下、生产成本较高、市场竞争激烈、技术水平和管理能力较弱、科研投入不足，农业产业化水平较低；农产品贸易方面，采购体系薄弱，主要以邻国市场为基础，价格及商业合同体系不健全，且进口国家多存在实施卫生和植物卫生措施协定的贸易壁垒；配套环境方面，支持农业发展的基础设施建设和现代化水平不足，物流体系不健全，打击森林和渔业违法犯罪的执法力度不足。

（3）与其他澜湄国家的农业合作情况

①柬埔寨与中国的农业合作

柬埔寨在与其他澜湄五国的合作中，与中国的农业合作最为紧密。中国长期以来都是柬埔寨重要的贸易伙伴，两国农产品贸易还存在巨大的发展空间。柬埔寨对中国农产品贸易曾长期处于贸易逆差状态，自2014年起，柬埔寨扩大对中国的农产品出口，柬埔寨对中国的农产品贸易由逆差转为顺差，且出口额逐年迅速扩大（图10-2）。2018年，柬埔寨对中国出口农产品1.99亿美元，自中国进口农产品0.57亿美元，贸易顺差1.42亿美元。从进出口农产品种类看，柬埔寨对中国（含香港与台湾地区）的主要出口农产品是稻米，占所有农产品出口额的42.73%，其他出口额较大的还有木薯、淀粉、离心粗糖等商品；进口额较大的有香烟、蒸馏酒饮等商品①。在农业投资方面，截至2017年底，中国对柬埔寨的农业投资

---

① 数据来源：http://www.fao.org/faostat/en/#data.

企业有 40 家左右，主要投资领域为水稻、玉米等粮食作物和天然橡胶、甘薯、油棕等经济作物种植①。

图 10-2　2001—2018 年柬埔寨与中国双边农产品贸易发展历程

数据来源：https://comtrade.un.org.

2018 年 6 月 27 日，柬埔寨农林渔业部部长文萨坤在首届"一带一路"农食品产业及贸易高峰论坛上呼吁中国大型投资公司加大对柬埔寨的投资，加大对农业、农食品加工业的投资力度，扩大柬埔寨农产品市场，加强柬埔寨中国农业双边合作。2018 年 10 月 18 日，中国国务院总理李克强在布鲁塞尔会见柬埔寨首相洪森。李克强指出，中柬应扩大双边贸易规模，中方愿继续进口柬优势农产品，鼓励有实力的中国企业赴柬投资兴业，更好实现互利共赢。

2018 年 8 月，中国与柬埔寨签署了《柬埔寨香蕉输华植物检验检疫要求议定书》，为柬埔寨香蕉进入中国市场开启大门。该议定书的签署标志着柬埔寨香蕉完成了对中国的检疫准入，成为柬埔寨首个输华水果品种。以前，柬埔寨香蕉如果想进入中国市场，只能选择"借道"越南。2019 年 5 月，首批输华的 100 吨柬埔寨香蕉已经成功抵达中国。柬埔寨

---

①　农业农村部国际合作司，农业农村部对外经济合作中心，2018. 中国农业对外投资合作分析报告［M］. 北京：中国农业出版社：26.

种植香蕉有着独特优势，基本上不受台风影响，光热条件适宜香蕉全年生长，特别是当地枯萎病发生率几乎为零，随着柬埔寨种植面积的扩大，未来有望成为最大的对华香蕉出口国。

②柬埔寨与泰国的农业合作

柬埔寨与泰国农产品贸易往来关系密切，柬埔寨对泰国出口的主要农产品有玉米、木薯、豆类等，而泰国对柬埔寨出口的主要产品有农用机械、食品等。近年，柬埔寨政治稳定、经济快速增长且农业资源丰富、劳动力充足，使许多的泰国公司、商人和投资者在柬埔寨进行投资。2015 年，柬埔寨狄皮公司和泰国乌汶生化乙醇有限公司（Ubon Bio Ethanol，UBE）签署无限量供应木薯合作协议，根据协议，泰国 UBE 公司将无限量购买柬埔寨木薯，并保障木薯的价格稳定①。2017 年，柬埔寨 AMRU Rice 公司与泰国 Thai Starch 公司签署谅解备忘录，按计划柬埔寨 AMRU Rice 公司在 2018 年向泰国 Thai Starch 公司供应 8 000 吨有机木薯，并预计在 2020 年将增长至 2 万～4 万吨有机木薯②。柬埔寨公司将木薯供应给泰国可以抵御与邻国木薯产品的竞争，提升种植木薯农民的经济收入。

除了农产品贸易，柬、泰还加强基础设施联通建设和政策沟通交流，共同促进双方农业合作。2019 年 5 月，柬泰签署斯登波口岸建设协议，柬埔寨通过泰国提供的 8 亿泰铢（约 2 600 万美元）优惠贷款，建设柬泰边境的斯登波口岸和连接柬埔寨 5 号公路的基础设施项目，该项目可缓解当前柬埔寨和泰国农产品等商品货运时间长的问题，有助于扩大柬泰两国的贸易规模③。2019 年 7 月，柬埔寨拜林省省长潘占托率领代表团一行访问泰国春武里府，柬泰双方领导人就增加农产品出口、提升两省贸易往来、打击跨境违法等方面的合作达成了共识④。

---

① 佚名，2015. 柬泰公司签署无限量供应木薯协议 [J]. 世界热带农业信息（12）：17-18.

② 陈本宗，2017. 柬泰公司合作推动有机木薯出口 [N/OL]. 柬华日报，11-23 [2020-12-22]. http://www.ccpit.org/Contents/Channel_4117/2017/1123/918941/content_918941.htm.

③ 焱鑫，2019. 柬泰签署斯登波口岸建设协议 [N/OL]. 高棉日报，05-24 [2020-12-22]. http://www.sohu.com/a/316303557_99978839.

④ 佚名，2019. 深化柬泰友好合作关系 拜林省省长潘占托访问泰国 [N/OL]. 华商传媒，07-28 [2020-12-22]. https://www.sohu.com/a/329895652_413350.

③柬埔寨与越南的农业合作

柬埔寨是越南农林水产品出口的临近且具有潜力的重要市场之一，农林水产品在柬埔寨和越南两国贸易总额中占较高比重，越南也曾经是柬埔寨农业领域的一流投资来源国，双方的农业合作往来密切。2017 年 12 月，柬埔寨政府与越南腰果协会达成了合作协议，利用柬埔寨 50 万公顷土地大规模开发腰果种植，越方向柬方提供了 2018—2022 年期间购买 100 万棵腰果树苗所需的经费，同时成立了越柬腰果开发研究工作组，由越南腰果协会和腰果企业向柬埔寨提供技术、供应树苗并收购腰果果实①。2019 年 7 月，越柬贸易投资促进论坛举办，越柬两国企业代表就关税、海关手续、投资优惠等具体问题进行交流，两国希望通过系列优惠政策进一步促进双方在农业投资、进出口贸易等方面的合作。

④柬埔寨与缅甸、老挝的农业合作

柬埔寨与缅甸、老挝同为传统的农业生产国，在自然资源禀赋和农业发展条件方面有较大的相似性，也存有一定的互补性。但在现阶段，三国之间的农业合作交往活动相对较少，存在较大的发展空间。2017 年 2 月，老挝湄公河委员会及柬埔寨湄公河委员会的代表在柬埔寨暹粒召开会议讨论联合渔业管理计划，旨在重建湄公河及色贡河流域内陆渔业资源，管理上述河流中长途迁徙的五种鱼类。据柬埔寨洪森总理称，2018 年柬埔寨与缅甸双方贸易额为 1 000 万美元，尚未符合两国的经济潜能，两国应继续深化经济方面的合作，两国的农业合作也有待进一步发展②。

10.3.2 成效与经验做法

（1）积极参与澜湄合作争取项目资金支持。柬埔寨充分利用其在农作物种植（如稻米）及水产养殖方面的资源禀赋优势，大力引导国际资金向农业领域投资，承接多项农业投资合作项目，积极争取澜湄合作专项基金

---

① 驻胡志明市总领馆经商室，2017. 越南与柬埔寨合作大规模开发腰果种植 ［N/OL］. 越南经济时报，12 - 08 ［2020 - 12 - 22］. http://hochiminh. mofcom. gov. cn/article/jmxw/201712/20171202682738. shtml.

② 佚名，2019. 柬缅 2018 年双边贸易额仅 1 000 万美元，应继续深化合作 ［N/OL］. 高棉日报，09 - 11 ［2020 - 12 - 22］. http://www. sohu. com/a/340217341_120133562.

支持，成为澜湄合作专项基金项目连续两年来获批最多的国家。迄今，柬埔寨从澜湄合作专项基金共收获 35 个项目，获得 1 496 万美元资金预算，涵盖农业、旅游、电信、教育、文化交流等多个领域。其中，柬埔寨共收获 5 个涉农项目，获得 217 万美元资金预算。柬埔寨副首相兼外交大臣布拉索昆认为澜湄合作专项基金项目体现了澜湄国家的需求，"增强澜湄区域航空互通，推动农业发展，解决湄公河区域土地退化、森林可持续利用和可持续渔业管理等问题，都将给域内国家带来实实在在的利益"[①]。

（2）促进澜湄国家在渔业共管、森林可持续管理等领域的交流。柬埔寨倡导农业领域的务实合作，以项目有效推动澜湄国家之间在渔业、林业等多领域的交流互动。通过评估当前澜湄流域非法、未报告和未登记捕捞的渔业问题、存在差距和最佳做法，制定有效的区域策略来打击上述违法捕捞活动，提升澜湄国家对解决违法捕鱼问题的共识。通过与泰国和越南举行技术会议、对泰国主要森林种植园和树种来源地的考察等活动，增进了柬埔寨与泰国、越南在树种资源共享、林业合作开发和森林可持续管理等方面的经验交流。

（3）深化与中、泰的农业合作关系。在澜湄国家中，中国和泰国的农业投资能力、科技水平相对较强，农业现代化程度相对较高。柬埔寨重点加强与中、泰的农业合作，通过引进农业投资，吸收先进农业生产技术和管理经验，改造传统农业，巩固农业的基础地位。柬埔寨与中国自 1958 年建交以来，友好合作关系不断发展，为两国农业合作发展创造了良好环境。澜湄合作机制下，柬埔寨与中国的农产品贸易规模不断扩大，双方在农业投资、园区建设、政策共识等多方面合作取得了显著的成效。柬埔寨与泰国在木薯等主要农产品供应及双边贸易、农产品物流互通、政策互信交流等领域也取得了较大突破。

（云南省农业科学院国际农业研究所　李忻蔚、郭文）

---

① 赵益普，郑美辰，2019. 澜湄合作为柬埔寨发展注入新动力 ［N］. 人民日报，02-23 (3).

11 老挝农业发展与澜湄农业合作进展

11.1 农业发展概况

11.1.1 资源环境与发展现状

（1）资源环境。 老挝位于中南半岛中部，是一个内陆国家，国土面积 23.68 万千米^2，地势北高南低，约 80％ 的地区由丘陵和山脉组成，境内多被森林覆盖，林地面积约占国土面积的 70％。老挝属热带、亚热带季风气候，5—10 月为雨季，11 月至次年 4 月为旱季，年平均降水量为 1 834 毫米，年平均气温约 26℃。有 90％ 的国土位于湄公河流域，水资源丰富。农业面积有 2.369 万千米^2，其中耕地面积为 1.694 万千米^2。2018 年全国总人口为 706.15 万，其中农村人口 458.97 万，约占全国总人口的 65％[1]。

根据联合国粮食及农业组织 2018 年数据统计，老挝收获面积排名前十的农作物如表 11-1 所示。

表 11-1 2018 年老挝收获面积前十的农作物及其产量

序号	农作物	收获面积（公顷）	产量（吨）	单产（千克/公顷）
1	水稻	848 174	3 584 700	4 226.4
2	蔬菜	170 840	1 460 530	8 549.1
3	玉米	165 620	981 680	5 927.3

---

① 数据来源：http://www.fao.org/faostat/en/#data；https://data.worldbank.org.cn。

（续）

序号	农作物	收获面积 （公顷）	产量 （吨）	单产 （千克/公顷）
4	根茎和块茎	115 915	2 956 867	25 508.9
5	咖啡豆	82 980	154 435	1 861.1
6	木薯	71 010	2 279 030	32 094.5
7	甘蔗	30 555	1 834 525	60 040.1
8	香蕉	23 120	970 985	41 997.6
9	花生	19 995	48 885	2 444.9
10	芝麻	13 035	16 235	1 245.5

数据来源：http://www.fao.org/faostat/en/#data.

老挝有较多畜牧草场，全国草山面积达 15 000 千米^2，且几乎所有农户都有畜禽饲养。目前老挝共有 1 370 个畜牧养殖场，在畜禽养殖中，水牛主要用于耕田，黄牛主要用于肉类加工，马、驴、骡主要用于驮运，其他畜禽供食用与上市交易。近年，老挝畜牧业发展迅速，且正由传统养殖向现代化养殖迈进，但目前的养殖技术还相对落后[1]。从养殖数量来看，老挝饲养较多的是猪牛羊和鸡鸭等（表 11 - 2）。

表 11 - 2　2018 年老挝畜牧业生产基本情况

序号	畜禽名称	养殖数量（头/只）
1	猪	3 824 663
2	牛	3 240 947
3	山羊	616 325
4	马	32 410
5	鸡	39 218 000
6	鸭	3 575 000

数据来源：http://www.fao.org/faostat/en/#data.

---

① 孔志坚，寸佳苾，2017. 老挝畜牧业、渔业发展现状及前景分析 [J]. 东南亚南亚研究
（4）：64 - 69.

水产方面，老挝境内水资源丰富，内陆水域面积约 6 000 千米²，渔业主要分布在湄公河及其 14 条支流①。水产品是老挝群众的重要消费食物之一，主要鱼类品种有罗非鱼、草鱼、巴勒鱼、印度野鲮等。据统计，老挝全国建有保护性池塘 765 处，水产养殖基地 199 处，且私人养殖基地发展较快。总体来说，老挝水产品产量及消费量逐年增加，但缺乏优质鱼苗和先进的养殖技术，大多苗种及饲料需从泰国进口②。

（2）农业发展现状。 2018 年老挝农业增加值为 28.47 亿美元（现价），同比增长 4.3%，占 GDP 的 15.7%。2000—2018 年老挝农业增加值（按 2010 年不变价统计）呈逐步上升的趋势，年均增长率为 3.17%；农业增加值占 GDP 比例逐年下降，年均下降率为 4.14%（图 11 - 1）。

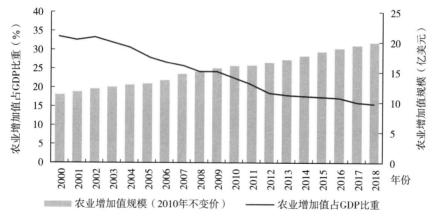

图 11 - 1　2000—2018 年老挝农业增加值变化情况

数据来源：https://data.worldbank.org.cn.

11.1.2　农产品进出口贸易

老挝无出海口，鉴于农产品物流运输的特殊性，农产品贸易主要合作伙伴为泰国、越南和中国，占比合计占其对外贸易总额的 90%。其中，泰

①　孔志坚，寸佳莅，2017. 老挝畜牧业、渔业发展现状及前景分析 [J]. 东南亚南亚研究（4）：64 - 69.

②　唐瞻杨，郭忠宝，梁军能，2019. 老挝渔业养殖现状调查及分析 [J]. 科学养鱼，355（3）：90 - 91.

国、越南与老挝文化习俗相近，拥有漫长陆地边境线，人文优势显著，深刻影响着老挝农产品贸易发展。2010—2016 年老挝农产品贸易发展成效突出，总体高速增长，但波幅大、缺乏平稳[1]。2017 年，老挝农业占进口份额比重为 13.3%，相比 2016 年增长 0.2 个百分点；占出口份额比重为 28.9%，相比 2016 年增长 1.4 个百分点[2]。根据东盟数据库数据统计分析，2018 年老挝对外农产品进口总额约为 3.22 亿美元，出口总额约为 6.53 亿美元，农产品贸易顺差约 3.32 亿美元。总体来说，老挝农产品贸易总量较小。

2018 年，老挝农产品贸易十大出口国分别为越南、泰国、中国、日本、比利时、德国、西班牙、美国、荷兰、柬埔寨（表 11-3）。其中越南是老挝农产品出口的第一大国。从出口的种类来看，出口额最大的农产品是水果和坚果，出口额达 1.7 亿美元；其次是蔬菜及块茎，出口额为 1.1 亿美元；第三是咖啡、茶、香料，出口额为 1.0 亿美元；此外，糖和糖果、谷物、畜禽动物出口额也较大。

老挝农产品贸易十大进口国（按出口金额排名）分别为泰国、越南、中国、美国、印度、日本、德国、澳大利亚、马来西亚、俄罗斯（表 11-4）。老挝从该十国进口的农产品金额占其农产品进口总金额的 99.2%，国别集中度明显较高。其中从泰国进口最多，约占全部进口额的 81%，明显多于其他进口国。从进口种类来看，进口额最大的农产品是畜禽动物，进口额为 9 886.7 万美元；其次是糖类，进口额为 5 153.3 万美元；第三是水果和坚果，进口额为 3 465.2 万美元；此外，制粉产品，谷类、面粉、淀粉或牛奶制品，蔬菜及块茎进口额也较大。

表 11-3　2018 年老挝十大农产品出口国家及出口金额

序号	出口国家	出口金额（美元）
1	越南	50 803 567
2	泰国	41 632 164
3	中国	36 031 825

① 郑国富，2018. 老挝农产品贸易发展特征及前景 [J]. 农业展望，151 (4)：70-73.
② 东盟秘书处，2018. 东盟统计年鉴 [M]. 东盟秘书处 [2020-12-22]. www.asean.org.

(续)

序号	出口国家	出口金额（美元）
4	日本	3 083 004
5	比利时	1 814 491
6	德国	749 896
7	西班牙	382 580
8	美国	341 822
9	荷兰	325 067
10	柬埔寨	253 550

注：根据 HS 两位编码的货物贸易数据（IMTS），选取 HS 01 - 20 数据整理得出。

数据来源：https://data.aseanstats.org.

表 11 - 4　2018 年老挝十大农产品进口国家及进口金额

序号	进口国家	进口金额（美元）
1	泰国	261 303 622
2	越南	27 086 030
3	中国	20 525 818
4	美国	4 683 623
5	印度	1 498 957
6	日本	1 256 375
7	德国	990 397
8	澳大利亚	719 057
9	马来西亚	543 823
10	俄罗斯	441 307

注：根据 HS 两位编码的货物贸易数据（IMTS），选取 HS 01 - 20 数据整理得出。

数据来源：https://data.aseanstats.org.

11.2　农业投资政策

11.2.1　宏观政策

老挝是传统的农业国，农业生产占据老挝国民经济三分之一的比重，整体农业生产力较低。自老挝人民民主共和国建立以来，老挝人民革命党和老挝政府特别注重农业发展，政府鼓励与国外的企业进行合作。老挝农业和林业部于 2015 年 2 月颁布了《老挝农业 2025 年发展战略和 2030 年愿景》，提出到 2030 年应用农业新技术，与市场机制相结合，推动农业朝着清洁高效的方向发展，朝着工业化、现代化、国际一体化的方向迈进。到 2025 年，农林部门的投资总量将达到 18.7 万亿基普（约合 233.75 亿美元），其中，国内和外国直接投资的私人投资为 16 万亿基普（约合 200 亿美元），占总投资的 85.56%（每年增加 25%），国内投资占 30%，外国直接投资占 70%。

11.2.2 相关法律制度

老挝政府鼓励外国公司及个人对各行业各领域投资。2009 年颁布了《投资促进法》，2011 年 4 月出台了《投资促进法实施条例》。老挝外商投资法律制度是以《投资促进法》为代表的包括一系列法律法规在内的完整法律体系，为投资者扩大特许权范围，最大限度提升老挝的投资效益。通过完善政策、规划、执行机制、信贷政策以及免税或减税政策等，吸引外商投资到农业和农村地区的基础设施、农产品加工、人力资源培训和市场开发、公共服务等，从而改善本国粮食及营养安全，构建可持续的产品和自然资源条件，增强抵抗自然及其他灾害风险的能力。

老挝现有的农业领域相关的法律有《宪法》《投资促进法》《土地法》《农业法》《合同及侵权责任法》《企业法》《税法》《增值税法》《环境保护法》《海关法》《野生动物和水生资源法》《渔业法》及《经济纠纷解决法》等基本法律。

11.2.3 市场准入及农产品贸易制度

(1) 农业领域外资管理法律制度及政策体系

外国投资者准入制度：《投资促进法》设置了外国投资者准入制度，规定外国投资者可以通过国内或国外独资、国内外合资或合同联营的方式进行投资。要求外国人进行一般经营公司注册的全部资金不低于 10 亿基普。农业类企业在获得企业注册登记证 90 个工作日内出资完成首期注册资本的 40% 并在一年内补足。涉及特许经营的要专门设立特殊目的公司和政府签署特许经营协议。《投资促进法》《对老挝公民有所保留的企业清单》对政府专控的行业类型和专为老挝公民保留的职业以及外国公民及法人不能投资的领域有明确规定。

农业用土地制度及政策：《土地法》规定老挝实行土地公有制，禁止买卖土地所有权，地产市场的交易仅为土地使用权交易。国家对老挝的所有土地拥有占有、使用、收益和处分的权利。外国人和无国籍人如果需要在老挝使用土地，只能向老挝的政府、公民以及其他组织租赁已经获得使用权的土地，并经过所在地方的政府机关批准。外资企业可以在老挝租赁土地进行经营，根据外国人投资的项目、产业、规模、特性，租赁期限最高不得超过 50 年，但可按政府的决定视情形续租。

涉农领域投资制度及政策：外资若投资粮食产品加工企业，注册资金不得低于 10 亿基普（约 80 万元人民币），外资股权占比不低于 20%。与农林业、农林及手工艺品加工有关的项目，企业注册资金应在 210 万元人民币以上。老挝政府对重点产业有税收优惠的政策，根据投资地区的偏远程度和经济社会基础设施条件不同，投资者可获十年、十五年免税优惠，在此基础上如投资清洁、无公害农业以及传统特色工艺品加工行业的，可另外获得四年、三年免税；在经济特区、工业区、边境贸易区以及某些特殊经济区等，按照各区的专门法律法规执行。

外汇管理制度及政策：《老挝外汇管理法》规定老挝国家银行奉行宽松的货币政策，实行外汇管制，央行对外汇流通依法进行监管，个人或企业在老挝境内应当使用老挝基普货币。外国来源的贷款和项目都要得到批准和许可，对任何法律或法规规定的豁免通常需要国会或国会常务委员会（针对法律和执行法令）或总理（针对普通法令）批准。项目发起人必须在老挝设立一个有限责任公司来承接项目，外国实体不被允许拥有项目的直接所有权。外国股东的贷款需要得到老挝人民银行的批准。任何注册资本（股权）仅限于通过老挝银行系统注入的注册资本（需要资本引进证书）。《外汇及贵金属管理条例》规定在注册资本未实缴到位前，投资者不得向老挝境内商业银行贷款。投资者将利润汇出老挝境外，需事先得到老挝国家银行的批准。

涉农劳动法律制度与政策：2013 年通过的现行《老挝人民民主共和国劳动法》分为总则、劳动技能培养与开发、促进就业、劳工保护、劳动合同、女工及童工、工资及薪水、劳工职业安全与健康、流动劳动力、劳工基金、劳工信息登记、禁止条款、劳动争议解决机制、三方组织、劳动管理及监察、奖励及处罚政策及附则十七部分。关于雇佣外籍员工有占比和办理用工手续的规定。

(2) 农资、农产品贸易制度。老挝是最后一个加入世界贸易组织的东盟国家，于 2013 年取得正式成员资格，获欧盟、美国及日本授予豁免进口关税等贸易优惠，其产品一般也可按较低关税率进入全球各地市场。

老挝的进出口事宜受《海关法》规管，财政部辖下的海关局为主要执法机关。老挝对不同商品制定有不同的贸易管理规定，仅允许已在当地注册营商的公司进出口货物，公司进出口货物前，须申领进出口许可证。老挝采用商品协调制度，进口货物及部分出口货物须缴纳关税。此外，所有进口货物均须缴纳增值税，出口货物获豁免增值税。老挝与贸易相关的法律法规还包括《老挝合同及侵权责任法》《老挝水果蔬菜质量管理标准》《牲畜及制品技术管理规范》《产品标准法》等。

11.3 澜湄农业合作进展与成效

11.3.1 主要进展

(1) 参与澜湄机制共建及交流活动①。自 2016 年澜湄合作机制正式建立以来，老挝积极参与机制共建及一系列交流活动，推动"3+5"合作框架下澜湄六国的农业合作。除领导人会议、外长会议等顶层机制下的农业合作共识，老挝还参与了许多农业领域的研讨、培训、互访等交流活动（表 11-5）。国际出访方面，全球湄公河研究中心老挝中心代表团于 2019 年 2 月到中国访问，老挝代表团与中国专家学者就澜湄合作框架下老中农业合作、水资源合作以及如何构建澜湄流域经济发展带等议题进行了深入交流。

---

① 根据 2019 年澜沧江—湄公河合作农业联合工作组第二次会议老挝代表的报告整理。

表 11 - 5　老挝近期参与澜湄合作机制下研讨培训活动情况

序号	活动名称	时间
1	现代农业产业园规划与农业信息科学应用研讨会	2018 年 7 月
2	热带农业畜牧规模化养殖与饲料作物种植技术培训班	2018 年 8 月
3	现代农业可持续发展一村一项目培训班	2018 年 9 月
4	澜沧江—湄公河国家植物品种保护研讨会	2018 年 10 月
5	澜沧江—湄公河水资源合作论坛水伙伴关系促进可持续发展研讨会（昆明）	2018 年 11 月
6	澜沧江—湄公河合作专项基金研讨会（北京）	2018 年 11 月
7	澜沧江—湄公河现代农业实用技术与减贫经验培训班	2019 年 6 月
8	澜湄合作机制协调培训	2019 年 5 月
9	老挝现代农业技术人才培训班、老挝杂交水稻技术人才培训班	2019 年 9 月
10	2019 澜湄农业农资合作峰会暨经贸洽谈会	2019 年 10 月

（2）澜湄合作专项基金项目执行情况①。2018 年，老挝向澜湄合作专项基金申报了 8 个农业项目，其中批准并实施了 3 个项目，分别是澜沧江—湄公河合作机制下农村发展和减贫领域共享和技术交流能力建设；社区推动发展方式对柬、老、缅、越和中国的农村发展影响联合研究项目；通过社区驱动发展路径减贫区域研讨会。2019 年，老挝向澜湄合作专项基金申报了 15 项农业相关项目，重点关注在农村发展、减贫、农村金融、农业合作等方面。

（3）与其他澜湄国家的农业合作

①老挝与中国的农业合作

农业领域是老中合作的重点领域，且呈现快速发展的势头，形成了援助与投资、园区项目与单个投资项目相互促进、共同发展的局面。2000 年，老挝和中国在万象签订《农业合作谅解备忘录》，标志着两国在农业领域开展多方面合作；2001 年，双方在云南签订了《农业合作纪要》，进一步加强了合作。

近年，中国向老挝给予许多农业方面的无偿援助，包括品种引进、农

---

①　根据 2019 年澜沧江—湄公河合作农业联合工作组第二次会议老挝代表的报告整理。

业技术培训、提供农业设备等，如由云南省农业科学院提供技术支撑、云南企业承担的老中农业技术示范中心。

在农业科技交流方面，双方在推进农业科技发展方面开展了频繁的交流合作，运用较多的一种模式是在老挝设立研究机构、农业园区、农业基地等合作平台，签订合作协议，在此基础上进一步开展农业科技合作。例如，云南省同老挝南塔省签订《中国云南省西双版纳州农业农村局与老挝南塔省农林厅合作框架协议》，在老挝南塔省设立了农作物联合育种中心、热带亚热带杂交玉米工程研究中心、低纬高原杂交玉米产业化工程研究中心，开展了玉米新品种试验示范测产、热带水果柚子技术指导及农业技术交流与合作等工作。在 2014 年中国—东盟技术对接洽谈会上，广西壮族自治区亚热带作物研究所与老挝国家农业与林业研究所签订农业科技合作协议，共同开展老挝沙拉湾省热带农业科技示范基地的建设，在热带果树技术（包括遗传学、生物技术、育种、种植和收获后技术等）方面加强合作研究。此外，还有重庆对外贸易经济委员会和老挝万象农林厅合作建立的老挝重庆综合农业园、广西与老挝占巴塞合作成立的中国果蔬新品种试种基地、云南与老挝乌多姆赛合作建立的农业科技示范园、河南长久农业技术有限公司与老挝国立大学合作建立的农林示范基地和农林业测试—科学研究中心等。

近年，老挝和中国的农业投资合作也逐渐增加，主要投资橡胶、中药材、木薯、大米、甘蔗、桉树及猪仔养殖等。截至 2017 年底，中国对老挝进行农业投资的企业有 80 家左右[①]。如云南昌盛达投资有限公司、重庆能源投资集团进出口有限公司与老挝丰沙里省在前期合作的基础上，于 2016 年共同签署了有关发展咖啡基地的合作协议，该项目通过创造就业和促进当地农民创收来减少罂粟种植活动，以减轻当地贫困[②]；湖南炫烨（老挝）有限公司在老挝投资种植水稻，该公司大米于 2015 年获得了中国市场准入；云南农垦集团云橡公司在老挝北部发展橡胶种植加工产业，截至

---

① 农业农村部国际合作司，农业农村部对外经济合作中心，2018. 中国农业对外投资合作分析报告 [M]. 北京：中国农业出版社.

② 佚名，2016. 滇企将在老挝建亚洲最大咖啡基地 [N/OL]. 昆明日报，07 - 28 [2020 - 12 - 22]. http://news. eastday. com/eastday/13news/auto/news/world/20160728/u7ai5876667. html.

2018 年已在老挝北部 4 省建有 21 处生产基地 13 万亩橡胶林，带动发展 50 万亩，建有 4 座橡胶加工厂，年产量 10 万吨。

《关于构建中老命运共同体行动计划》中明确提出，要大力加强民生、减贫合作，推动老挝早日摆脱欠发达状态。中老双方在减贫方面采取了一系列有效合作措施。比如，双方在万象和琅勃拉邦各选一个村实施减贫示范项目，涉及 16 项工程，覆盖基础设施、公共服务、农户生计等多个方面；由广西外资项目管理中心实施的老挝万象市金花村产业减贫示范项目，通过与企业合作，在金花村成功开展了大棚有机蔬菜种植示范，已完成的一期工程大幅提高了当地农民的收入，起到了良好的产业带动作用；2016 年 12 月，在老挝万象启动了东亚减贫合作示范项目，通过项目的实施，改善了项目区村民的生产生活条件，增加了村庄的发展活力。

②老挝与柬埔寨的农业合作情况

老挝与柬埔寨的农业合作详见本书柬埔寨相关章节（10.3.1）。

③老挝与缅甸的农业合作

2008 年缅甸与老挝合作实施小规模内陆养鱼计划，该计划受日本资助，为期 3 年。此外，两国之间在橡胶跨境种植方面保持着合作。老挝与缅甸在农业领域的合作交流较少，未来两国的合作将有较大发展空间。

④老挝与泰国的农业合作

泰国是老挝主要农产品贸易国之一，也是老挝农产品第一大进口国，2017 年老挝有 87.5% 的农产品来自泰国，主要农产品种类有糖、谷物、养殖动物、水果等。2013 年 3 月，老泰两国签署了农业合作备忘录，泰国将在老挝种植甜玉米、芝麻、栗、蓖麻、黄豆、花生、绿豆、木薯、桉树及饲料玉米等作物。该合作备忘录的签订，为泰国进口老挝农产品提供更多的便利。

⑤老挝与越南的农业合作

老越建交已有 55 年，近年，双方在政府层面和企业层面的农业投资、合作、交流等方面都得到了良好发展。2019 年 2 月，老、越两国领导人签署了 9 份合作协议，其中包括《老挝越南政府关于华潘省农业技术中心建设项目的移交备忘录》。2019 年 6 月，老挝和越南的规划和投资部之间在老挝万象召开交流会议，签署了两部委 2019—2021 年合作协议。会上，越南规划和投资部部长阮志勇提出了两国在未来应重点推动的领域为农业和旅游业。

越南是老挝农产品第一大出口国，老挝主要向越南出口糖、咖啡、谷物、水果等，越南市场在老挝农产品对外贸易中占据重要地位。近年，两国间的农业投资合作也不断增多，如老挝最大的企业集团 Dao‐Heuang Group 与越南正蓝星经销股份公司签署合作协议，分销越南的咖啡产品[1]；老挝占巴塞省政府与越南咖啡总公司签署合作协议，在波罗芬高原种植咖啡，这一合作项目不仅促进越南与老挝两国之间的投资合作，还为当地数千名劳动者提供了就业机会，帮助老挝南部加快实现减贫致富计划目标[2]。

11.3.2 成效与经验做法

(1) 积极参与澜湄农业合作。 2019 年 6 月，老挝农林部参加了在柬埔寨举办的澜沧江—湄公河合作农业联合工作组第二次会议，就推动澜湄农业合作快速发展的重大问题同其他澜湄国家交换了意见，达成一系列共识，并表达了对 2020 年举办澜湄合作农业联合工作组第三次会议的意愿。2018 年 1 月，老挝农林部正式提名农业联合工作组组长及中心成员，为建立健全澜湄合作机制及落实《澜沧江—湄公河农业合作三年行动计划（2020—2022）》奠定了工作基础。

(2) 有序推进专项基金项目的申报和实施。 老挝先后向澜湄合作专项基金申报了 23 项农业项目，其中 2018 年申报了 8 项，2019 年申报了 15 项。2019 年老挝申报的澜湄合作专项基金农业项目数量增多，接近 2018 年申报数的 2 倍，且涉及范围更广，对农村金融、服务和经营模式等方面也增加了关注。

(3) 深化与其他澜湄国家的农业合作。 老挝是东南亚唯一的内陆国，

---

① 古小玲，2014. 越南与老挝公司签署新的贸易协议 [J]. 世界热带农业信息 (5)：20‐21.
② 佚名，2013. 越南老挝合作发展咖啡生产与出口 [J]. 世界热带农业信息 (11)：26‐27.

从进出口贸易额看,老挝对外贸易额在澜湄六国中最低,价格上也不具优势,但随着近年老挝对外开放程度的加深,农产品贸易额也逐年上升,对外贸易不断加强。自 2002 年建成首个经济特区以来,老挝目前已有 12 个经济特区,投资企业约有 351 家,投资额达到 16 亿美元。老挝政府积极为现有经济特区和专区吸引投资,努力改善特区和专区投资环境,这些经济特区与专区为政府创造了收入,为老挝人民创造了就业工作岗位。此外,澜湄合作机制建立以来,老挝同其他澜湄五国的交流合作也日益深入,农产品贸易、农业技术、农村发展等不断得到了改善。

（云南省农业科学院国际农业研究所　芮艳兰、郭文）

12 | 缅甸农业发展与澜湄农业合作进展^①

缅甸农业发展与澜湄农业合作进展①

12.1 农业发展概况

12.1.1 资源环境与发展现状

(1) 资源环境。缅甸位于中南半岛西部，与中国、老挝、泰国、孟加拉国和印度相连，濒临孟加拉湾和安达曼海，南望国际黄金水道马六甲海峡。国土面积 67.66 万千米^2，可耕地 18 万多千米^2，目前只有 12.06 万千米^2 进行作物耕种。缅甸属于热带季风气候，全年气温变化不大，年平均气温 27℃。大部分地区都位于北回归线以南，降水丰沛，内陆干燥区年降水量 500~1 000 毫米，山地和沿海多雨区年降水量 3 000~5 000 毫米。

水稻、豆类和芝麻是缅甸三大主要农作物。水稻是缅甸最重要的农作物，也是缅甸第一大对外出口作物，伊洛瓦底江三角洲、锡当河河谷以及实皆省伊洛瓦底江流域是水稻主产区。此外，缅甸主要的作物还有橡胶，尼塔伊州、孟邦、克伦邦、伊洛瓦底地区、仰光地区、若开邦和勃固省是橡胶主产地。根据联合国粮食及农业组织数据显示，2018 年缅甸收获面积排名前十的农作物如表 12-1 所示。

畜牧业在缅甸农业结构中占有很重要的比例，以家庭饲养为主。2018 年缅甸主要养殖的牲畜为鸡、鸭、牛、猪、羊和马（表 12-2）。其中鸡鸭年养殖量达 3 亿多只，近几年缅甸也大力发展牛羊养殖业。

---

① 本章得到缅甸农业、畜牧与灌溉部的大力支持。

表 12 - 1　2018 年缅甸收获面积前十的农作物及其产量

序号	农作物	收获面积 （公顷）	产量 （吨）	单产 （千克/公顷）
1	水稻	71 49 311	27 573 589	3 856.8
2	干菜豆	3 165 311	5 592 419	1 766.8
3	芝麻籽	1 491 788	715 437	479.6
4	带壳花生	1 057 482	1 562 428	1 477.5
5	玉米	519 227	1 984 136	3 821.3
6	豌豆	444 450	358 545	806.7
7	新鲜水果类	402 021	1 433 845	3 566.6
8	鹰嘴豆	382 578	534 602	1 397.4
9	天然橡胶	329 702	275 487	835.6
10	新鲜蔬菜类	286 948	3 798 803	13 238.6

数据来源：缅甸农业、畜牧与灌溉部。

表 12 - 2　2018 年缅甸畜牧业生产基本情况

序号	畜禽名称	养殖数量（头/只）
1	鸡	361 243 000
2	鸭	28 407 000
3	牛	21 786 000
4	猪	19 779 000
5	羊	11 051 000
6	马	96 811

数据来源：缅甸农业、畜牧与灌溉部。

　　缅甸拥有 2 230 多公里海岸线，捕捞水域专属经济区达 48.6 万千米^2，内陆水域约 810 万千米^2。主要渔业为水产养殖、租赁渔业、开放渔业和海洋渔业，其中海洋渔业产量占缅甸整体渔业产量的一半以上，水产养殖约占五分之一[①]。

　　（2）农业发展现状。 近年，缅甸逐渐成为亚洲经济发展最快的国家之

---

　　① 缪苗，陈军，刘晃，王佳迪，2019．"一带一路" 视域下的中缅渔业合作潜力分析与发展策略 [J]．热带农业科学（8）：104 - 110.

一，GDP 增长率 2016 年达 8.4%、2017 年达 5.9%，成为外资最有吸引力的国家之一①。缅甸政府高度重视农业发展，农业是国民经济发展中的主导力量，以农业为基础的各行业在国内发挥着重要作用，国内 70% 左右人口直接或间接从事农业生产。虽然农业规模不断扩大，但缅甸农业发展相对缓慢，据世界银行统计数据，2000—2009 年缅甸农业增加值年均增长率为 11%，但是 2010—2018 年缅甸农业增加值增长速度开始放缓，年均增长率仅为 2%。同时，缅甸农业增加值在 GDP 中的占比持续下降，由 2000 年的 58% 下降到 2017 年的 22%，2018 年回涨到 25%（图 12-1）。

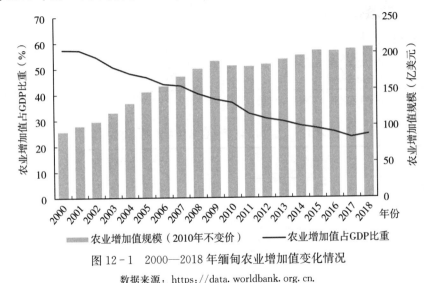

图 12-1　2000—2018 年缅甸农业增加值变化情况

数据来源：https://data.worldbank.org.cn.

为推动农业经济发展，改善农业生产环境和条件，近年缅甸政府及农业部门出台了一系列农业发展政策，鼓励私营企业发展，寻求国际合作，寻求技术支撑等。

12.1.2　农产品进出口贸易

2018—2019 年，缅甸外贸进出口总额达 292.11 亿美元。其中，出口 140.47 亿美元，进口 151.64 亿美元。其中，农产品出口额为 28.15 亿美

---

① 杨德荣，曾志伟，周龙，2018. 缅甸农业发展现状分析 [J]. 营销界：农资与市场，504 (22)：39-43.

元，畜牧产品出口额为 3.29 亿美元，水产品出口额为 6.42 亿美元，林产品出口额为 1.43 亿美元①。

缅甸出口量第一的农作物是大米，是世界第五大稻米出口国。2016—2017 年，出口大米 170 万吨，2017—2018 年则创纪录地达到了近 360 万吨。2018—2019 年，缅甸出口大米（含碎米）已有 200 多万吨，创汇 5.7 亿多美元。其中，中国及其他邻国市场占 32.89%，欧盟国家的市场则占 21.03%，非洲国家市场占 26.04%，其他国家占 20.04%。② 豆类是缅甸第二大出口商品，2017—2018 年，共出口大豆 132 万吨，出口额为 8.87 亿美元。芝麻是第三大出口作物，主要出口到日本、韩国和中国。除上述作物，缅甸橡胶也是重要出口作物之一，90% 的橡胶出口目的地为中国。

2018 年缅甸农产品贸易十大出口国如表 12 - 3 所示，该十国出口农产品总金额占缅甸农产品出口总额的 87.87%。

表 12 - 3　2018 年缅甸十大农产品出口国家及出口金额

序号	出口国家	出口金额（美元）
1	中国	2 790 725 328
2	印度	410 236 263
3	泰国	324 190 432
4	新加坡	130 320 587
5	比利时	80 973 069
6	孟加拉国	75 856 597
7	科特迪瓦	59 523 649
8	几内亚	56 781 175
9	日本	54 845 794
10	马来西亚	47 201 066

注：根据 HS 两位编码的货物贸易数据（IMTS），选取 HS 01 - 20 数据整理得出。
数据来源：https://data.aseanstats.org.

---

① 佚名，2019. 本财年前 10 个月缅甸外贸进出口同比减少 [N/OL]. （缅甸）镜报，08 - 21 [2020 - 12 - 22]. http://www.sohu.com/a/335661078_99924424.
② 缅甸稻谷协会，2019. 本财政年度内缅甸大米及碎米出口情况 [N/OL]. （缅甸）缅甸之光，08 - 06 [2020 - 12 - 22]. https://finance.sina.com.cn/money/future/agri/2019 - 08 - 08/doc - ihyt-cerm9383243.shtml.

2018 年缅甸农产品贸易十大进口国如表 12-4 所示。缅甸在该十国进口金额为 17.35 亿美元，前十大国家农产品进口额占缅甸农产品进口总额的 93.50%。进口额最多的农产品为糖及糖食，动、植物油脂及其分解产品，谷物，粮食粉，糕饼点心；麦芽，淀粉，菊粉，麦麸等制粉工业产品；其余进口金额较大的产品有乳品，蛋类，天然蜂蜜，食用蔬菜、根及茎块，食用水果及坚果，谷物等。

表 12-4 2018 年缅甸十大农产品进口国家及进口金额

序号	进口国家	进口金额（美元）
1	印度尼西亚	558 712 745
2	泰国	460 450 204
3	印度	204 106 381
4	马来西亚	140 818 218
5	澳大利亚	101 686 303
6	中国	86 353 902
7	巴基斯坦	72 874 817
8	新加坡	50 743 060
9	新西兰	33 367 021
10	越南	26 854 816

注：根据 HS 两位编码的货物贸易数据（IMTS），取 HS 01-20 数据整理得出。

数据来源：https://data.aseanstats.org.

12.2 农业投资政策

12.2.1 宏观政策

为了实现将缅甸大部分传统农业经济转变为生产性和可持续的农业经济目标，缅甸政府鼓励民众及外资投资农业，并将农业及相关服务、农产品增值行业列为十大优先投资行业之首，将畜牧、水产养殖业列为十大优先投资行业的第二位。同时，由于与农业配套的生产资料（如化肥、农用机械等）均依靠进口，缅甸政府鼓励投资替代进口的制造业，比如鼓励建设化肥生产厂和农机制造厂等。至于林业，虽未在十大优先投资行业之列，但缅甸政府通过投资法律规定，将森林种植、保护以及其他与森林有关的业务纳入鼓励投资的范围。缅甸政府在农业宏观政策的要求下，努力改善投资环境，积极吸引外资，出台了保障投资者权益的投资法，为了提高工作效率，重新组建了投资委员会，以快捷的一站式服务方式，在短期内办结外资审批。此外，还调整了汇率制度，以稳定汇率、降低投资者的外汇风险。

12.2.2 相关法律制度

缅甸具有较深远的普通法传统。目前，仅缅甸农业、畜牧与灌溉部已颁布了 24 项法律和 155 项法规，主要包括《种子法》《淡水养殖法》《渔业养殖法》《动物健康与发展法》《兽医法》等农业法律法规。

缅甸与农业生产资料有关的法律法规有《农地法》《闲置地、休耕地和未垦地管理法》《经济特区法》《投资法》《水产养殖法》《淡水渔业法》《海水渔业法》《种子法》《农药法》《肥料法》等；生产经营法律、法规有《公司法》《合伙法》《特别公司法》《国有经济企业法》等；与农产品市场流通有关的法律、法规有《商品销售法》；涉农保护制度有《环境保护法》《环境保护法实施细则》及与环境保护有关的标准等。

12.2.3 市场准入及农产品贸易制度

（1）农业领域外资管理法律制度及政策体系

外国投资者准入制度：2017 年 4 月发布的限制投资行业分为四类：只允许国营的行业、禁止外商经营的行业、外商只能与本地企业合资经营的行业、必须经相关部门批准才能经营的行业。禁止外商经营的行业包括：淡水渔业及相关服务、建立动物进出口检疫站（畜牧兽医部门负责动物检查和发放许可证）、宠物护理、林区和政府管理的天然林区域的林木产品生产、小型超市和便利店（占地面积小于 929 米²）等 12 项。外商只能与本地企业合资经营的行业共有 22 项，其中涉农领域包括：渔业码头及渔业市场建设，与渔业相关的调查活动，兽医诊所，农业种植及销售和出口、部分食品生产、加工等。必须经相关部门批准才能经营的行业共有 10 类，其中需经农业、畜牧与灌溉部批准才能经营的行业共有 18 项，涉及种植业、养殖业、渔业、农药化肥等领域的诸多方面。经自然资源与环境保护部批准才能经营的行业共有 15 项，其中涉农的林地、木材、转基因生物及转基因活性生物、珍珠养殖等方面。其中，涉及进出口的投资还应当符合商务部的相关政策。

农用土地、房屋买卖和租赁制度及政策：根据缅甸法律规定，外国人和外国投资者不能取得缅甸土地的所有权，但可以通过租赁方式使用土地。根据《缅甸投资法》的规定，投资者可与缅甸政府、企业、个人租赁土地及建筑物。在经济特区的投资者可通过租赁特区土地和建筑物方式使用土地和建筑物 75 年，特区以外的土地和建筑物，投资者可通过租赁方式使用 70 年。

涉农领域融资制度及政策：在缅甸融资的方式非常有限。缅甸中小企业及大部分外资企业很少从缅甸银行获得贷款，缅籍企业一般通过民间高利贷融资，外资企业多数从境外金融机构或母公司等获得贷款。依据《外汇管理法》，凡是在缅甸投资委员会和投资与公司局办理注册的国内公司以及外资公司，若向国外银行或金融机构贷款，在事先取得缅甸央行的审核和批准后才能向外国相关银行贷款。

外汇管理制度及政策：缅甸尚未完全解除外汇管制，但随着对外开放力度的加大，外汇汇进汇出与前几年相比自由度增加，外国企业可通过银行将美金汇进缅甸。根据《外汇管理法》的规定，外国人或外资公司可以在有关部门授权下开立外汇账户。外国投资者可以将符合规定的与投资有关的资金汇出境外。

涉农劳动法律制度与政策：缅甸有着完善的法律体系，工会也有较强的法律意识，同时，缅甸《劳动法》特别注重保护劳工权益。《缅甸经济特区法》（2014 年）及实施细则还规定，第 1 年聘用缅籍员工的比例不低于 25％、第 2 年不低于 50％、第 3 年不低于 75％。但规定投资者经管委会同意可以不受聘用比例限制。所有雇主必须依法与员工签订劳动合同并为员工按法律规定投保，雇主对其解雇行为应向雇员支付的相应遣散费。

(2) 农资、农产品贸易制度。现行与贸易管理相关的法律和规定有：《缅甸联邦贸易部关于进出口商必须遵守和了解的有关规定》（1989 年）、《缅甸进出口法》（2012 年）、《缅甸联邦关于边境贸易的规定》（1991 年）、《缅甸联邦进出口贸易实施细则》（1992 年）、《缅甸联邦进出口贸易修正法》（1992 年）、《关税法》以及缅甸商务部最新规范性文件等。

12.3 澜湄农业合作进展与成效

12.3.1 主要进展

（1）参与澜湄机制的活动。缅甸积极参与澜湄合作机制下各类交流活动，参加了领导人会议、外长会、高官会、农业联合工作组会议以及各类农业论坛、培训活动。2019 年，在中国商务部和国务院扶贫办牵头下，中国国际扶贫中心组织有关专家赴缅甸选择适合乡村，通过传授大棚有机蔬菜和有机水稻种植技术，开展了农业减贫示范合作项目。2019 年 3 月"澜湄周"在缅甸首都内比都召开，缅甸各界澜湄合作意识不断增强。

（2）澜湄合作专项基金项目执行情况[①]。2017 年 11 月 28 日，缅甸与中国签署了第一批澜湄合作专项基金项目共 10 项，资金预算 240 万美元，其中农业项目 5 项，农业项目总预算资金 109.29 万美元，实施期为2018—2020 年。此次专项基金项目涉及咖啡品质提高、农产品加工技术培训等。目前专项基金项目正在顺利实施中，项目资金使用最高已完成78.21％，平均已使用资金 37％。此批项目涵盖缅甸多个地区，主要针对选定地区的农民开展研讨交流会议，推进加工等基础设施建设，组织开展技术培训，建立示范基地。通过该批专项基金项目，推动了缅甸果蔬农产品由民间小额互市向大额国际进出口贸易转变；创新了农业国际合作运营模式，从整体上推动了缅甸农业的发展，提升了缅甸农业技术水平。

2019 年 1 月 23 日，中国和缅甸双方代表在内比都签署第二批澜湄合作专项基金缅方项目协议，中国将对涉及农业、教育等领域的 19 项中小型项目向缅方提供支持，其中农业项目 7 项，农业项目预算资金约为 328万美元，相较于第一批澜湄合作专项基金项目，此批项目涉及范围更广、辐射地区更多、合作层次更深。此批合作项目将针对蚕业、橡胶、优质种质资源收集示范、渔牧业合作等方向展开。2019 年 5 月缅甸已收到专项基金全部预算，目前 7 项农业专项合作基金项目顺利进行中。此批项目将

---

① 根据 2019 年澜沧江—湄公河合作农业联合工作组第二次会议缅甸代表的报告整理。

致力加强缅甸与中国及澜湄其他国家间的合作、增加缅甸建立生物技术实验室所需的基础设施、提供优质的种质资源、建立研发中心、提升缅甸农产品质量、开展农业技术培训、助力农产品加工技术水平的提升，有效防控动植物疫病的传播，同时加强对网络信息化的利用。

（3）与其他澜湄国家的农业合作

①与中国的农业合作

中国是缅甸最大的贸易伙伴及投资来源国，2015 年两国农产品贸易总额为 3.55 亿美元，相较于 2006 年的 0.72 亿美元，十年间两国农产品贸易增长率为 393.06％[①]。其中稻米是主要贸易作物，据缅甸稻米联盟（MRF）称，MRF 与中粮（COFCO）达成协议，2019 年缅甸向中国出口 10 万吨大米。豆类是中国对缅甸需求量第二大的农作物，2018—2019 年，缅甸共向国外出口 47 万多吨绿豆，出口总额为 3.4 亿多美元（约合 5 151 亿缅币），其中出口至中国市场 10 万多吨，占出口总量的 21％。2017 年中国海关总署与缅甸农业、畜牧与灌溉部等部门高效协作，先后消除中国烤烟、苹果、梨等 6 种农产品对缅出口市场准入障碍，2018 年又成功推动玫瑰、百合、康乃馨 3 种鲜花顺利对缅出口。2019 年 9 月，中缅两国政府签署了缅甸大米、玉米出口中国植物检验检疫议定书，缅甸大米、玉米出口中国检验检疫准入问题得以解决。目前中缅双方主管部门正积极推动缅甸部分农畜产品检验检疫及对华出口。

2014 年 11 月，缅甸畜牧水产和农村发展部与中国农业部共同签署了《中缅畜牧渔业合作谅解备忘录》，推动了中缅农业合作深入发展。

②与泰国的农业合作

2017 年 3 月，缅甸—泰国边境贸易联合工作委员会达成共同合作发展两国贸易、重点发展两国边贸的决议，决定设立单一窗口检查站为两国边境商品通关提供便利。同时缅方代表提出向泰国出口橡胶的要求，希望泰方给予更加宽松的管理措施。泰方代表答应予以研究，争取在按照泰国检疫标准进行检验的前提下，提供更多的便利条件[②]。2019 年 9 月 3 日，

---

① 联合国贸易和发展会议统计数据库（https：//archives. un. org）。

② 驻清迈总领馆经商室，2017. 加强边贸合作泰缅将设单一窗口［EB/OL］. http://chiang mai. mofcom. gov. cn/article/jmxw/201703/20170302541489. shtml.

泰国总理兼国防部部长巴育在曼谷会见缅甸国防军总司令敏昂莱，双方同意共同致力解决边境问题，在海上安全以及渔业等方面加强合作[1]。

③与越南的农业合作

2017 年 8 月 25 日，缅甸与越南双方在缅甸首都内比都发表联合声明，决定建立全面合作伙伴关系。未来，双方将重点关注交通运输基础设施、旅游业的合作，扩大农业、林业、电信和银行业的合作。双方将采取措施改善投资环境、鼓励相互投资[2]。2018 年，两国在仰光工商联合总会举行企业见面会，表示未来两国企业将加强对农业与农村、橡胶等领域的合作，根据工商会数据，2018 年越南在缅甸投资 20 个项目，投资额达到 21.06 亿美元，在缅投资的国家和地区中排名第七位，其中农业投资较前几年有较大上涨。

④缅甸与柬埔寨、老挝的农业合作

详见各国相应章节（柬埔寨 10.3.1、老挝 11.3.1）。

12.3.2 成效与经验做法

澜湄合作开展以来，缅甸不断扩大与其他澜湄国家合作领域，并取得了丰硕成果。澜湄合作专项基金项目的实施，在很大程度上促进了缅甸农业的发展。如澜湄合作机制下的缅甸咖啡产量和质量的提高项目，让缅甸的咖啡产业加快了和世界接轨的脚步。在实施澜湄合作咖啡增产项目之后，咖啡的产量和品质都有了很大的提升，也进一步增加了缅甸咖啡的出口额，增加了咖啡农的收入。同时，围绕澜湄合作五个优先领域，缅甸逐渐加强了与其他澜湄国家间的联系，全面推动缅甸经济发展。

（云南省农业科学院国际农业研究所　徐璐、李露）

---

[1] 王国安，2019. 泰缅双方同意共同致力于解决边境问题 [EB/OL]. （09 - 03）［2020 - 12 - 22］. https://www.sohu.com/a/338473083_123753.

[2] 涂赞，2017. 缅甸与越南建立全面合作伙伴关系 [EB/OL]. （08 - 26）［2020 - 12 - 22］. http://news.cri.cn/20170826/51534702 - 8f24 - e07f - 8eac - 32d0344c3995.html.

13 | 泰国农业发展与澜湄合作进展

13.1 农业发展概况

13.1.1 资源环境与发展现状

(1) 资源环境。泰国位于中南半岛中部，西北部、西部与缅甸接壤，东北部与老挝交界，东部与柬埔寨为邻，南部与马来西亚相连。东南临泰国湾，西南濒安达曼海，海岸线长约 2 705 千米，国土面积 51.31 万千米^2。全境大部分为低缓的山地和高原，按地形特征可分为北部山区丛林、东北部高原的半干旱农田、中部平原的广袤稻田和南部半岛热带岛屿四个区域。全国总农业用地面积 22.11 万千米^2，占国土面积的 43.09％。其中，可耕土地面积 16.81 万千米^2，永久性农作物用地 4.50 万千米^2，永久牧场 0.80 万千米^{2①}。森林面积 14.40 万千米^2，占国土面积的 28％，主要木材资源有橡胶木和桉木。泰国属于热带季风气候，季节划分明显，3—6 月为热季、7—10 月为雨季、11 月至次年 3 月为旱季，年平均气温 24～30℃，年均降水量约 1 000 毫米，降水充沛。2018 年全国总人口 6 942.85 万，农村人口占比 50.05％，农业就业人员占全部就业人员的 30.67％^{②}。

丰富的自然资源为泰国农业生产奠定了良好的基础。种植业是泰国农业最重要的组成部分，并不断向多元化方向发展，形成了以水稻、橡胶、

---

① 东盟秘书处，2018. 东盟统计年鉴 [M]. 东盟秘书处 [2020-12-22]. www.asean.org.
② 数据来源：https://data.worldbank.org.cn.

甘蔗、木薯、玉米这五大农作物为主，以油棕果、热带水果、蔬菜、花卉为辅的多种作物全面发展的种植业态。其中，水稻是泰国最重要的农作物，稻田占全国耕地面积的52.0%，从事水稻生产的农户占总农户的77.5%[1]，年产超过3 000万吨，泰国米在国际市场上享有盛誉，泰国享有"东南亚粮仓"的美誉。天然橡胶是泰国第二大农作物，全国77个府中有52个府种植橡胶，年产约460万吨，其出口量长年稳居世界第一位。甘蔗是泰国主要经济作物之一，年产超过1亿吨，位居世界前列。据联合国粮食及农业组织统计，2018年泰国收获面积排名前十的农作物如表13-1所示。

表13-1　2018年泰国收获面积前十的农作物及其产量

序号	农作物	收获面积（公顷）	产量（吨）	单产（千克/公顷）
1	水稻	10 647 941	32 348 114	3 038.0
2	天然橡胶	3 203 696	4 813 527	1 502.5
3	甘蔗	1 790 208	135 073 799	75 451.5
4	木薯	1 332 379	29 368 185	22 041.9
5	玉米	1 103 147	5 069 143	4 595.2
6	油棕桐果	856 422	15 534 984	18 139.4
7	热带鲜果	577 890	2 551 900	4 415.9
8	芒果、山竹、番石榴	207 758	1 576 419	7 587.8
9	鲜菜豆	154 482	291 846	1 889.2
10	椰子	121 248	858 235	7 078.3

数据来源：http://www.fao.org/faostat/en/#data.

泰国是世界主要鱼类产品供应国之一，也是仅次于日本和中国的亚洲第三大海洋渔业国。泰国湾和安达曼海是两大海洋渔业产区，渔场面积达34.28万千米^2[2]。同时泰国有湖泊面积30多万公顷，有近1 100千米^{2}的淡水养殖面积。曼谷、宋卡、普吉等地是重要的渔业中心和水产品集散

① 王禹，李哲敏，雍熙，等，2017. 泰国农业发展现状及展望 [J]. 农学学报（11）：100-105.
② 张成林，王健，刘晃，等，2018. 泰国渔业及养殖工程发展现状与思考 [J]. 科学养鱼，352（12）：60-61.

地。目前，泰国渔业已从小规模、沿海捕捞发展为深海大规模作业，从单纯捕捞发展成为捕捞和养殖并重的商品化生产。淡水水产养殖主要供国内消费，主要种类有尼罗罗非鱼、杂交鲇鱼、银无须鲃、罗氏沼虾、蛇皮毛足鲈。咸淡水水产养殖通常生产供出口的优质产品，主要种类有斑节对虾、南美白对虾、翡翠股贴贝、泥蚶和牡蛎。据联合国粮食及农业组织统计数据，2018 年泰国水产养殖总产量达 89.1 万吨，其中，海水养殖产量 9.3 万吨，淡水养殖产量 41.2 万吨，咸淡水养殖产量 38.6 万吨[①]。

泰国主要畜牧品种有鸡、鸭、猪、牛、羊和马（表 13-2），全国分为 9 个畜牧区。其中猪、肉牛和种牛主要分布在北部，蛋鸡、肉鸡、蛋鸭、肉猪和奶牛等主要分布在中部。泰国畜牧业在过去十几年里取得了很大成就，主要畜牧品种的产量显著增加，尤其是肉鸡产业发展迅速，使泰国一度成为世界第三大肉鸡加工品出口国，其在牲畜和肉类加工出口总值中的占比达 80% 以上。2017 年，泰国肉鸡出口额达 26.5 亿美元，同年牲畜和肉类加工出口总值 32 亿美元，比 2016 年增长 4.5%[②]。

表 13-2　2018 年泰国畜牧业生产基本情况

序号	畜禽名称	养殖数量（头/只）
1	鸡	277 994 000
2	鸭	12 309 000
3	猪	7 847 507
4	牛	5 576 993
5	羊	511 500
6	马	6 142

数据来源：http://www.fao.org/faostat/en/#data.

（2）农业发展现状。农业是泰国的传统产业，也是泰国的支柱产业之一。近 20 年来，泰国农业保持了长期稳定的增长，年平均增长率保持在 2% 左右，农业增加值占 GDP 的比重维持在 8%～12%（图 13-1）。2018

---

① 泰国水产养殖部门概况，http://www.fao.org/fishery/countrysector/naso_thailand/zh.
② 陈格，汪羽宁，韦幂，等，2019. 泰国农业发展现状与中泰农业科技合作分析 [J]. 广西财经学院学报（3）.

年，泰国农业经济同比增长 4.6%，其中，农作物同比增长 5.4%，禽类同比增长 1.9%，渔业同比下滑 1%，农业管理类同比增长 4%，林木类同比增长 2%[①]。

图 13 - 1　2000—2018 年泰国农业增加值变化情况

数据来源：https://data.worldbank.org.cn.

　　泰国农业的稳定增长得益于政府行之有效的政策支持。泰国政府长期致力发挥本国农业资源优势，发展多元化、外向型农业以支持和推动其他产业发展。早在 20 世纪 90 年代，泰国政府就开始发展有机农业，并以有机农产品作为主导大力发展农产品出口贸易。目前，泰国已建立较为完善的有机农业产业链，包括有机农业技术研发和应用、有机农业生产、有机食品加工、销售网络及质量保证体系。此外，泰国也是澜湄国家中农业科技基础较好、科研水平较高、科技实力较强的国家，在农业科技政策制定、科研资金管理和科技管理体制建设方面形成了从中央到地方，含政府机构、科研院所、高校、农民合作组织、企业等多元主体参与的完整运作体系。

---

　　① 中国驻宋卡总领馆经商室，2018. 泰国明年农业 GDP 增速预计为 2.5% ～ 3.5% [EB/OL].（12 - 27）[2020 - 12 - 22]. http://songkhla.mofcom.gov.cn/article/jmxw/201812/20181202820695.shtml.

13.1.2 农产品进出口贸易

泰国是世界五大农产品出口国之一,是世界上主要的大米、天然橡胶出口国,也是亚洲第三大海洋渔业国及世界第一大产虾大国。大米是泰国出口农产品中的重中之重,占全球大米贸易 25% 以上,长期在世界市场上保持第一位,目前泰国大米主要出口市场包括亚洲、非洲、北美和中东地区。天然橡胶也是泰国自 20 世纪 90 年代以来主要的出口商品之一,泰国生产的 90% 以上橡胶用于出口,橡胶产品主要有烟片胶、20 号标准胶、5 号恒粘标准胶和浓缩胶乳等。泰国还是仅次于巴西的世界第二大木薯出口国家,每年约 80% 的木薯被加工后出口到国外。此外,罐装金枪鱼、罐装菠萝、冻虾、鸡肉制品、罐装海鲜和罐装水果等加工类的食品也是泰国出口的主要产品。

据东盟数据库统计,2018 年泰国十大农产品贸易出口国如表 13－3 所示。泰国对这十个国家出口的农产品金额总计 171.19 亿美元,占其出口农产品总额的 61.33%。除了这十大农产品出口贸易国家,泰国还与老挝、柬埔寨、韩国、荷兰、加拿大、南非共和国、新加坡、菲律宾等国家建立了良好的农产品出口贸易伙伴关系,对这些国家的农产品出口额都在 4 亿美元以上。从出口的商品种类看,泰国出口的农产品主要有肉及其他水生无脊椎动物制品;谷物;糖及糖食;食用水果及坚果;蔬菜、水果、坚果;鱼及其他水生动物等。

表 13－3 2018 年泰国十大农产品出口国家及出口金额

序号	出口国家	出口金额（美元）
1	中国	3 819 540 639
2	日本	3 811 995 524
3	美国	2 797 713 351
4	印度尼西亚	1 406 403 374
5	越南	1 348 977 711
6	马来西亚	930 439 948
7	英国	856 822 195

（续）

序号	出口国家	出口金额（美元）
8	菲律宾	776 274 128
9	缅甸	698 329 950
10	澳大利亚	672 726 570

注：根据 HS 两位编码的货物贸易数据（IMTS），选取 HS 01－20 数据整理得出。

数据来源：https：//data. aseanstats. org.

2018 年泰国十大农产品贸易进口国如表 13－4 所示。泰国从这十个国家进口的农产品金额总计 52.97 亿美元，占其进口农产品总额的 61.54%。除了这十大农产品进口贸易国家，泰国还从缅甸、韩国、日本、新加坡等国家进口农产品，从这些国家的农产品进口额都在 2 亿美元以上。从进口的商品种类看，泰国进口的农产品主要有鱼及其他水生动物；含油的籽，果仁和果实，药用植物；食用水果及坚果；食用蔬菜、根及茎块；乳品，蛋类，天然蜂蜜等。

表 13－4　2018 年泰国十大农产品进口国家及进口金额

序号	进口国家	进口金额（美元）
1	中国	1 343 930 583
2	美国	1 026 727 429
3	越南	458 582 395
4	印度尼西亚	426 497 695
5	印度	410 430 888
6	巴西	382 987 497
7	新西兰	357 351 889
8	澳大利亚	348 077 798
9	马来西亚	289 164 178
10	日本	253 359 362

注：根据 HS 两位编码的货物贸易数据（IMTS），选取 HS 01－20 数据整理得出。

数据来源：https：//data. aseanstats. org.

13.2 农业投资政策

13.2.1 宏观政策

泰国现为中等收入的发展中国家，实行较为自由的经济政策。作为东南亚地区传统的农业国家，农业作为该国重点的基础产业，有效支撑了泰国整体经济的发展。

泰国的农业发展宏观政策，从短期来讲，其"第十二份国家发展规划（2017—2021）"明确指出将把"摆脱中等收入国家陷阱、维持经济稳定增长、减少贫穷和缩小社会贫富差距，同时继续大力推动国家交通和物流体系的基础"作为现阶段包括农业在内的产业发展目标；从长期来讲，其"20年农业发展规划（2017—2036）"明确泰国长期发展目标为"农民稳定、农业富余、农业资源可持续发展"，同时，"泰国4.0战略"将农业发展重点定位于"培养智慧农民，把新发明和现代科技运用于农业，包括信息研究、确定种植计划以及在整个供应链有效管理农产品等方面"。可见，泰国农业未来的发展方向集中于农业科技升级与高附加值农业产业发展，并让农民阶层走向高收入群体。

13.2.2 相关法律制度

泰国制定了完善的农业法律、政策和法规。与生产要素有关的法律法规有《土地法典》《渔业法案》《泰国水资源法》《植物品种保护法》《植物检疫法》《动物饲料质量控制法案》《肥料法案》《有害物质法案》等；与农业环境保护有关的法律法规有《提高和保全自然环境质量法案》《国家环境促进和保护条例》等；与农产品流通销售有关的法律法规有《农产品规格法》《农业期货交易法》《出口和进口商品法》等；与生产经营有关的法律法规有：《食品法》《饲料管理法》等；与涉农投资有关的税收制度及政策有《税法典》等；与涉农保护和金融支持有关的法律法规有《劳动保护法》《劳动关系法》《社会保险法》《合作社法案》《农业和农业合作社银行法》等。泰国以各个单行法案或条例对农业全周期中的各个要素分类进行规制，同时将相关农业各环节的支持政策通过农业合作社制度惠及每个具体的农业生产主体，以实现立法者对农业中各个细分领域的精确化规制。

13.2.3　市场准入及农产品贸易制度

（1）**农业领域外资管理法律制度及政策体系**。泰国在外资农业投资领域的规制方式包含了限制与促进两个方面：一方面，外商投资管理的纲领性法律——《外商经营企业法》（1999）对外商投资领域设立了负面清单，该清单包括三类禁止或限制外商投资经营的业务，分别为"因特殊原因限制投资业务""因对自然资源、生态环境造成不良影响而限制投资的业务"以及"因泰国国内尚未做好准备、无法平等竞争而限制投资的业务"（如需获得豁免，则需要提请泰国中央政府相关部门的批准），上述负面清单涵盖了包括种植业、捕捞业在内的农业生产中大部分的上游产业。另一方面，泰国政府通过泰国投资促进委员会等外资投资管理与促进部门落实农业外资投资优惠政策，以此匹配泰国短期与中长期的农业发展规划。此种规制方式表明，泰国政府希望在保护本国农民利益的基础上，利用外国资本投资农业的下游产业，建立高附加值的产业链，从而拉动泰国国内农业经济增长，提高农业发展程度，增加农民收入，缓解泰国因社会发展不均、贫富差距较大所产生的社会矛盾。

外国投资者准入制度：虽在泰国成立，但 50% 以上的股份由外国人或外国公司持有的公司，将被《外商经营企业法》视为外国（外籍）公司，受到《外商经营企业法》行业准入限制。泰国严格禁止外资进入农业、林业投资领域，不允许外资获得农业耕地、林业耕地所有权和承包经营权。

外国人在泰国开始商业经营的最低投资额不得少于 200 万泰铢（约合 38 万元人民币），当涉及经批准方可从事的行业时，最低投资额不得少于 300 万泰铢（约合 58 万元人民币）。泰国没有专门针对外资并购及外国国有企业投资并购进行安全审查方面的法律规定。

农产品关税限制：在进出口管理方面，泰国对多数商品实行自由进口政策，任何开具信用证的进口商均可从事进口业务。泰国仅对部分产品实施禁止进口、关税配额和进口许可证等管理措施。关税配额产品包括桂圆等 24 种农产品，如大米、糖、椰肉、大蒜、饲料用玉米、棕榈油、椰子油、龙眼、茶叶、大豆和豆饼等。这些产品在配额内实行低关税，在配额外实行高关税。但关税配额措施不适用于从东盟成员国的进口。在出口管理方面，泰国除通过出口登记、许可证、配额、出口税、出口禁令或其他限制措施加以控制的产品，大部分产品可以自由出口，受出口管制的产品目前有 45 种，其中征收出口税的有大米、皮毛皮革、柚木与其他木材、橡胶、钢渣或铁渣、动物皮革等。

外汇管理制度及政策：泰国财政部授权泰国央行负责外汇管制工作。《外汇管理法》提出了外汇管制相关指导原则。

泰国公司及跨国公司可在泰国设立资金中心，从而为其集团公司管理外币。泰国对非居民在泰利息收入征收 15% 的预提税。商业银行可办理外汇贷款偿还业务，且不受任何限制，但如汇入的贷款金额超过 5 万美元或相当金额，则应提供汇入证明。外币可以自由汇入泰国境内，但必须在收到外币现钞 360 日内将外币出售或存入外币账户。

涉农劳动法律制度与政策：《外籍人工作法》是泰国政府管理外籍人在泰国工作的基本法，于 1978 年制订，2008 年修订。泰国劳工部就业厅是外籍人在泰国工作许可的归口管理部门。2017 年 1 月，泰国总理巴育在巡视劳工部时签署了一项总理特赦令，将全面放开在泰国外籍劳工从业工种限制。即在泰国外籍劳工今后将和泰国人享受同等的择业机会，但外籍劳工流动性方面仍未全面放开，须就近选择就业。

（2）农资、农产品贸易制度。泰国主管贸易的政府部门是商业部（Ministry of Commerce），其主要职责分为两部分，对内负责促进企业发展、推动国内商品贸易和服务贸易发展、监管商品价格、维护消费者权益和保护知识产权等；对外负责参与 WTO 和各类多、双边贸易谈判、推动促进国际贸易良性发展等。

农产品和食品市场制度分为几个层次：农贸市场、批发市场、零售市场、终端市场以及期货市场。与贸易相关的主要法律法规有《出口商品促进法》（1960 年）、《出口和进口商品法》（1979 年）、《部分商品出口管理条例》（1973 年）、《出口商品标准法》（1979 年）、《反倾销和反补贴法》（1999 年）、《海关法》（2000 年）和 2007 年《进口激增保障措施法》等。

13.3　澜湄农业合作进展与成效

13.3.1　主要进展

在澜湄机制下，泰国积极参与澜湄农业合作，大力推进外向型农业发展，不断拓宽合作领域，在诸多合作领域取得显著成果。

（1）参与澜湄机制共建及交流活动。 在澜湄机制下，中、老、泰等国通过澜沧江—湄公河的水上贸易更有活力，来自中国的新鲜水果借助运输船顺江而下，在泰国清盛港上岸。泰国借此将清盛港打造为一个互联互通的国际港和物流中心，建立了大量的仓库以承接各国运输来的货物，促进澜湄流域国家的商品贸易往来。2018 年 4 月，中泰双方共同签署澜湄合作专项基金泰方首批项目合作协议。根据双方签署的协议，中国将资助泰方开展包括跨境经济特区联合发展、贸易和物流边境设施升级改造、澜湄商务论坛以及次区域农村电子商务发展在内的 4 个项目。2019 年 3 月，澜湄合作专项基金"澜湄合作国家协调员能力建设"合作谅解备忘录签约仪式在曼谷举行，该项目将有效提升澜湄六国官员参与澜湄各领域合作的能力，为澜湄合作有序推进、提质升级提供人力资源保障[①]。2019 年 7 月，泰国湄公学院与中国热带农业科学院签署了合作谅解备忘录，双方将在澜湄国家农业科技政策、农业政策等方面进行大数据合作研究，联合申报农业国际合作项目，共享区域农业数据、信息资源，共建澜湄国家农业发展研究基地等领域开展实质性合作。2019 年 10 月，泰国副总理兼商业部长朱林在曼谷会见了到访的中国农业农村部部长韩长赋一行，双方就中泰关系、农业双边及多边合作、农业专家互访、人员交流培训等交换了意见[②]。此次会晤将进一步推进中泰两国农业的务实合作。

---

① 杨舟，2019. 中泰签署澜湄合作专项基金项目合作协议［EB/OL］.（03 - 20）［2020 - 12 - 22］. http://www. xinhuanet. com/2019 - 03/19/c - 1124255694. htm.

② 李敏，2019. 泰国副总理朱林会见中国农业农村部部长韩长赋 中泰深化农业合作［EB/OL］（10 - 20）［2020 - 12 - 22］. http://news. cri. cn/uc - eco/20191020/3f0cce69 - b4d9 - 837b - 62a3 - 317b25797236. html.

（2）澜湄合作专项基金执行情况[①]。2018 年，泰国开始计划执行 5 个澜湄专项基金项目，分别为：澜湄次区域气候变化下水稻病虫害及自然灾害监测预报预警中心的发展对水稻可持续生产的影响，执行时间为 2019—2021 年，项目将以澜湄国家的水稻种植农民、水稻相关管理人员和部门为目标受益人，开展人员培训、会议及研讨、联合研究等活动；湄公河—澜沧江国家通用稻米产品标准的制定与实施，执行时间为 2019—2021 年，项目将以澜湄国家的水稻种植农民、水稻管理人员、稻米行业的贸易商为目标受益人，开展人员培训、会议及研讨等活动；促进澜沧江—湄公河国家农业系统的一体化和可持续发展，执行时间为 2018—2021 年，项目将以澜湄国家农业部门为目标受益人，开展技术交流、人员培训和平台建设等活动；饲料种子贸易合作的拓展与发展，执行时间为 2018—2021 年，项目将以泰国、缅甸及柬埔寨的农业生产部门和中国、缅甸及越南的消费部门为目标受益人，开展人员培训、实地考察和商贸配对等活动；适应气候变化与小农的粮食安全，执行时间为 2019—2021 年，项目将以澜湄国家为目标受益人，开展人员培训、会议及研讨、平台建设等活动。

（3）与其他澜湄国家的农业合作

①泰国与中国的农业合作

中泰同为农业大国，有着长期合作的历史。2009 年 8 月，中泰签署自贸协定，促进双方投资与贸易合作。2010 年，中国—东盟自由贸易区正式启动后，中泰两国农业合作加快推进，合作水平不断深化，合作相关领域不断拓展。2013 年以来，中国成为泰国第一大贸易伙伴，两国之间进出口农产品种类日益丰富，泰国的大米、橡胶、热带水果等产品受到中国消费者的欢迎。相关数据表明，两国农业贸易一直保持在中泰两国双边贸易的首位，中国与泰国在农业领域的密切合作已经发展到一个新的高度[②]。目前，中泰农业合作主要涉粮食、渔业和养殖业、动物疾病预防和控制、经济作物以及农村能源五大领域。2019 年 11 月，中国国务院总理

---

① 根据 2019 年澜沧江—湄公河合作农业联合工作组第二次会议泰国代表的报告整理。
② 吴勇，2006. 中泰农业合作研究 [D]. 武汉：华中农业大学.

李克强赴泰国出席东亚合作领导人系列会议并对泰国进行正式访问，双方就加强两国发展战略对接，扩大贸易、投资、产能等领域合作达成广泛共识，将推动两国企业在农业、科技等领域的创新合作。

②泰国与越南的农业合作

泰国与越南在农业生产方面有长期的往来合作。2003 年 4 月，泰国在东盟特别领导人会议上提出了涉及柬老缅泰四国的"伊洛瓦底江—湄南河—湄公河（三河流域）经济合作战略"（ACMECS）。2004 年 2 月，越泰两国政府在岘港举行会议，就在农业、经济、教育和社会等各领域扩大双边合作广泛交换了意见，并就越南加入由 ACMECS 达成一致意见。除政府间开展的农业合作，泰国与越南还频繁开展农业企业间的相互投资。

③泰国与柬埔寨、老挝和缅甸的农业合作

详见各国相应章节（柬埔寨 10.3.1、老挝 11.3.1、缅甸 12.3.1）。

13.3.2　成效与经验做法

（1）**以科技助力农业发展，加强与其他澜湄国家的合作。**泰国在促进澜湄国家间农业科技创新、加强澜湄国家间农业科技人员交流、促进农业可持续发展方面取得了一定成绩。澜湄流域国家的农业都具有相似性，加强泰国和澜湄国家间的农业科技合作，通过农业科技交流，推动澜湄地区农业共同发展。目前，泰国政府与中国科技部重点研发的大湄公河次区域稻飞虱合作防控研究已取得明显成效。

（2）**拓宽合作领域，深化澜湄合作层次。**借助澜湄合作的不断推进，开拓创新型农业合作领域。泰国一直是世界主要稻米出口国，随着近年世界人口的增多和社会经济的发展，对稻米产量和质量的要求也越来越高。泰国通过申请澜湄合作专项基金项目，助力减少稻米病虫害，提升稻米质量。未来，泰国会联合具有相同需求或互补优势的其他澜湄国家，开展多边合作，不断深化农业科技合作层次，增强与澜湄国家有机农业、生态农业、农业生物技术、农业新能源开发与应用，深化农业生物多样性和农业生态系统保护等前沿科研领域的交流与合作。

（3）**以合作共赢为目标，多项战略融合发展。**目前泰国致力打造对外开放的"东部经济走廊"和以数字化智慧农业为导向的"泰国 4.0 战略"，这些发展政策与中国"一带一路"倡议高度契合，也完全符合澜湄合作在农业等领域的优先发展方向。泰国通过将国内外多项战略相互融合形成政策合力，推进了泰国与其他澜湄国家的相互合作与协调发展。

（云南省农业科学院国际农业研究所　李忻蔚、徐璐、李露）

14 | 越南农业发展与澜湄农业合作进展

14.1 农业发展概况

14.1.1 资源环境与发展现状

（1）**资源环境。**越南位于中南半岛东部，国土总面积 33.123 万千米^2，北与中国广西、云南接壤，西与老挝、柬埔寨交界，划分为 64 个行政省。越南四分之三以上的地区为高山和丘陵，气候炎热、潮湿且多雨，北方四季分明，南方分为雨季和旱季。水资源丰富，拥有 2 360 条河流的密集水网，年均降水量约 1 820 毫米，雨季从 4—5 月持续到 10—11 月。越南农业用地面积 12.178 万千米^2，其中耕地面积为 11.536 万千米^2。2018 年全国总人口 9 554.04 万，其中农村人口为 6 123.32 万，约占全国总人口的 64%[①]。

根据联合国粮食及农业组织数据统计，2018 年越南收获面积排名前十的农作物如表 14-1 所示。

近年，随着越南经济的快速发展，畜牧业和渔业也受到重视并得以快速发展，水产养殖业、猪肉集约化养殖等已具规模。水产养殖以虾为主，养殖区域主要集中在南部湄公河流域，多为粗放式养殖[②]。2014 年越南政府提出畜牧业重组方案，采取集中发展九龙江平原畜牧业、为养殖户提供资金支持、提高畜牧业科技水平等措施，实现畜牧业的重组优化。2018 年畜牧业生产基本情况如表 14-2 所示。

[①] 数据来源：http://www.fao.org/faostat/en/#data；https://data.worldbank.org.cn.

[②] 韦锦益，赖志强，潘仲团，2010. 越南畜牧业考察报告 [J]. 广西畜牧兽医，26（3）：140-142.

表 14-1　2018 年越南收获面积前十的农作物及其产量

序号	农作物	收获面积 （公顷）	产量 （吨）	单产 （千克/公顷）
1	水稻	7 570 741	44 046 250	5 818.0
2	玉米	1 032 598	4 874 054	4 720.2
3	蔬菜	865 681	14 879 631	17 188.4
4	天然橡胶	689 486	1 137 725	1 650.1
5	咖啡豆	618 879	1 616 307	2 611.7
6	木薯	513 021	9 847 074	19 194.3
7	腰果	283 986	266 388	938.0
8	甘蔗	269 434	1 7945 204	66 603.3
9	鲜果	245 374	2 801 751	11 418.3
10	花生	185 899	456 762	2 457.0

数据来源：http://www.fao.org/faostat/en/#data.

表 14-2　2018 年越南畜牧业生产基本情况

序号	畜禽名称	养殖数量（头/只）
1	猪	28 151 948
2	牛	8 228 012
3	山羊	2 683 942
4	马	53 473
5	鸡	316 916 000
6	鸭	76 911 000

数据来源：http://www.fao.org/faostat/en/#data.

（2）农业发展现状。 2018 年越南农业增加值为 356.97 亿美元（现价），占 GDP 的 14.6%。总体上，2000—2018 年越南农业增加值变化情况（按 2010 年不变价统计）呈逐步上升的趋势，年均增长率为 3.22%；但农业增加值占 GDP 比例呈现波动下降的趋势，年均下降率为 2.85%（图 14-1）。

14.1.2　农产品进出口贸易

越南是东盟 10 国经济发展速度最快的国家，加入 WTO 后农产品贸

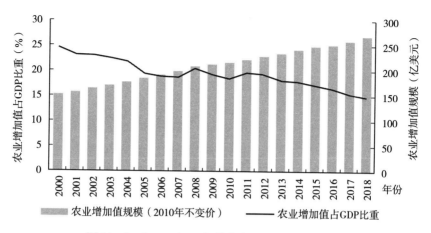

图 14-1 2000—2018 年越南农业增加值变化情况

数据来源：https://data.worldbank.org.cn.

易不断增长[①]。目前农业已成为越南产品出口比例最高的行业之一，每年越南生产的 1/3 的大米、90％的天然橡胶、90％的咖啡和超过 50％的水产品都用于出口[②]。越南是世界 15 个主要农产品出口国之一，根据联合国粮食及农业组织统计数据，2017 年越南腰果、黑胡椒出口总量在全球均排名第一，咖啡、木薯均排名第二，水稻排名第三，橡胶排名第四，茶叶排名第五。

2017 年，越南农业占进口份额比例为 8.0％，相比 2016 年增长 0.7 个百分点；占出口份额 12.1％，相比 2016 年增长 0.9 个百分点[③]。根据东盟数据库数据统计分析，2018 年越南对外农产品进口总额约 142.38 亿美元，出口总额约 249.67 亿美元，农产品贸易顺差达 107.29 亿美元。

2018 年越南农产品贸易十大出口国分别为中国、美国、日本、韩国、荷兰、德国、菲律宾、英国、泰国、印度尼西亚（表 14-3）。越南向该十国出口的农产品金额占其农产品出口总金额的 68.9％。其中，有近四成

---

① Huy N T，夏云，谭砚文，等，2015. 越南农业利用外国直接投资及其对中国的启示 [J]. 世界农业，440 (12)：177-180.

② 冯怀宇，2015. 我国农业标准化示范区模式在越南的应用探索 [R]. 成都：市场践行标准化质量推进强国梦：第十一届中国标准化论坛：758-762.

③ 东盟秘书处，2018. 东盟统计年鉴 [M]. 东盟秘书处 [2020-12-22]. www.asean.org.

的出口农产品去往中国和美国。中国是越南农产品出口第一大国，对中国出口额约占越南全部农产品出口总额的 24.9%。从出口的种类来看，出口额最大的农产品是水产鱼类，出口额达 64.1 亿美元；其次是水果和坚果等，出口额为 59.9 亿美元；第三是咖啡、茶、香料，出口额为 40.7 亿美元；此外，谷物和肉类出口额也较大。

表 14-3　2018 年越南十大农产品出口国家及出口金额

序号	出口国家	出口金额（美元）
1	中国	6 210 352 288
2	美国	3 663 892 842
3	日本	1 818 305 598
4	韩国	1 310 815 387
5	荷兰	871 315 302
6	德国	828 098 034
7	菲律宾	791 333 244
8	英国	600 071 109
9	泰国	587 245 666
10	印度尼西亚	527 607 820

注：根据 HS 两位编码的货物贸易数据（IMTS），选取 HS 01-20 数据整理得出。

数据来源：https://data.aseanstats.org.

越南农产品贸易十大进口国分别为美国、中国、阿根廷、泰国、澳大利亚、俄罗斯、巴西、科特迪瓦、印度尼西亚、柬埔寨（表 14-4）。越南从该十国进口的农产品金额占其农产品进口总金额的 66.2%。其中最大进口国为美国，自美国农产品进口额约占越南农产品进口总额的 11.9%。从进口种类来看，进口额最大的农产品是谷物，进口额达 33.8 亿美元；其次水果和坚果，进口额为 31.5 亿美元；第三是水产鱼类，进口额为 15.2 亿美元；此外，动植物油，油料、杂粮和种子、工业或药用植物、稻草和饲料，蔬菜及块茎谷类、面粉、淀粉或牛奶制品，乳制品、鸟蛋、蜂蜜等动物来源的可食用产品的进口额也较大。

表 14-4　2018 年越南十大农产品进口国家及进口金额

序号	进口国家	进口金额（美元）
1	美国	1 687 732 273
2	中国	1 113 096 037
3	阿根廷	1 094 528 280
4	泰国	1 050 671 063
5	澳大利亚	934 020 787
6	俄罗斯	789 400 473
7	巴西	731 555 581
8	科特迪瓦	726 949 157
9	印度尼西亚	687 822 473
10	柬埔寨	607 052 432

注：根据 HS 两位编码的货物贸易数据（IMTS），选取 HS 01-20 数据整理得出。
数据来源：https：//data. aseanstats. org.

14.2　农业投资政策

14.2.1　宏观政策

越南 1986 年开始施行革新开放。2001 年越共九大确定建立社会主义市场经济体制。2016 年 1 月，越共十二大明确，2016—2020 年越南经济社会发展总体目标是继续夯实基础，早日基本建设成为现代工业国家。

农业是越南国民经济的支柱产业，农业产值约占国内生产总值的 30％。越南政府于 2019 年 7 月 17 日颁布了关于"鼓励和促进企业对农业领域进行有效、安全和可持续地投资"的第 53 号决议，该决议提出了一个愿景，即到 2030 年推动农业朝着现代化、可持续、大规模生产、应用科学技术、创新的方向发展，致力提高农业生产力、质量、效率和竞争力，改善人民的生活，建设现代文明的农村。到 2030 年，越南农业跻身世界 15 个最发达国家之列，其中农业加工业跻身世界十大国家之列。

14.2.2　相关法律制度

农业在越南属于可以获得投资优惠的产业领域。越南政府 2018 年颁布了《关于促进企业投资农业和农村地区的机制和政策》，政府通过豁免和减少土地使用费、豁免和减少政府土地租赁和水面租金，投资农业和农村地区的基础设施，支持土地集中、人力资源培训和市场开发、公共服务等，优先直接扶持企业进行农业科学研究、采购转让先进技术直接投入生产，发展高科技农业园，参与生产—加工—产品销售供应链建设，并对投资程序和手续进行了规定。

农业领域的投资涉及很多部基本法律法规，如《投资法》《土地法》《商法》《林业保护和开发法》《灌溉法》《中小企业扶持法》《科学技术法》《贸易法》《海关法》《进出口税法》《知识产权法》《企业法》《外贸管理法》《环境保护法》《劳动法》《越南社会保险法》等。

14.2.3 市场准入及农产品贸易制度

(1) 农业领域外资管理法律制度及政策体系

外国投资者准入制度：越南政府已将几乎所有外资项目审批权下放至省级部门，仅维持对少数行业的审批。对于国家重大项目，由国会决定项目的投资立项和项目标准，政府负责制定项目审批程序和颁发投资许可证。限制投资的领域包括经营大米出口在内的《投资法》第6条和附件4的修正中共35项。鼓励投资包括行业鼓励和区域鼓励两类，农业行业主要是种、养及加工农林水产，制盐，培育新的植物、畜禽和种子；区域鼓励根据行政区划，分别对社会经济条件特别艰苦地区和艰苦地区两类地区进行鼓励投资。

农业用土地、房屋买卖、租赁政策：越南2013年11月29日颁布了第四部《土地法》，规定土地所有权属于国家，不承认私人拥有土地所有权，集体和个人可对国有土地享有使用权。土地使用期限分为长期稳定使用和有期限使用两种情况。土地使用权的转移必须在国家主管部门办理相关手续。外国投资者不能在越南购买土地，可租赁土地并获得土地使用权，使用期限一般为50年，特殊情况可申请延期，但最长不超过70年。

涉农投资的税收制度及政策：根据越南《投资法》规定，外国投资企业和越南内资企业都采用统一的税收标准，对于不同领域的项目实施不同的税率和减免税期限。自2016年1月1日起，越南企业所得税的基本税率为 20%。为鼓励外商投资企业，越南政府出台相关优惠政策，对于在特别贫困地区、高科技农业区、"大农田"、原料集中产地、农业机械、盐业、水利灌溉、畜牧养殖、食品加工等地方和行业投资的项目，给予税收等优惠。另外，个人所得税、增值税、非农土地使用税、农业土地使用税等在农业生产方面均有减免。

外汇管理制度及政策：越南货币为越南盾，不可自由兑换。2016 年初越南引入新的汇率管理机制，以每日公布"中央参考汇率价格"取代长期实行的固定汇率机制，商业银行在中央参考汇率价格基准上下浮动 3% 制订各自的汇率价格。外国投资者可在越南金融机构开设越盾或外汇账户。如需在国外银行开设账户，需经越南国家银行批准。外国投资者可向从事外汇经营的金融机构购买外汇，以满足项目往来交易、资金交易及其他交易的需求。如外汇金融机构不能满足投资者的需要，政府将根据项目情况，解决其外汇平衡问题。在资本和利润汇回方面，投资项目结束后，外国投资者可以将在外国投资机构中享有的股份或在商务合作合同中享有的资本份额自越南汇出。

涉农劳动法律制度与政策：越南不允许外籍人员持旅游签证在越南务工。在越南工作 3 个月以上的外籍劳务人员须办理劳动许可证。从 2018 年 1 月 1 日起，在越南工作 1 个月以上的外籍劳务人员必须参加强制社会保险。外国劳动者应当按月工资标准缴纳 8% 的退休与死亡金。用人单位按月工资标准最高缴纳 18% 的强制社会保险，包括 3% 疾病险和生育险，1% 工伤险和职业病险，14% 退休和死亡金。与越南政府达成政府间避免劳动者双重征收社会保险的国家的劳动者除外。

（2）农资、农产品贸易制度。 越南主要贸易法律法规包括：《贸易法》《对外贸易法》《民法》《投资法》《电子交易法》《海关法》《进出口税法》《知识产权法》《信息技术法》《反倾销法》《反补贴法》《企业法》《会计法》《统计法》等。根据加入世界贸易组织的承诺，越南逐步取消进口配额限制，基本按照市场原则管理。关于出口，越南主要采取出口禁令、出口关税、数量限制等措施进行管理。越南进出口商品检验检疫工作根据不同商品种类由不同部门负责，食品和药品检验由卫生部负责，动植物和其他农产品检验由农业与农村发展部负责。

14.3 澜湄农业合作进展与成效

14.3.1 主要进展

(1) 参与机制共建及交流情况。2019 年 3 月 18 日，澜湄合作与区域合作新机遇研讨会在越南首都河内举行，越南重视澜湄合作，各部门积极参与这一框架下的相关合作。目前越南正在研究澜湄合作提出的一些新理念以确定澜湄合作专项基金的具体合作项目。

(2) 澜湄合作专项基金申请情况①。目前越南尚未执行澜湄合作专项基金农业项目。在基金申请方面，越南向澜湄合作专项基金提出了"在下一次工业革命背景下越南、中国、老挝、柬埔寨和缅甸农业部门的机遇和挑战""越南、中国、老挝、柬埔寨和缅甸之间边境农业贸易效率提升""加强和促进塞桑—斯雷博克—塞孔河流域水资源和干旱风险的管理能力""越南松拉省 Sop Cop 区社区减贫旅游项目""越南广宁省海下区促进性别平等的农业和旅游业减贫项目"等农业项目建议。

(3) 与其他澜湄国家的农业合作

①越南与中国的农业合作

当前，越中双方就"两廊一圈"构想与"一带一路"倡议的战略对接合作达成共识，自然条件及发展水平的差异造就了两国农产品、农业科技及农业生产要素等方面的互补性。近年，两国政府及地方政府、农业机构在作物生产与品种推广、农机生产、农产品加工、农业人力资源开发、动植物疫病防控、渔业等领域不断加强合作，并签署了《中越农业合作谅解备忘录》《动植物检验检疫合作协议》《北部湾渔业资源增殖放流与养护合作谅解备忘录》等文件，打下了良好的合作基础。2018 年 1 月，中越两国农业部副部长共同主持召开中越农业合作联委会第一次会议，确定了渔业增殖放流与养护、中越水稻杂交研制联合中心、畜禽废弃物处理及沼气、植物保护和农药及跨境动物疫病防治等领域和项目的合作，并讨论通过了联委会的组织结构，意味着中越农业合作新机制的形成。

---

① 根据 2019 年澜沧江—湄公河合作农业联合工作组第二次会议越南代表的报告整理。

在农产品贸易方面,自 20 世纪 90 年代起,中越两国就签订了多项双边经贸协定。2000 年两国签署《关于新世纪全面合作的联合声明》,明确了积极推动两国农、林、渔业的互利合作,鼓励支持两国有关企业和部门在农作物、家畜家禽良种培育、农林产品加工、农业机械制造、海洋捕捞、水产养殖等方面加强交流和合作。2015 年两国签署《农业合作备忘录》,将合作范围拓展至农业研究、技术、贸易和动植物品种的培育、追踪和疾病防控、农业机械设备的生产、农产品加工、专家交流和信息互通领域。2019 年 6 月,越南农业与农村发展部同中国海关总署联合举行会议,以寻求措施促进两国农产品贸易更好、更快发展。

②越南与柬、老、缅、泰四国的农业合作

详见各国相应章节(柬埔寨 10.3.1、老挝 11.3.1、缅甸 12.3.1、泰国 13.3.1)。

14.3.2 成效与经验做法

(1)**扩大农产品对外贸易,推动农业经济共同增长。**越南在其他澜湄国家的农业对外贸易中扮演了重要角色,比如越南是柬埔寨主要农产品贸易对象国家之一,在柬埔寨农产品十大进口国与十大出口国中均排名前列,同时也是老挝农产品出口的第一大国。近年,通过同中国、柬埔寨等签订农产品贸易相关合作协议,越南同其他澜湄国家的农产品贸易合作得到加强,在农业领域的合作关系得到了进一步加强。

(2)**广泛开展国际农业投资合作,促进农业和农村发展。**越南广泛开展与其他澜湄国家之间的农业投资活动,如:通过与中国签署多项农业合作备忘录,将中国的资金吸引到越南的农业和农村发展领域①;在老挝 400 多个越南企业投资项目中有很多项目投资于农业②;与柬埔寨共同举

---

① 越通社,2019. 越中促进农产品贸易[EB/OL].(06 - 19)[2020 - 12 - 22]. https://zh. vietnamplus. vn/%E8%B6%8A%E4%B8%AD%E4%BF%83%E8%BF%9B%E5%86%9C%E4%BA%A7%E5%93%81%E8%B4%B8%E6%98%93/98386. vnp.

② 佚名,2019. 越南与老挝提升投资贸易合作关系实质性[EB/OL].(09 - 11)[2020 - 12 - 22]. https://yuenan. zhaoshang. net/2019 - 09 - 11/724741. html.

办贸易投资促进论坛，共同交流企业投资优惠[1]；在缅甸的农业投资较前几年有较大上涨；与泰国之间也频繁开展农业企业间的相互投资。近年，越南加大了农业领域的国外资金引进力度，为鼓励更多国际农业投资，越南制定了一系列优惠政策，对于直接投资农产品加工、林业种植、畜牧养殖、水产养殖及加工等领域的外资企业提供税收等方面的优惠支持，并修订了相关法律法规，对于农业和农村投资领域最高降低 50% 的外商投资土地租金，为其他澜湄国家企业对越南农业投资创造便利[2]。

（云南省农业科学院国际农业研究所　芮艳兰、郭文）

---

① 越通社，2019. 2019 年越柬贸易投资促进论坛在柬埔寨首都金边举行 ［EB/OL］. （07 - 10）［2020 - 12 - 22］. https://zh. vietnamplus. vn/2019%E5%B9%B4%E8%B6%8A%E6%9F%AC%E8%B4%B8%E6%98%93%E6%8A%95%E8%B5%84%E4%BF%83%E8%BF%9B%E8%AE%BA%E5%9D%9B%E5%9C%A8%E6%9F%AC%E5%9F%94%E5%AF%A8%E9%A6%96%E9%83%BD%E9%87%91%E8%BE%B9%E4%B8%BE%E8%A1%8C/99344. vnp.
② 宫玉涛，2014. 近年来越南的农业改革新举措及评析 ［J］. 农业经济（5）：14 - 16.

Report on the Development of Lancang–Mekong Agricultural Cooperation 2019

Foreign Economic Cooperation Center, Ministry of Agriculture and Rural Affairs, P.R.C

International Agriculture Research Institute, Yunnan Academy of Agricultural Science, P.R.C

China Agriculture Press
Beijing

澜沧江—湄公河农业合作发展报告 2019

Report on the Development of Lancang-Mekong
Agricultural Cooperation

Preface ////////////////

Lancang-Mekong Cooperation (LMC) mechanism was officially established when the first LMC Leaders' Meeting was convened in March 2016. Agriculture is one of the five LMC's priorities. Since the LMC Joint Working Group on Agriculture (JWG-A) was set in 2017, Lancang-Mekong agricultural cooperation has borne fruits in many aspects including the improving mechanisms, strategic alignment, planning and research, scientific and technological exchanges, project implementation as well as investment and trade, which has contributed to building Lancang-Mekong Economic Development Belt.

The Lancang-Mekong Agricultural Cooperation Center (LMAC), set in the Foreign Economic Cooperation Center, Ministry of Agriculture and Rural Affairs of the People's Republic of China, is a coordinating, facilitating and supporting agency for promoting agricultural cooperation in the Lancang-Mekong subregion under LMC mechanism after LMC Water Center, Global Center for Mekong Studies and Lancang – Mekong Enviormental Cooperation Center. In order to collect and disseminate achievements on the cooperation, LMAC has begun to organize the professionals to edit *Report on the Development of Lancang-Mekong Agricultural Cooperation* (hereafter referred to as *Report*) since 2019. The *Report* is intended to update the cooperation progress, present outcomes, experiences and practices of Lancang-Mekong agricultural cooperation for the exchange and reference of agricultural departments and relevant institutions of the six Lancang-Mekong countries.

The *Report* 2019 was co-edited by the Foreign Economic Cooperation Center, Ministry of Agriculture and Rural Affairs of the People's Republic of China, along with the International agricultural Research Institute, Yunnan Academy of Agricultural Science (YAAS). It reviewed almost three-year progress and achievements made in Lancang-Mekong agricultural cooperation from a multi-leveled and comprehensive perspective, containing "General Report", "Special Topics", "Province and Country Reports". The "General Report" analyzes Lancang-Mekong agricultural cooperation on its current situation and development prospect. The "Special Topics" includes the action plan, science and technology cooperation, project implementation, rural revitalization, etc. The "Province and Country Reports" concludes the agricultural cooperation development in five Mekong countries, and three provinces and regions in China.

During writing and editing the *Report*, we have been guided and supported by Department of International Cooperation of Ministry of Agriculture and Rural Affairs of the People's Republic of China, Department of Agriculture and Rural Affairs of Yunnan Province, Department of Agriculture and Rural Affairs of Guangxi Zhuang Autonomous Region, Department of Agriculture and Rural Affairs of Hainan Province. Meanwhile, backing and assistance are from agricultural departments of five Mekong countries as well. In thinking of these, we are indebted and would like to extend our heartfelt appreciation to all of them. For omissions and deficiencies, valuable comments and advice are warmly welcome. With non-stop working and improving, the *Report* is supposed to be a credible and authoritative knowledge product on Lancang-Mekong agricultural cooperation.

Editorial Board

December, 2020

Contents ///////////////

Preface

I General Report

1 Progress and Prospects of Lancang-Mekong Agricultural Cooperation ·· 143

    1. 1 Current Situation and Latest Progress ····························· 143

    1. 2 Opportunities and Challenges ··································· 149

    1. 3 Priorities and Development Prospects ······················ 153

II Special Topics

2 Mission and Working Progress of LMAC ······················ 159

    2. 1 Background ··· 159

    2. 2 Terms of Reference ·· 159

    2. 3 Work Progress ·· 161

3 Three-Year Plan of Action on Lancang-Mekong Agricultural Cooperation (2020 - 2022) ······························· 164

    3. 1 Background ··· 164

    3. 2 Development Goals ··· 165

    3. 3 Fundamental Principles ·· 165

3. 4   Key Areas and Tasks ·· 166

3. 5   Organization and Implementation ······················· 172

4   Progress and Effectiveness of Agricultural Science and Technology Exchange and Cooperation in Lancang-Mekong Subregion ············ 174

4. 1   Background ··· 174

4. 2   Establishment of the Platform and Mechanism for Agricultural Science and Technology Exchange for LMC ····················· 176

4. 3   Achievements of Agricultural Science and Technology Exchange and Cooperation ·· 178

5   Progress and Effectiveness of the Chinese Projects Supported by the LMC Special Fund ··· 183

5. 1   Agricultural Cooperation Mechanism and Foundation Was Improved ··· 183

5. 2   Key Support for Industrial Cooperation Was Created by Experimental Demonstration ······························· 185

5. 3   Agricultural Support Service System Was Improved by Establishment of Information and Technology Platform ····· 186

5. 4   Joint Research and Action Were Conducted to Build Innovative and Green Lancang-Mekong Subregion ·············· 188

5. 5   Cooperation of Capacity Building Were Carried out to Build Talent Cultivation Support System ··························· 191

6   Regional Rural Revitalization ······································ 194

6. 1   Sharing of the Experience of Rural Revitalization ·············· 195

6. 2   Poverty Alleviation Demonstration Cooperation Carried Out to Promote Comprehensive and Sustainable Development of Rural Areas ·· 197

6. 3   Enhance Infrastructure Construction and Improve People's Livelihood to Promote Rural Development ····················· 204

6. 4 Technology Extension and Industry Development to Promote
from Poverty to Prosperity in Rural Areas ······················ 209

Ⅲ Province and Country Reports

**7 Agricultural Development and the Progress of Lancang-Mekong
Agricultural Cooperation in Yunnan Province of China** ·············· 217

7. 1 General Situation of Agricultural Development ················· 217
7. 2 Lancang-Mekong Agricultural Cooperation ···················· 221
7. 3 Future Cooperation ·· 227

**8 Agricultural Development and the Progress of Lancang-Mekong Agricultural
Cooperation in Guangxi Zhuang Autonomous Region of China** ············ 231

8. 1 Overview of Agricultural Development ······················· 231
8. 2 Agricultural International Cooperation ······················· 232
8. 3 Lancang-Mekong Agricultural Cooperation ··················· 235
8. 4 Future Cooperation Prospect ································· 242

**9 Agricultural Development and the Progress of Lancang-Mekong
Agricultural Cooperation in Hainan Province of China** ················ 247

9. 1 Overview of Agricultural Development ······················· 247
9. 2 International Agricultural Cooperation ······················ 248
9. 3 Lancang-Mekong Agricultural Cooperation ··················· 252
9. 4 Future Cooperation ·· 258

**10 Agricultural Development and the Progress of Lancang-Mekong
Agricultural Cooperation in Cambodia** ··························· 262

10. 1 Overview of Agricultural Development ······················ 262
10. 2 Agricultural Investment Policy ···························· 269

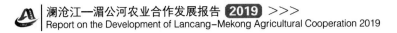
10. 3　Progress and Results of Lancang-Mekong
　　　Agricultural Cooperation ·················· 273

11　Agricultural Development and the Progress Lancang-Mekong Agricultural Cooperation in Laos ·················· 284

11. 1　Overview of Agricultural Development ·················· 284
11. 2　Agricultural Investment Policy ·················· 290
11. 3　Progress and Results of Lancang-Mekong
　　　Agricultural Cooperation ·················· 295

12　Agricultural Development and the Progress of Lancang-Mekong Agricultural Cooperation in Myanmar ·················· 304

12. 1　Overview of Agricultural Development ·················· 304
12. 2　Agricultural Investment Policy ·················· 310
12. 3　Progress and Results of Lancang-Mekong
　　　Agricultural Cooperation ·················· 314

13　Agricultural Development and the Progress of Lancang-Mekong Agricultural Cooperation in Thailand ·················· 320

13. 1　Overview of Agricultural Development ·················· 320
13. 2　Agricultural Investment Policy ·················· 328
13. 3　Progress and Results of Lancang-Mekong
　　　Agricultural Cooperation ·················· 333

14　Agricultural Development and the Progress of Lancang-Mekong Agricultural Cooperation in Vietnam ·················· 340

14. 1　Overview of Agricultural Development ·················· 340
14. 2　Agricultural Investment Policy ·················· 346
14. 3　Progress and Results of Lancang-Mekong
　　　Agricultural Cooperation ·················· 350

I

General Report

1 | Progress and Prospects of Lancang-Mekong Agricultural Cooperation

In March 2016, the first Lancang-Mekong Cooperation (hereinafter referred to as LMC) leaders' meeting was held in Hainan Province, China, and the LMC mechanism was officially established. Agriculture is one of the five priority areas of LMC. Lancang-Mekong agricultural cooperation has good foundation, great potential, and remarkable results. With the development and change of the international situation, Lancang-Mekong agricultural cooperation also faces new opportunities and challenges. The six countries should work together to strengthen cooperation in the fields such as improving mechanisms, planning and research, strategic alignment, scientific and technological exchanges, investment and trade, and jointly implement the key projects to promote the deepening of subregional agricultural cooperation and help the building of Lancang-Mekong Economic Development Belt.

1.1 Current Situation and Latest Progress

1.1.1 Initial Achievements in Building the Cooperation Mechanism and System

(1) **LMC Joint Working Group on Agriculture (JWG-A) was established to discuss cooperation plans.** On September 11, 2017, the first meeting of JWG-A was held in Guangxi Zhuang Autonomous Region, China. This meeting discussed concept paper of JWG-A, and the

Lancang-Mekong agricultural cooperation mechanism was officially launched. On June 12-13, 2019, the second meeting of JWG-A was held in Siem Reap, Cambodia, under the joint chairmanship of the heads of delegations of Cambodia and China. At the meeting, the Chinese delegation proposed several initiatives such as the establishment of Exchange and Cooperation Consortium for Agricultural Science and Technology in the LMC (ECCAST-LMC), the joint construction of the Lancang-Mekong Technology Extension and Information Sharing Platform, the joint establishment of Lancang-Mekong Agricultural Cooperation Center as a regional agency for Lancang-Mekong agricultural cooperation, and formulating *the draft Three-Year Plan of Action on Lancang-Mekong Agricultural Cooperation (2020 – 2022)*. The initiatives were supported by the representatives of all countries.

（2）**Lancang-Mekong Agricultural Cooperation Center was established to serve regional agricultural cooperation.** In order to implement the consensus of the Establishing Lancang-Mekong Agricultural Cooperation Center at the second LMC leaders' meeting, Ministry of Agriculture and Rural Affairs of the People's Republic of China set up the Lancang-Mekong Agricultural Cooperation Center (hereinafter referred to as LMAC) at the Foreign Economic Cooperation Center at the end of January 2019. Basing on the Belt and Road Initiative and LMC mechanism, focus on the key areas, create the platform for agricultural technology exchange, joint research, investment and trade cooperation in the Lancang-Mekong subregion, and promote the experience sharing, position coordination, and practical cooperation in the agricultural and food sectors in this region. At the second meeting of JWG-A held in June 2019, the representative of China introduced the background, responsibilities and plans of LMAC to all the delegates, and put forward the goal and vision of building LMAC into a permanent executive organization for JWG-A. The proposal received the support of all participants.

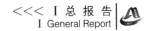

(3) **The Exchange and Cooperation Consortium for Agricultural Sciences and Technology in the LMC (ECCAST-LMC) and the Water Ecological Cooperation Group was established to improve the support system of Lancang-Mekong agricultural cooperation.** In order to implement the cooperation consensus reached by the six countries at the second meeting of JWG-A held in Cambodia in June 2019, and in response to the initiative of "Expand exchanges and cooperation in agricultural science and technology, support research institutions to enhance information sharing, communication and exchange of visits", proposed in *Five-Year Plan of Action on LMC* (2018 – 2022), based on the original "Exchange and Cooperation Consortium for Agricultural Science and Technology in Great Mekong Subregion (ECCAST-GMS)", China Yunnan Academy of Agricultural Sciences took the lead in the establishment of the ECCAST-LMC in August 2019, with a wider scope and richer cooperation content. In the next step, the ECCAST-LMC will actively expand the scope of its members, cooperate with more agricultural research and education institutions in the Lancang-Mekong region, to carry out scientific and technological exchanges and cooperation in a wider range of fields such as planting, animal husbandry and fishery. In order to improve the cooperation mechanism for the protection of aquatic organisms in the Lancang-Mekong subregion, promote the cooperation in the capacity-building of aquaculture, and establish a cooperation platform for the ecological conservation of water resources, the Water Ecological Cooperation Group initiated by the Yangtze River Basin Fishery Administration and Management Office of the Ministry of Agriculture and Rural Affairs of China will be established soon.

(4) **The LMC Village Head Forums were held to promote exchanges at the grassroots level.** In April 2017, the Lancang-Mekong Agricultural Cooperation and the China-Cambodia-Laos-Myanmar-Thailand Village Head Forum were held in Mengla County, Yunnan Province, China. The

forums focused on "strengthening rural cooperation and benefiting grassroots farmers", provided a platform of villages cooperation, rural construction, and agricultural development for the village heads in LMC countries, and promoted rural exchanges, summarizing development experiences, sharing cooperation achievements and tapping cooperation potential in participating countries. The second LMC Village Head Forum was held in Mangshi, Yunnan Province, China in April 2018. The six LMC countries shared the experience and made discussions on the theme of promoting rural vitalization. The forum issued *Mangshi Initiative on Cooperation between LMC Villages and Cooperatives*, and eight cooperation agreements were signed during the exhibition and matchmaking activities, with a contract amount of about 120 million CNY.

1. 1. 2 Initial Progress in Carrying out Planning and Research on Lancang-Mekong Agricultural Cooperation

（1）*Three-Year Plan of Action on Lancang-Mekong Agricultural Cooperation* （2020－2022） was formally approved. *Five-Year Plan of Action on LMC* （2018－2022） proposed that "Strengthen policy coordination, and strengthen coordination to ensure food and nutrition security, and food safety, promote investment opportunity and enhance cooperation on sustainable · agricultural development". In order to strengthen the integration of the agricultural strategies of the LMC countries and promote the Lancang-Mekong agricultural cooperation in a pragmatic and orderly manner, LMAC led the drafting of *Three-Year Plan of Action on Lancang-Mekong Agricultural Cooperation* （2020－2022）, which was submitted to the representatives of the second meeting of JWG-A in June 2019 for discussion. All the representatives from the six countries fully affirmed the significance of formulating the plan, and fed back their opinions and suggestions on the plan at the end after the meeting. The plan was formally approved in early 2020.

146

（2）The "Report on Lancang-Mekong Agricultural Cooperation Development" is being compiled. In order to track the progress, effectiveness and experience of Lancang-Mekong agricultural cooperation in various fields, countries, and provinces in time, LMAC launched the compilation work of "Report on Lancang-Mekong Agricultural Cooperation Development" for the first time in September 2019, with the support from the Yunnan Academy of Agricultural Sciences and other institutions and experts. It is planned to issue the report regularly for the references of the LMC JWG-A, relevant departments and scientific research institutions.

（3）The research on key agricultural cooperation sectors of LMC countries is being carried out. For purposes of promoting the advantageous industries cooperation in the LMC countries, LMAC has started to establish partnerships with relevant scientific research institutions and enterprises to strengthen the research on key agricultural sectors of LMC countries, such as rice, natural rubber, sugar, palm, and fruits, as well as information collection and research on the current situation of agricultural development, industry characteristics, investment policies and environment of LMC countries, so as to provide basic support for promoting the integration of Lancang-Mekong agricultural cooperation strategies, project design and implementation, and enterprises' economic and trade cooperation.

1.1.3 Remarkable Achievements in Expanding Agricultural Trade and Investment Cooperation

（1）The scale of agricultural trade has been continuously expanding. In recent years, China's agricultural products trade with the five Mekong countries has been continuously expanding, with imports growing faster than exports. In 2018, the total agricultural trade volume between China and the five Mekong countries was 18.918 billion USD, accounting for 8.7% of China's total agricultural trade, which increased by 15.8% over the previous year, and a nearly 10-fold increase from the beginning of the establishment of China-ASEAN Free Trade Area in 2002. Among them, the import value of agricultural products was 9.652 billion USD, which increased 19.1% over the previous year, while the export value was 9.266 billion USD, which increased by 12.5% over the previous year.

(2) **Foreign investment in agriculture is going to grow.** The Mekong countries are the important region for China's agricultural foreign investment. By the end of 2018, China's agricultural investment stocks in the five Mekong countries reached 3.16 billion USD, accounting for 62.7% of China's agricultural investment stock in ASEAN, and 16% of China's total foreign agricultural investment stock. China has invested more than 280 companies in the five Mekong countries, accounting for nearly 30% of the total number of Chinese overseas investment enterprises. The overseas investment areas have developed from direct cultivation to processing, warehousing, logistics and other industrial chain links, involving a variety of agricultural products such as grain (rice), economic crops (rubber, palm, cassava, sugarcane).

(3) **The agricultural cooperation parks are jointly built for foreign economic and trade cooperation.** China has jointly established a number of agricultural cooperation parks with Cambodia, Laos and other countries by earnestly implements the initiative of *Five-Year Plan of Action on LMC (2018-2022)*, carried out rice, natural rubber, tropical fruits and other advantageous agricultural product cooperation of the whole industrial chain including varieties cultivation, technology demonstration, production and processing, trade and logistics. Furthermore, it helps promote the establishment of a standard system of the production of advantageous agricultural products in the LMC countries, form the agglomeration effects of industry, capital, technology, and build a platform for expanding trade and investment cooperation in LMC countries.

1. 1. 4　Smooth Progress in the Implementation of Agricultural Technology Exchange Projects

（1）**Lancang-Mekong agricultural technology exchange have achieved remarkable results.** On various platforms, such as the ECCAST-GMS, overseas crop improved variety experiment stations, agricultural science and technology demonstration bases, and joint laboratories, LMC countries carried out joint research and cooperation on agricultural technology issues of common concern to cultivate, demonstrate and promote varieties suitable for local planting, prevention and control of animal and plant diseases, personnel training, etc.

（2）**The Lancang-Mekong Agricultural Cooperation projects have been implemented successfully.** China fully utilized the LMC Special Fund, the Asian Regional Cooperation Special Fund and other fund channels, mobilized resources from all parties to implement the important initiatives of the LMC leaders' meeting, created cooperation highlights and model projects, and improved agricultural science and technology level and comprehensive production capacity in LMC countries. From 2017 to 2018, Ministry of Agriculture and Rural Affairs of the People's Republic of China organized and implemented 15 projects supported by LMC Special Fund, with a total budget of 26. 98 million CNY. The agricultural cooperation and exchanges have achieved initial results by developing overseas demonstrations and technical cooperation, capacity building, joint research and action, etc.

1. 2　Opportunities and Challenges

1. 2. 1　Opportunities

（1）**The Belt and Road Initiative promotes the integration of agricultural development strategies in LMC countries.** The Lancang-Mekong countries are good neighbors enjoying geographical proximity and cultural affinity. They are important parts of the Belt and Road, China-Indochina Peninsula Economic Corridor and the Bangladesh-China-India-Myanmar Economic Corridor. In May 2017, the Ministry of Agriculture of the People's Republic of China and other three ministries and commissions jointly issued *Vision and Action on Jointly Promoting Agricultural Cooperation on the Belt and Road*, which clarified the cooperation goals, principles, ideas and priorities, planed the action steps. It is stated the requirements included "strengthening the existing multilateral agricultural-related mechanisms of LMC" and "jointly devising the plan of bilateral cooperation on agricultural investment, increasing agricultural investment in least developed countries". The Belt and Road Initiative has provided a major historic opportunity for promoting integration of mutual strategies, developing agricultural cooperation with complementary advantages and mutual benefits.

(2) There is a strong demand for international cooperation in agriculture in LMC countries. LMC countries regard agriculture as a basic industry, and developing agriculture and solving food security issues have always been the top priorities. These countries have strong complementarity in agricultural resources, technology, and industrial structure, etc. , and they have strong demands for cooperation with each other. Especially, in improving agricultural infrastructure, developing modern agriculture, expanding agricultural exports, attracting foreign investment, and developing international agricultural cooperation have strong demands. China attaches great importance to the basic status and role of agriculture, and has successively made major strategic plans for promoting agricultural development and agricultural opening-up. In 2016, the General Office of the State Council issued several opinions on promoting agricultural foreign cooperation, which has provided guarantees for developing international agricultural cooperation and Lancang-Mekong agricultural cooperation. In 2018, China began to implement the Rural Vitalization Strategy. It is

urgent to expand the space for agricultural development and build a mutually beneficial and win-win situation with complementary resource endowments, technological advantages, product flows, and industrial patterns with neighboring countries.

(3) The East Asian Integration Process provides a good regional environment. At present, the East Asian regional integration is making progress steadily. Regional Comprehensive Economic Partnership (RCEP) agreement has been officially signed. The China-Japan-South Korea Free Trade Area negotiations have been fully accelerated, and it was agreed to build a "RCEP+" free trade agreement on the basis of RCEP and vigorously promote the cooperation among the three countries in the fourth party. The relationship between China and ASEAN has continuously achieved new developments, and jointly issued *the China-ASEAN Strategic Partnership Vision* 2030. The protocol for upgrading the China-ASEAN Free Trade Area has come into full force, and the revised version of the rules of origin of products have been officially implemented. The relationship between China and ASEAN has achieved a leap from quantitative accumulation to qualitative contributions, resulting in important contributions to the prosperity and stable development in East Asia. As a new link of China-ASEAN cooperation, LMC countries are all members of the RCEP, and also are the key areas for trilateral and quadrilateral cooperation carried out by China, Japan and South Korea. In the new era, the stable and positive situation in East Asia provides a great macro environment for Lancang-Mekong agricultural cooperation.

1. 2. 2　Challenges

(1) Global trade protectionism and unilateralism are on the rise. At present, the international situation is undergoing profound and complex changes. Since the global financial crisis, the recovery of major global economies has been anemic, the world economy has even run into recession risks, which brings new and severe challenges to countries around the world, including the Lancang-Mekong subregion. Meanwhile, the intensifying global protectionism, the impact of multilateral rules and international order, further aggravated the external environment of agricultural international cooperation. Facing many complex, uncertain factors and downward pressure on the world economy, China and the Mekong countries should jointly maintain the international system with the United Nations as the core and the multilateral trading system with the WTO as the core, jointly safeguard the valuable achievements of cooperation in various fields and the great situation of deepening subregional cooperation, and eventually benefit the countries and people in the region.

(2) **Climate change, natural disasters and international factors exacerbate the vulnerability of subregional cooperation.** With the aggravation of global climate change and the frequent occurrence of extreme weather, the food security and sustainable development of the social economy in the Lancang-Mekong subregion are exposed to threats. Natural disasters occur frequently, and the loss of the disasters intensified from time to time in the Lancang-Mekong subregion. Especially, floods and droughts, the distribution of water resources, and ecological and environmental problems bring direct impacts on the agricultural production and cooperation in the Lancang-Mekong subregion. In addition, as an important production and supply base of rice and natural rubber in the world, the agricultural production and international cooperation in the Lancang-Mekong subregion are also affected by the supply and demand, macro policies, and the exchange rate changes in the world market.

(3) **The construction of agricultural infrastructure is relatively lagging.** To promote the Lancang-Mekong agricultural cooperation, sound infrastructure construction are needed as a strong support. The infrastructures such as water, electricity, transportation, and communications in the Lancang-Mekong subregion are relatively backward. Furthermore, less investment

in construction of farmland water conservancy facilities, dependence on the weather, and backward development of the agricultural industry, have restricted the smooth implementation of agricultural cooperation projects and increased the difficulty of foreign investment.

1.3 Priorities and Development Prospects

1.3.1 Establishing and Improving the Mechanism and System

We will improve the inter-governmental cooperation mechanism, and gradually expand and establish the mechanism of the Lancang-Mekong Agricultural Cooperation High-level Officials and Ministerial Meetings on the basis of the LMC JWG-A. We will give full play to the coordination and service role of LMAC as the permanent executive organization of the JWG-A, and promote the establishment of the Lancang-Mekong Agricultural International Cooperation Center with LMAC currently established by China as the core. Also we will give full play to the leading role of ECCAST-LMC in the subregional agricultural science and technology exchange, gradually build the Lancang-Mekong cooperation mechanism for plant disease and insect pest prevention and control, animal epidemic disease prevention and control, promote the establishment of the Water Ecological Cooperation Working Group and the LMC Agricultural Sector Development Group, and continuously improve the mechanism and system of Lancang-Mekong agricultural cooperation.

1.3.2 Deepening Research on Agricultural Cooperation Plan

We will track and analyze the agricultural development environment, international investment dynamics of key sectors and agricultural cooperation needs of LMC countries, promote to build the Lancang-Mekong Agricultural Cooperation Institute, strengthen exchanges with agricultural research institutions of LMC countries, carry out joint research, build experts database on agricultural sector research, planning, technology of LMC countries, and gradually form a support system for agricultural cooperation research in LMC countries. We will regularly summarize the progress and achievements of Lancang-Mekong agricultural cooperation, and compile the Report on Lancang-Mekong Agricultural Cooperation. Based on *Three-Year Plan of Action on Lancang-Mekong Agricultural Cooperation* (*2020 - 2022*), we will study the key agricultural cooperation projects and policy suggestions in detail, improve the top-level design of Lancang-Mekong agricultural cooperation, and promote practical cooperation.

1.3.3 Continuously Deepening Exchanges and Cooperation at All Levels

We will give play the functions role of LMAC as a subregional coordination and support institution, continue to deepen agricultural cooperation and exchanges at all levels, strengthen horizontal and vertical strategic integration. On the one hand, we will strengthen the agricultural strategic coordination and cooperation exchanges among the LMC countries, and jointly promote cooperation in the fields of agricultural science and technology, economy and trade, and cross-border epidemic prevention and control in the subregion. On the other hand, we will strengthen the agricultural strategic coordination among agricultural cooperation departments, such as the governments (ministries, provinces, counties, etc.), enterprises and research institutions. We will strengthen the plan interpretation and policy publicity to make all the departments to find the matching points and promote collaborative linkage.

1.3.4 Gradually Optimizing Agricultural Trade Cooperation

Under the background of Lancang-Mekong subregion integration and the community of common destiny, agricultural trade in LMC countries is facing the great development opportunities. We will gradually play the role and service functions of the government, rationally guide the optimization and upgrading of the structure of agricultural trade, change the extensive model, upgrade levels, expanding the value chains, and improve the market competitiveness of agricultural products. We should tap the resource potential and complementary advantages of each country, and optimize the distribution of benefits and the structure of agricultural trade to narrow the differences among countries. We will strengthen and improve the construction of agricultural trade facilities, deepen cooperation in inspection, quarantine and supervision of agricultural products, and improve the facilitation of agricultural trade.

1. 3. 5 Raising the Level of Agricultural Investment Cooperation

The level of agricultural investment cooperation in LMC countries will continue to expand and upgrade with the overall growth of agricultural investment cooperation in recent years. The investment fields and ways will be more diversified, from the planting of grain, natural rubber, cassava, sugarcane and tropical fruit to variety value chains, such as research, processing and logistics. And the cooperation of the quality and safety of agricultural products will be strengthened. We will support and promote the construction of the agricultural cooperation park to create the investment cooperation platform in LMC countries, which can attract the related domestic and foreign companies to enter the park to form the collective effects. The agricultural cooperation parks will share resources, achieve mutually beneficial and win-win results, enhance the competitiveness, and promote the development of local related industries and the employment of farmers.

1. 3. 6 Gradually Focusing and Establishing Key Project Brands

Combined with the development needs of LMC countries, we will focus on the implementation of the LMC Special Fund project, especially gradually strengthen the projects about agricultural technology promotion and information exchanging, testing and demonstration, capacity building, agricultural parks construction, quality and safety of agricultural product. We should integrate resources, create cooperation highlights and form a cluster effect to improve the agricultural competitiveness and serve the construction of the Lancang-Mekong Economic Development Belt.

(Written by Jiang Ye and Zhu Zidong,
Foreign Economic Cooperation Center,
Ministry of Agriculture and Rural Affairs, China;
Translated by Mo Nan,
International Agriculture Research Institute,
Yunnan Academy of Agricultural Sciences, China)

II

Special Topics

2 | Mission and Working Progress of LMAC

2.1 Background

In January 2018, at the second LMC Leaders' Meeting, China proposed to jointly establish the LMAC, which was recognized by all the LMC countries. At the end of January 2019, Ministry of Agriculture and Rural Affairs of the People's Republic of China officially established the LMAC. Under the Belt and Road Initiative (BRI) and LMC mechanism, with a focus on the key areas, LMAC aims to perform as a platform for technological exchange, joint research and investment and trade cooperation in the Lancang-Mekong subregion, and promote the experience sharing, position coordination, and pragmatic cooperation in agricultural and food sectors in the region, which can help the building of Lancang-Mekong Economic Development Belt.

2.2 Terms of Reference

The establishment of the LMAC in the Ministry of Agriculture and Rural Affairs of the People's Republic of China was a preliminary step to implement the proposals at the Second LMC Leaders' Meeting. In the future, LMAC will be gradually upgraded to a coordination and service agency which is co-established and co-managed by the six LMC countries, and it will become the permanent executive organization of LMC JWG-A to promote rapid and sustainable development of the Lancang-Mekong agricultural cooperation.

The terms of reference of LMAC are:

(1) To enhance the complementarity between the development strategies on agricultural cooperation, strengthen research exchanges, and disseminate research outcomes among Lancang Mekong countries, LMAC will:

-track and analyze the agricultural development environment, international investment trends of key industries and the demands for agricultural cooperation in LMC countries;

-research and propose the initiatives, policies and project proposals for subregional agricultural cooperation;

-organize and compile reports on Lancang-Mekong agricultural cooperation research.

(2) To maintain the LMC Mechanism on Agriculture, LMAC will:

-ensure the smooth operation of LMC Mechanism on Agricultural and improve it gradually;

-coordinate in the implementation of work plans and other already signed agreements, protocols and MOUs in agricultural cooperation, as a permanent executive agency of the LMC JWG-A;

-develop partnerships and working networks and expand the friends circle for LMC countries.

(3) To assist with establishment, argumentation, implementation, management and other relevant work of the LMC agricultural project and giving priority to the LMC Special Fund projects, LMAC will:

-assist with the establishment, argumentation, implementation and management of the projects on agricultural investment cooperation, technological cooperation and joint research within Lancang-Mekong subregion;

-promote the implementation of major agricultural cooperation projects

to boost subregional agricultural and rural development.

2.3 Work Progress

Since its establishment, LMAC has discussed and drafted its mandate, vision, mission and work plans. It has held extensive discussions with the agricultural departments of Mekong countries, relevant ministries, commissions, governments in key provinces, scientific research institutions, and enterprises of China. LAMC has also developed the partnerships and work networks of Lancang-Mekong agricultural cooperation work network, and disseminated the new image of LMAC. Over the past year, LMAC achieved the expected results to serve as a regional support service organization, focused on the tasks of promoting mechanisms, strengthening foundations and methods.

(1) **Improving mechanism and working networks of Lancang-Mekong agricultural cooperation.** LMAC supported the Ministry of Agriculture, Forestry and Fisheries of Cambodia to successfully hold the second meeting of JWG-A of the LMC in Cambodia. At the meeting, LMAC discussed its working plans with the delegates and proposed several initiatives such as formulating *the draft Three-Year Plan of Action on Lancang-Mekong Agricultural Cooperation（2020 - 2022）*, establishing of ECCAST-LMC and the Lancang-Mekong Agricultural Extension and Information Platform, which have received great attention and recognition from the delegates of the Mekong countries. LMAC promoted the establishment of the ECCAST-LMC and the Water Ecological Cooperation Group, as a window unit of Lancang-Mekong agricultural cooperation, which is playing the role of the permanent executive agency of JWG-A, including planning, coordination, implementation and publicity.

(2) **Organizing the planning research and top-level design of Lancang-**

Mekong agricultural cooperation. LMAC drafted *Three-Year Plan of Action on Lancang-Mekong Agricultural Cooperation* (2020 – 2022) and submitted it to the second meeting of the JWG-A of the LMC for consideration. The plan is included in the outcome document of the fifth LMC Foreign Ministers' Meeting. LMAC organized the preparation of "Report on Lancang-Mekong Agricultural Cooperation Development (2019)" for the exchange and reference of the JWG-A, relevant departments and scientific research institutions of LMC countries. Also LMAC investigated the experience and practices of Lancang-Mekong agricultural cooperation in relevant provinces and regions in China and jointly discussed working plans.

(3) **Assisting with the management and the implementation of the key projects in Lancang-Mekong agricultural cooperation projects of China.** LMAC assisted with the management of Chinese agricultural projects of the LMC Special Fund. LMAC is implementing the project of the Lancang-Mekong Agricultural Extension and Information Platform supported by the LMC Special Fund, which utilized information technology to build and improve the agricultural public information sharing and agricultural technology promotion service system (mobile App) in the LMC countries. Also LMAC is keeping track of the progress of the implementation of the Lancang-Mekong agricultural cooperation projects, and established the projects and experts database.

(4) **Actively conducting external publicity and establishing the cooperation network.** LMAC carried out the exchanges and cooperation with the agricultural departments, research institutes, and enterprises in the LMC countries to build cooperative relationship. LMAC organized to design the LOGO and prepared the promotional video to display the new image to the public.

（Written by Zhu Zidong，Yang Guang and Jiang Ye，
Foreign Economic Cooperation Center，
Ministry of Agriculture and Rural Affairs，China；
Translated by Mo Nan，
International Agriculture Research Institute，
Yunnan Academy of Agricultural Sciences，China）

3 Three-Year Plan of Action on Lancang-Mekong Agricultural Cooperation (2020—2022)[①]

3.1 Background

Agriculture plays an important role in improving people's livelihood and promoting sustainable economic and social development in the six Lancang-Mekong countries.

The first Lancang-Mekong Cooperation (LMC) Leaders' Meeting determined that agriculture is one of the key priority areas of the LMC and identified the direction of Lancang-Mekong agricultural cooperation. In September 2017, the first Meeting of the LMC Joint Working Group on Agriculture (JWG-A) was held in Guangxi, China, where the LMC mechanism for agricultural cooperation was formally established. The Concept Paper of JWG-A notes that its terms of reference include identifying priorities and modalities of agricultural cooperation and developing agricultural cooperation plans.

In January 2018, the second LMC Leaders' Meeting issued *Five-Year Plan of Action on LMC* (*2018 – 2022*), which further clarified the priorities and overall requirements of agricultural cooperation.

To enhance practical agricultural cooperation among the six countries

---

① Officially approved by LMC countries in January 2020.

in the next few years, taking into account their respective strategies, plans and needs of agricultural development, this Plan is prepared in line with the Sanya Declaration, the Phnom Penh Declaration and *Five-Year Plan of Action on LMC* (2018–2022) adopted by the Leaders' Meetings, as well as relevant documents of JWG-A.

This Plan of Action consists of the development goals, fundamental principles, key areas and tasks, and implementation mechanisms of Lancang-Mekong agricultural cooperation. It is aimed at facilitating the implementation of strategies covering the Lancang-Mekong region such as the Vision and Action on Jointly Promoting Agricultural Cooperation on the Belt and Road and the ASEAN Community Vision 2025, and promoting the building of the LMC Economic Development Belt.

3.2 Development Goals

This Plan of Action is intended to promote closer agricultural exchanges and cooperation among member countries, advance the protection and utilization of agricultural resources, improve food security and nutrition, sustainable natural resource, ensure food safety, enhance agricultural competitiveness and export, promote logistic infrastructure, trade facilitation, contribute to the realization of the agriculture-related goals of the United Nations 2030 Agenda for Sustainable Development, revitalize the rural areas, and secure common development in the region.

3.3 Fundamental Principles

This Plan of Action follows the principles in the Sanya Declaration adopted at the First LMC Leaders' Meeting. The implementation of this Plan of Action will be based on the principles of consensus, equality, mutual consultation and coordination, voluntarism, common contribution and shared benefits, and respect for the United Nations Charter and international laws, as well as in accordance with domestic laws, rules, regulations and procedures of each member country.

In the spirit of openness and inclusiveness, the Plan of Action complements and develops in synergy with existing agricultural initiatives under other Mekong sub-regional cooperation mechanisms, and strengthens exchanges and collaboration with other sectors under the LMC framework such as poverty reduction and environment.

3.4   Key Areas and Tasks

3.4.1   Agricultural Policy Dialogue

Policy coordination is the premise and guarantee of practical and effective agricultural cooperation among member countries. Therefore, on the basis of respect for the national conditions and agricultural development stages of each country, member countries will actively improve the policy dialogue platform, strengthen consultation and cooperation, exchange with and learn from each other, and give full play to their respective features and strengths to narrow the gap in agricultural development.

The cooperation includes but is not limited to:

(1) **Improving the Lancang-Mekong agricultural cooperation mechanisms.** Hold the LMC JWG-A Meetings regularly; and create ad hoc groups within the JWG-A as needed, such as on crop disaster monitoring and control, forestry, livestock and veterinary cooperation, fisheries and water ecological cooperation, tropical agriculture industry upgrading, and rural human resources development.

Hold the LMC Village Head Forums regularly.

Hold the LMC Agriculture Ministers' Meetings as appropriate.

Turn Lancang-Mekong Agricultural Cooperation Center into a subregional cooperation center for supporting services of the six countries.

（2）**Encouraging multi-level and multi-agent participation.** Maintain regular contacts among government officials of member countries through bilateral visits; ensure unimpeded exchanges of policy information; and promote the alignment and coupling of agricultural development strategies of countries.

Enhance exchanges and cooperation through multilateral platforms by gradually increasing and diversifying dialogues with agriculture-related international organizations, global and regional financial organizations, and non-governmental organizations （NGOs） on policy exchange, technology transfer and investment promotion.

Support the establishment and improvement of dialogue mechanisms among subnational agricultural authorities of member countries to facilitate their regular policy exchanges and experience sharing, and connect them for cooperative projects.

Strengthen the think tank network of agricultural cooperation and hold science forums regularly to facilitate the discussions of experts and academics in relevant fields; and issue the "Report on Lancang-Mekong Agricultural Cooperation Development" on a regular basis.

3.4.2 Enhancing the Development of the Agricultural Industry

Agricultural production capacity has a direct impact on food security. Therefore, member countries will strengthen cooperation on agricultural production, ensure regional food security by working on quantity, quality and the ecosystem, and promote sustainable agricultural development.

The cooperation includes but is not limited to:

（1）**Strengthening exchanges and cooperation in agricultural science and technology.** Enhance cooperation between agriculture-related universities, colleges and research institutes, so that they can carry out joint research and technology development on issues of common interest and make collaboration proposals; encourage exchange visits of agricultural professionals;

and intensify joint programs on higher education.

Co-build joint laboratories, network laboratories, technology testing and demonstration bases, technology promotion centers and science and technology demonstration parks to integrate, create, demonstrate and deploy efficient, safe, low-carbon, circular and intelligent technologies relating to genetic resources, crop management, crop disaster prevention and control, animal disease prevention and control, agricultural machinery and equipment, agricultural information technology, agricultural resources and environment, climate change adaptation and mitigation, and the extension of tropical crop value chain.

Establish a group for Lancang-Mekong agricultural science and technology exchanges and collaboration.

(2) Improving agricultural supporting services systems. Facilitate exchanges of experience on agricultural technology extension to share good practices and improve the agricultural technology extension services systems.

Establish a Lancang-Mekong agricultural database, technology extension and marketing information system sharing platform.

Deepen cooperation in joint prevention and control of transboundary animal and plant diseases, enhance information sharing, improve monitoring, early warning and joint prevention and control, strengthen laboratory capacity building, build the traceability system for animal movement, jointly carry out cross-border movement management of animals and animal products, and promote the safety and facilitation of trade in livestock and livestock products.

Establish the mechanism of exchange and cooperation on ecological conservation along the Lancang-Mekong River and jointly set up wild fish breeding and rescue centers for information sharing, for example, information on fish diversity, fish abundance and fish migration, etc. , as well as possibility and opportunity on fishery cooperation, such as strengthening capacity building in aquaculture development.

Enhance conservation and use of forest resources; promote integrated management of forest ecosystem along the LMC Countries.

(3) Ensuring the quality and safety of agricultural products. Promote experience sharing to improve the regulatory mechanism for agricultural products quality and food safety from farm to fork, collaborate on the whole process traceability for agricultural products promotion, and enhance inspection and testing capacities.

Collaborate on the development, harmonization, mutual learning and mutual acceptance of standards relating to seeds and seedlings, plant variety protection, animal and crop management, quality grading of agricultural products, preservation and post-harvest loss reduction of agricultural products, agricultural inputs, and geographical indications.

(4) Promoting small and medium scale of agro-processing. Develop the regulations and policies to support and encourage the new and existing small and medium scale of agro-processing and young entrepreneur.

Facilitate and provide the capacity building, technical supports to meet the requirement and standard such as GAP, GHP, GMP and HACCP.

Establish the demonstration of agro-processing in order to transfer technology and share experiences.

Promote the research study on products development, food science, technology and innovation.

3.4.3 Agricultural Trade and Investment Cooperation of Private Sectors

Fully leveraging their respective advantages in the agriculture sectors, member countries will further the cooperation on intraregional trade of agricultural products and investment in the whole range of the agricultural industry chain, expand the global market with joint efforts and enhance the agricultural competitiveness of the region.

The cooperation includes but is not limited to:

(1) Agricultural trade. Improve the infrastructure for storage, processing, supply chain and logistics of agricultural products, promote cooperation in entry-exit inspection and quarantine of agricultural products, and advance agricultural trade facilitation.

Facilitate the development of cross-border e-commerce, and explore the possibility of creating a Lancang-Mekong agricultural e-commerce platform.

Enhance producers and processors' awareness of the branding, labeling and packaging of agricultural products, increase the products' added value, and intensify branding and advertising efforts, so as to improve their competitiveness in the market and export.

Make full use of all kinds of fairs and exhibitions to promote agricultural products.

Work towards the establishment of a Lancang-Mekong agricultural investment and trade data sharing platform, so as to enhance the exchange of information in this regard.

Strengthen the quality control system and share information of agricultural inputs through border trade amongst LMC countries.

(2) Investment cooperation of agricultural private sectors. Encourage the governments of member countries to optimize business environment in order to direct more foreign direct investment to agricultural business development.

Encourage the private sectors of member countries to play an active role in the development of all links of the value chain, including production, processing, storage, transportation and distribution, and collaborate on bilateral investment that is complementary and mutually beneficial for a win-win result.

Make joint efforts in building agricultural industry parks where private sectors are welcomed to take part in their construction and operation.

Work towards the establishment of a Lancang-Mekong agricultural industry collaboration group to foster partnerships among enterprises and industry associations, extend the industry chain, and engage smallholder farmers in the market and promote the contract farming model implementation mechanism to agricultural products amongst the LMC countries.

3.4.4　Capacity Building and Knowledge Sharing

Member countries will continue to advance agricultural information exchange, knowledge sharing, technology transfer and human resources development in the region.

The cooperation includes but is not limited to:

Improve the capacity of all kinds of personnel, including farmers, technicians and officials, by sending technical experts to other member countries and organizing training courses, seminars and field studies.

Make more joint efforts in building agricultural training bases, personnel training centers and technology transfer centers, and support the sharing of existing training resources in the sub-region.

Share experience in poverty reduction and rural development to underpin the comprehensive development of agriculture and rural areas.

Strengthen the capacity in preserving agricultural heritage, share experience in its discovery and preservation, and promote the exchange and mutual learning of farming culture among member countries.

3.4.5　Collaboration with Other Sectors

Under the LMC framework, agricultural initiatives are closely related to those of other fields, such as connectivity, production capacity, investment and trade, poverty reduction, water resources, forestry, environmental protection, customs and quality inspection. Therefore, member countries will actively search for cooperation opportunities with relevant sectors.

The cooperation includes but is not limited to:

Work together to improve agricultural infrastructure, trade and investment.

Exchange information on agriculture-related standards, enhance the sharing of standards information resources, facilitate the improvement of standard systems, and improve the connectivity of standards.

Jointly apply for and implement international agricultural projects.

3.5 Organization and Implementation

3.5.1 Institutional Arrangements

The Plan of Action is subjected into force after adopted by JWG-A. It may be revised, amended or modified by consensus.

JWG-A coordinates the implementation of this Plan, including but not limited to designing, advising, liaison, communication, coordination, monitoring and reporting activities. JWG-A will annually update the Foreign Ministers' Meeting on the implementation of this Plan through the LMC Senior Officials' Meeting. JWG-A may propose and organize LMC Agriculture Ministers' Meetings as necessitated by the cooperation, during which the progress of the Plan will be reviewed and guidance will be given on the next steps.

The national Heads of JWG-A are mandated to: (i) Propose projects and activities to implement the Plan of Action; (ii) Coordinate, execute and supervise the above-mentioned projects and activities; (iii) Report progress in the implementation to their Ministers of Agriculture, seeking their support and instructions; (iv) Maintain liaison with the LMC national secretariats/agencies for close communication; and (v) Update JWG-A regularly on the progress.

The Lancang-Mekong Agricultural Cooperation Center serves as a coordination and service agency of Lancang-Mekong agricultural cooperation. It supports the implementation of this Plan of Action in coordination with JWG-A.

Member countries may invite experts and scholars in related fields to provide technical, knowledge and intellectual support as necessitated by projects and activities so as to facilitate the implementation of the Plan of Action.

3.5.2 Funding

The funding mechanism follows a government-guided and multi-participation model. The governments of member countries are encouraged to provide financial support while seeking funds from other sources. Funds may include, but are not limited to, capital and resources from:

Governments of member countries;

The LMC Special Fund set up by the Chinese government;

Global and regional cooperation agencies;

Countries outside the region;

The private sector, including businesses and individuals.

3.5.3 Partnership

An extensive network of partnership will be developed, where all stakeholders are encouraged to take part and collaborate in appropriate forms to contribute to the goals of this Plan.

Partners may include but are not limited to government agencies, research institutes, financial institutions, businesses, non-profit organizations and civil society organizations of member countries, and government agencies and private sectors of countries outside the region, as well as international agricultural agencies, global and regional financial organizations and non-governmental organizations.

4 | Progress and Effectiveness of Agricultural Science and Technology Exchange and Cooperation in Lancang-Mekong Subregion

4.1 Background

The wide application of modern science and technology in agricultural field has greatly promoted the improvement of agricultural productivity. Agricultural science and technology have increasingly become the main driving force for the modern agricultural development. With the acceleration of the process of world multi-polarization, economic globalization and regionalization, the relevance of world agriculture is increasing, and countries are increasingly attaching importance to agricultural science and technology cooperation to enhance their agricultural competitiveness in the world market. Most LMC countries are rich in agricultural resources, but the degree of development and utilization is relatively low. It is urgent for LMC countries to deal with climate change, food security, poverty reduction, environment protection and to realize agricultural upgrading and sustainable development through the cooperation of agricultural science and technology on introducing advanced and applicable technologies and equipment that meet the requirements of high yield, high quality, high efficiency, and environment friendly and food safety.

174

Comparatively speaking, China's Yunnan, Guangxi, Hainan and other provinces (autonomous regions), which are adjacent to the Mekong countries, rely on the mainland of China and have export competitive advantages in meat products, fruits, vegetables and processed products; while relying on the Mekong countries in rice, coconut, dried coconut, canned pineapple, pepper, vanilla, natural rubber, palm oil, coconut oil and palm kernel oil, and tropical fruit, etc. , they have strong import competitive advantage. More importantly, China's Yunnan, Guangxi, Hainan and the Mekong countries face together the challenges of small-scale manual agriculture, low development level, poor farmers, underdeveloped rural areas, and the urgent need to protect the ecological environment and biodiversity. Compared with the most of the Mekong countries on agricultural science and technology, China's Yunnan, Guangxi and Hainan have commonalities and complementarities, and they are also advanced in many respects. Over the years, China's Yunnan, Guangxi, Hainan and other provinces (autonomous regions) have made remarkable achievements in continuously introducing technologies, products and talents to the five Mekong countries by increasing the intensity of investigation, visit and various kinds of scientific and technological training, promoting bilateral and multilateral cooperation and exchanges. However, while LMC countries have made important progress in agriculture and agricultural science and technology cooperation, they must also face more and more common problems. Challenges are constantly emerging. The past bilateral cooperation and exchanges between countries can no longer meet the needs of sustainable development, especially in the aspect of agricultural science and technology cooperation and exchange. The need for countries to establish regional and multilateral cooperation platforms and mechanisms was very urgent.

4.2 Establishment of the Platform and Mechanism for Agricultural Science and Technology Exchange for LMC

In order to meet the urgent needs of regional agricultural economic development and agricultural science and technology cooperation among the LMC countries, in March 2008, the Yunnan Academy of Agricultural Sciences, on the basis of years of exchanges and cooperation with the five Mekong countries, approved by the Yunnan Provincial People's Government, with the support by Perez-Guerrero Trust Fund and Ministry of Agriculture, the P. R. China, jointly held the Workshop on Agricultural Science and Technology Exchange and Cooperation in GMS in Kunming. During the workshop, Yunnan Academy of Agricultural Sciences led to establish the Exchange and Cooperation Consortium for Agricultural Science and Technology in GMS (ECCAST-GMS) after Joint Statement (Kunming Statement) signed by the representatives from Cambodian Agricultural Research and Development Institute (CARDI), Yunnan Academy of Agricultural Sciences (YAAS), the People's Republic of China, National Agriculture and Forestry Research Institute (NAFRI), Lao P. D. R., Myanmar Academy of Agricultural, Forestry, Livestock and Fishery Sciences (MAAFLFS), Myanmar, Department of Agriculture (DOA), Ministry of Agriculture and Cooperatives, Kingdom of Thailand and Vietnam Academy of Agricultural Sciences (VAAS), Vietnam. After more than 10 years of operation and development, the ECCAST-GMS has gradually become a regional cooperation platform with functions such as testing, demonstration, communication, and training, and the long-term cooperation mechanism has been gradually improved. In promoting the coordinated development of agriculture and agricultural science and technology in the Lancang-Mekong subregion, and in the construction of the Asian community of "Shared River, Shared Future", the influence of the ECCAST-GMS in the subregion has gradually expanded, and it has become the main platform and mechanism for agricultural science and technology exchange and cooperation in the subregion.

In June 2019, at the second meeting of JWG-A held in Cambodia, the LMC countries agreed to establish the ECCAST-LMC on the basis of the original ECCAST-GMS, with a wider coverage and richer cooperation content.

In August 2019, the ECCAST-LMC was announced to be established during the tenth Steering Committee Meeting of ECCAST-GMS in Zhaotong, Yunnan Province, China. Representatives of 13 national agricultural scientific research institutions from Southeast Asian and South Asian countries, as well as representatives of the Ministry of Agriculture and Rural Affairs of China, the Chinese Academy of Agricultural Sciences and 18 provincial agricultural sciences academies of China jointly witnessed the establishment of the ECCAST-LMC. The members of the ECCAST-LMC discussed and approved the Charter of the ECCAST-LMC.

The ECCAST-LMC is rooted in the principle of joint efforts, co-manage and shared interests. The ECCAST-LMC will focus on the relevant action plans of Lancang-Mekong agricultural cooperation, actively expand the scope of members, cooperate with more agricultural scientific research and education institutions in the Lancang-Mekong subregion, carry out scientific and technological exchanges and cooperation in a wider range of fields such as planting, animal husbandry and fishery, help LMAC to build a support system for agricultural cooperation among LMC countries, create a platform for scientific and technological exchanges and joint researches in agriculture, and gradually establish a joint prevention and control mechanism for cross-border plant diseases and insect pests, animal diseases, cooperation mechanism for fisheries ecological conservation, promote the implementation of the agriculture related goals of the UN 2030

Agenda for Sustainable Development and the building of Lancang-Mekong Economic Development Belt.

4.3 Achievements of Agricultural Science and Technology Exchange and Cooperation

Over the years, some of China's provinces and autonomous regions, especially Yunnan, Guangxi and Hainan, have carried out fruitful exchanges and cooperation in agricultural science and technology with the five Mekong countries. The relevant contents were described in detail in the regional section of this book. This section only covers the achievements of the ECCAST-GMS in the past decade. At the same time, the necessity, existing foundation and development prospect of establishing the mechanism and platform of agricultural science and technology exchange and cooperation in the Lancang-Mekong subregion are explained.

The ECCAST-GMS is composed of steering committee, secretariat and working groups. The Steering Committee is in charge of the strategic governance of the ECCAST-GMS, approving plans, budgets and working reports, etc. The chairman of the Steering Committee is taken turns by the leader from academy or department of each GMS country. The secretariat is in charge of managing and coordinating the consortium, handling daily work, carrying out the resolution of steering committee organizing and coordinating relevant cooperation projects and activities, etc. The secretariat of ECCAST-GMS location is in Kunming, Yunnan Province, the P. R. China. The coordinator and permanent secretariat are permanently taken by staff of YAAS, and the working groups are composed of research and development personnel from the 6 countries. Under the leadership of the Steering Committee, the working groups carry out their research work according to the requirements of cooperation content. From 2008 to 2019, the ECCAST-GMS formed six working

groups on upland rice, soybean, sugarcane, potato, plant protection and agricultural economics.

4.3.1 Initial Achievements of Scientific and Technological Cooperation in Major Food and Cash Crops

Over the past decade, on the platform of the ECCAST-GMS, the working groups have jointly exchanged and screened 543 crop varieties, 124 varieties (materials) suitable for different countries were preliminarily selected. One upland rice variety has been approved and released in Vietnam. In addition, two upland rice varieties, two soybean varieties and one sugarcane variety are expected to be approved or widely promoted in Myanmar, Vietnam and Cambodia. Among the suitable varieties, the average yield increased by 31.1% for upland rice, 11.1% for soybean, 33.3% for sugarcane and 10.5% for potato. The highest yield increase of upland rice was 146.8%, soybean was 105.3%, and sugarcane was 49%. Hybrid rice, upland rice, hybrid wheat, barley, corn, soybean, sugarcane, potato, flowers, vegetables and other food and cash crop varieties bred by YAAS have been introduced and demonstrated by Southeast Asian countries, with an area of more than 2 million mu[①]. It has contributed to the food security, poverty reduction and income increase of farmers in the mountainous areas of LMC countries, and laid a scientific and technological foundation for the diversification of China's source countries of soybean import.

4.3.2 Establishment of Joint Prevention and Control Mechanism for Cross-border Plant Diseases and Insect pests

Since 2011, the plant protection working group of the ECCAST-GMS has carried out joint research on diseases, insects and weeds of rice,

---

① Fifteen mu equal one hectare.

vegetables, fruits and other cash crops, and has fully grasped the occurrence, harm and prevention and control of major diseases, pests and weeds in the Lancang-Mekong subregion. Especially, the joint investigation, sample collection and isolation and preservation of bacterial resources were carried out in the major rice production areas of the Lancang-Mekong subregion. These cooperative research work have laid a solid foundation for further study the co-evolution of *Magnaporthe grisea* and its host, the evolution and long-distance transmission of *Magnaporthe grisea*, the origin of pathogenic bacteria, the genetic diversity of the white-backed planthopper population and its possible migration routes and disaster characteristics and causes of invasive weeds in Lancang-Mekong subregion. These research results have greatly promoted the joint monitoring, early warning and control of major diseases, pests and weeds in the main rice production areas in the subregion. In August 2019, the plant protection working group carried out joint monitoring, early warning and prevention and control technology cooperation research in view of the increasingly serious situation of Fall armyworm in most countries of Southeast Asia in recent years, to master the occurrence characteristics and laws of Fall armyworm population, share research results and experience, and improve the regional control level.

4.3.3　Capacity Building

Over the past decade, YAAS has successively sent 9 young scientists and technicians to CARDI, MAAFLFS, DOA and VAAS to carry out learning and cooperation research. One Myanmar researcher and eight talent young scientists have been awarded funding by China government to YAAS on postdoctoral work and one-year of study and cooperative research respectively. Their capabilities have been improved, and the scope and space of cooperation have been expanded, which laid a solid foundation for future cooperative research.

From 2008 to 2019, with the joint efforts of all members, YAAS convened ten sessions of steering committee meeting of the ECCAST-GMS, more than 50 seminars. About 770 agricultural scientists and officials from member countries visited each other, participated in training and attended seminar and workshop with over 500 academic reports were made and exchanged, about 7,000 farmers, technicians and managers participated in exchange visits, training and on-site observation. The capabilities of a large number of researchers and officials from YAAS, CARDI, MAAFLFS, NAFRI, DOA and VAAS have been improved by yearly continuous participation in cooperation.

4. 3. 4 Promotion of the Agricultural Economic and Trade Cooperation by Integration Industry, Education and Research

While promoting agricultural science and technology cooperation, YAAS paid attention to the cooperation with enterprises and led to establishing Yunnan Agriculture Oversea Development Technology Innovation Alliance, which is composed of 42 agricultural related enterprises, scientific research institutes. Over the past decade, YAAS has promoted more than 150,000 hectares of suitable new varieties, such as hybrid rice, hybrid corn, upland rice, soybean, sugarcane and potato, and exported more than 8,000 tons of potato seed.

The ECCAST-GMS held four academic exchange meetings on the themes of food security in mountainous areas, marketization of agricultural production and structural adjustment of agricultural production. It proposed to create a community of interests in agricultural production through agricultural demonstration zones, exchange of science and technology, technology promotion, and agricultural products trade, and reached a consensus with all countries on the construction of cross-border agricultural economic belt.

4.3.5 Giving Full Play to the Role of the ECCAST-GMS

Over the years, the ECCAST-GMS has built a platform for negotiation and cooperation with the five Mekong countries for scientific research institutions from 17 countries and international organizations, 19 provinces, autonomous regions and municipalities directly under the central government (including Guangdong, Guangxi, Hainan, Fujian, Sichuan, Chongqing, Guizhou, Xinjiang, Zhejiang, Jiangsu, etc.), as well as the Chinese Academy of Agricultural Sciences, China Academy of Tropical Agricultural Sciences, and more than 40 enterprises. The influence at home and abroad is expanding day by day.

In 2008, Asian Development Bank (ADB) formally accepted the ECCAST-GMS as the partner of the GMS Working Group on Agriculture (WGA). The International Fund for Agricultural Development (IFAD) sent representatives to attend the meeting when the ECCAST-GMS was established, and listed YAAS as its supporting institution for technical cooperation in LMC countries. The Bioversity International and YAAS signed an agreement to jointly use the ECCAST-GMS to work for Southeast Asian countries. The International Rice Research Institute (IRRI) and YAAS are actively promoting the establishment of integrated pest control laboratory in Yunnan.

(Written by Li Lu,
International Agriculture Research Institute,
Yunnan Academy of Agricultural Sciences, China)

5 | Progress and Effectiveness of the Chinese Projects Supported by the LMC Special Fund

In 2017 – 2018, the Ministry of Agriculture and Rural Affairs of China had organized and implemented 15 projects supported by the LMC Special Fund with a total budget of 26.98 million CNY. All the projects mainly focused on technology cooperation, included seminars and exchange, test and demonstration, capacity building, etc. Among them, there were 5 projects about mechanism platform building, 4 projects about technical cooperation, 3 projects about personnel training, 2 projects about joint research and action, and 1 project about media publicity. The implementation of these projects had played a positive role in improving agricultural cooperation mechanism, implementing the important initiatives of the Leaders' Meeting, strengthening technical support, exporting Chinese agricultural technology, equipment and talents, sharing Chinese agricultural development experience, publicizing the progress and achievements of agricultural cooperation, and promoting the construction of the Lancang-Mekong Economic Development Belt.

5.1 Agricultural Cooperation Mechanism and Foundation Was Improved

(1) **Holding the LMC Village Head Forum, and building a new platform for Lancang-Mekong agricultural and rural cooperation.** The Ministry of Agriculture and Rural Affairs of China and Yunnan provincial

government held the LMC Village Head Forum in Yunnan for two consecutive years. The forums issued *Mangshi Initiative on Cooperation between LMC Villages and Cooperatives*, which proposed to establish the Lancang-Mekong Village Community Development Union, facilitated the cooperation and matching of 19 organizations, and 8 cooperation agreements signed on site. The experience and practice of China in promoting rural vitalization had aroused strong interest and desire for cooperation among participants, which contained industries development, three industries integration of agricultural production, agricultural product processing industry and agricultural product market service industry, electronic commercial, ecological protection and revenue-sharing. All these deeds prepared a good start for promoting agricultural cooperation, rural and farmers' cooperation among LMC countries.

(2) **Holding the JWG-A meeting of the LMC, and establishing the partnership network of Lancang-Mekong agricultural cooperation.** The Ministry of Agriculture and Rural Affairs of China actively implemented the results of the JWG-A first meeting, which promoted the involved countries to reach a consensus on concept documents. Each country has clarified the head and focal point of JWG-A, determined the contact mechanism, and made close contact on agricultural development policies, application and implementation of the projects supported by LMC Special Fund and other matters. From the perspectives of government, enterprise, industries and research, it has established good cooperation relationships with the management departments, business departments, diplomatic channels, scientific research institutions, organized and established an expert team to lay solid foundation for subsequent cooperation.

(3) **Carring out research on Lancang Mekong agricultural cooperation.** *Three-Year Plan of Action on Lancang-Mekong Agricultural Cooperation* (*2020 - 2022*), has been drawn up and approved by the agricultural departments of LMC countries and officially adopted in early 2020, which

clarified the direction and priority of Lancang-Mekong agricultural cooperation. Some researches on natural rubber, banana and other industries, as well as the research on LMC countries have been carried out.

5.2　Key Support for Industrial Cooperation Was Created by Experimental Demonstration

The Project of the experimental demonstration of Mekong River rice yield green increasing technology, which was organized and implemented by the Department of Agriculture and Rural Affairs of Guangxi Zhuang Autonomous Region of China, which was focused on the concept of green and efficiency, highlighting the leading and demonstration function, strengthening technology introduction and test. This project optimized and assembled new technology suitable for the local reality, increased production and income under protecting the local ecological environment, provided an effective technical support for improving the quality and efficiency of local rice production, also provided a scientific basis for rice breeding research. During the implementation of the project, there were 44 rice varieties introduced from China, 15 excellent varieties selected suitable for local conditions and 8,655 mu experimental demonstration base established for rice yield green increasing technology. According to the local actual situation, China introduced comparatively matured rice production technologies, such as seedling raising, cultivation, water and fertilizer management and green prevention and control of diseases and insect pests, and the promotion and application area reached more than 45,000 mu, and the local rice yield was increased by more than 25%, the average income per mu was increased by 200 CNY. They carried out technology demonstration and promotion of six modes of integrated planting and breeding in the paddy field, such as rice-shrimp, rice-fish and rice-duck polyculture. According to the calculation result, the economic income per mu by rice-duck polyculture mode was increased by 220 CNY, and the rice-fish polyculture mode was increased by 413 CNY, the rice-shrimp (*Macrobrachium rosenbergii*) polyculture mode was increased by 3,000 CNY. The demonstration base became an important platform for local agricultural technicians and farmers to visit and train.

On the base of the China-Cambodian Tropical Ecological Agricultural Demonstration Zone, the project of the Lancang-Mekong Tropical Agricultural Industry Cooperation Demonstration Zone had been launched by Hainan Province of China. The enterprises built the zone with the support of the Chinese Academy of Tropical Agricultural Sciences and other institutes. Chinese enterprises were supported to build 1,000 mu coconut industry cooperation demonstration base in Cambodia, Among which, the coconut germplasm resources nursery is 50 mu. 15 participants from Cambodia, Laos, Myanmar, Thailand and Vietnam were invited to Hainan for 20 days of training study tour. Some experts from the Chinese Academy of Tropical Agricultural Sciences were invited to hold training courses at the Royal Agricultural University of Cambodia and the zone onsite.

5.3 Agricultural Support Service System Was Improved by Establishment of Information and Technology Platform

The Lancang-Mekong agricultural extension and information platform adopted Chinese latest mobile internet technology, integrated all kinds of agricultural scientific and technological resources and market information, to build a comprehensive agricultural service platform (mobile App) for agricultural technology extension and information sharing in LMC countries. The platform could transfer Chinese advanced agricultural practical technology and agricultural information service mode, and innovate the means of agricultural information services in Mekong countries and enhance the exchange of agricultural policies, information sharing and achievement transformation. At present, the application framework of Chinese-English and Cambodian-English versions of the platform has been developed and entered the test operation stage. The platform intends to achieve two functions. One is information release. The agricultural departments, scientific research institutions and agricultural related enterprises can issue agricultural policies, technologies, conditions, market situation and public information, etc., in order to guide agricultural production, processing, storage and sales. The other one is agricultural technology services, hiring experts to answer questions raised by farmers and technicians online.

According to the technical requirements of green prevention and control of crops diseases and insect pests in the region, the project of the green prevention and control cooperation platform construction for crops diseases and insect pests mainly carried out seminars, exchange and training on policy, models, academic research and management. The crops green prevention and control platform was jointly set up by the Plant Protection Institute of Chinese Academy of Agricultural Sciences (CAAS) and relevant plant protection research and management institutions of the five Mekong countries, namely the Crop Diseases and Insect Pests Green Prevention and Control Cooperative Laboratory, headquartered in Beijing (Plant Protection Institute of CAAS). The establishment of the platform is of great significance for enhancing the ability of joint monitoring, early warning and joint prevention and control of cross-border pests and diseases in the subregion, as well as improving the comprehensive agricultural production capacity of the subregion and the level of food security, and has a far-reaching effect on the promotion of agricultural products trade and the construction of economic development belt.

The project of the Southeast Asia smart agriculture monitoring platform construction set an agricultural intelligence system in Laos,

Cambodia and other countries, which builds a "Internet + agriculture" platform covering the subregion for intelligent agriculture information exchange and database. The platform construction can utilize agricultural climate analysis, which contain land and appropriate cropping system, collect meteorological data on important agricultural activities, conduct climate prediction and environmental monitoring of pest information and land conditions, and can provide timely and accurate first-hand environmental data for agricultural production. It will play a positive role in promoting agricultural production in the subregion.

Depending on the second "the Belt and Road" Tropical Agricultural Science and Technology Cooperation Forum held by the Chinese Academy of Tropical Agriculture Sciences and other platforms, the project of the agricultural research institutions cooperation platform construction of the LMC countries invited relevant experts in charge of universities and research institutions of the Mekong countries to visit China, such as Maejo University of Thailand, Kasetsart University of Thailand, Department of Agriculture of Ministry of Agriculture and Cooperatives of Thailand, Economic, Social and Cultural Commission of Cambodia, Ministry of Labor and Vocational Training of Cambodia, Ministry of Agriculture, Forestry and Fisheries of Cambodia, and signed three cooperation agreements including the Memorandum of Understanding between Chinese Academy of Tropical Agricultural Sciences and Maejo University of Thailand, and established contact channels with 7 institutions, including Agriculture Department of Ministry of agriculture of Thailand.

5.4　Joint Research and Action Were Conducted to Build Innovative and Green Lancang-Mekong Subregion

Office of Fisheries Law Enforcement for Yangtze River Basin of the Ministry of Agriculture and Rural Affairs of China (hereinafter referred to as "Yangtze River Office") conducted joint law enforcement and proliferation activities several times with relevant institutions of Laos, Cambodia, Thailand and other Mekong countries, of which China-Laos jointly released *Mystus wyckioides* 120,000, *Barbodes daruphani luosuoensis* 65,000 and *Clarias fuscus* 200,000, and donated to Louang Namtha of Laos cumulative 614,000 fries for propagation and release for five consecutive years, including carp 560,000, *Mystus wyckioides* 44,000 and *Barbodes daruphani luosuoensis* 10,000; China-Thailand also jointly released 500,000 indigenous *Carassius auratus* and *Macrobrachium rosenbergii* 1 million; China-Cambodia jointly released more than 700 kg of parents and more than 1 million rare and endangered indigenous fish, turtles, frogs and other aquatic adults and fries into city moat of Angkor Wat, which had played a positive role in rapid conservation of fisheries resources and the maintenance of ecosystem stability of Lancang-Mekong river basin. In 2019, China and Laos held joint law enforcement and fisheries stock enhancement activities, collected and destroyed 60 sets of electric fishing machines, 36 ground cages, 110 fishing nets, electric trawls, enchanted array and other illegal fishing tools on site. On the Lancang-Mekong River, law enforcement officers of the two countries carried out joint cruise for fishery administration, ensuring the effect of fisheries stock enhancement. In addition, publicity activities for aquatic biological protection were organized and carried out. Through such publicity channels as signs, publicity materials, newspapers, TV media, etc., issued the current situation and importance of fisheries stock enhancement activities to the public of the countries participating in the implementation of the project to improve the influence of the events and enhance public awareness of ecological protection. The implementation contents, effects and achievements of the joint fisheries stock enhancement project were shown by the background materials, technical manuals and exhibition boards of project achievements to the relevant departments of

LMC countries, FAO and other international organizations. In November 2018, Yangtze River Biological Resources Conservation Forum invited the Lancang-Mekong fisheries authorities to participate. The representatives from the Mekong countries highly affirmed Chinese achievements in the protection of aquatic organisms in Lancang-Mekong river basin and reached a consensus on strengthening cooperation in the protection of aquatic organisms. In May 2019, Yangtze River Office sought the opinions from Mekong countries on the preparation plan for the Lancang-Mekong Fishery and Aquatic Ecology Cooperation Working Group (proposal draft by China). A preparatory meeting will be held to establish an exchange and cooperation mechanism of aquatic ecological conservation along the Lancang-Mekong river basin. Organized twice scientific investigations of Mekong dolphins in Cambodia section of Mekong River, and estimated the population was about 80 individuals.

The impact of rubber planting on biodiversity in Lancang-Mekong River Basin joint research project carried out the investigation of the plant diversity of rubber forest in Lancang River (rubber planting area in Yunnan Province, China) and Mekong River region (Vietnam, Cambodia, Laos, Thailand and Myanmar), obtained a large number of rubber field observation data, and mastered the species composition characteristics, diversity and regional distribution of rubber forest. This project strengthened the cooperation with rubber production and research institutions such as the Asian Branch of the International Tropical Agricultural Center and the National Agricultural University of Vietnam, and proposed the development of rubber suggestions on joint scientific and technological research, solving key technologies, and building an environment-friendly ecological rubber garden. By the end of 2018, the joint research project had completed 247 field surveys of rubber forest community quadrats, also investigated from various aspects, the management mode, tapping system and latex output of the rubber plantation, which is of great significance to promote the healthy development of the natural rubber industry.

5. 5 Cooperation of Capacity Building Were Carried out to Build Talent Cultivation Support System

Chinese Academy of Tropical Agricultural Sciences and other 3 institutions implemented 4 training programs, including the tropical agricultural talent cultivation project in LMC countries, cross border animal epidemics disease prevention and control technology exchange and cooperation project, biogas technology training course and the Seminar on pesticide risk management of LMC Countries, which held 10 foreign training sessions in China, with 185 participants; sent more than 20 expert teams to carry out technical exchange and on-site training, and trained 2,500 local farmers and technicians.

The tropical agricultural talents cultivation project has built talents training experts pool (currently 163 experts in the pool), training practice pool (9 bases in the pool) and 13 supporting quality training courses, and held 6 training sessions on tropical agricultural harmful organisms epidemic monitoring, early warning, comprehensive prevention and control in China, with 124 participants of government officials, agricultural technicians and scientific researchers from the five Mekong countries. Ruminant Feeding Standard Research and Development Center of the Ministry of Animal Husbandry and Development of Thailand and the School of Animal Science and Technology, Meizhou University, Thailand, held two trainings in the field of animal husbandry, trained 67 technicians. Focusing on the core of the training work, it steadily promoted science and technological research and cooperation with the return visit of students as the starting point, and signed cooperation agreements or reached cooperation intentions with Cambodian Ministry of

Labor and Vocational Training, Mekong University, Khon Kaen University, Meizhou University, Chiang Mai University and other Thai institutions, to write proposal report on agricultural sustainable development projects of LMC countries and the analysis report on the demand technical talents of LMC countries, to provide support for the construction of tropical agricultural talents cultivation project.

The cross border animal epidemics disease prevention and control technology exchange and cooperation project taught the live cattle Foot and Mouth Disease (FMD) virus detection technology through the training, which improved the diagnosis and monitoring ability on FMD in LMC countries' veterinary laboratory, carried out the cross-border animal disease diagnosis technology training through the training, which improved the detection ability and technical level of live cattle FMD virus in Laos, deepened the close relationship with China-Myanmar-Thailand laboratory, and provided technical support for joint prevention and control of cross-border animal epidemic diseases and safety trade of livestock products in Lancang-Mekong subregion.

The biogas technology training course had completed the technical exchange, achievement demonstration, enterprises introduction and the experience sharing for trainees from the Mekong countries, encouraged the trainees to apply for the cooperation projects, and submitted cooperation intention of the suggestions on the construction of cooperation platform for livestock and poultry waste treatment and biogas technology between China and Vietnam. The experts of the project were invited by Cambodian students to operate 2 training sessions on commercial biogas technology in Cambodia supported by the United Nations Industrial Development Organization, and was invited to bid for a capacity building project of biomass energy in Cambodia-Laos which was initiated by United Nations Industrial Development Organization.

The Seminar on pesticide risk management of LMC countries aimed to further strengthen the experience exchange of risk management among LMC countries, and to improve the risk management ability of regional pesticide, to implement the achievement list of the second "the Belt and Road" Summit Forum, and to promote international mutual recognition of agricultural standards. The training was divided into three stages: Beijing, Guangxi and Yunnan, and 28 trainees participated in theoretical exchange and practical learning on the biodiversity and pest control, plant disease biological control, Chinese pesticide management policy and environmental risk control, and visited the insecticide factory in Fumin, Dounan, Chenggong, Yiliang, Anning in Yunnan Province and Suining in Guangxi Autonomous Region, and studied at demonstration bases for prevention and control of diseases and insect pests such as flowers, fruits and crops. This project provided an opportunity to strengthen exchanges in the field of pesticides and promoted international trade cooperation in the pesticide industry.

(Written by Zhang Yun[1] and Xu Yubo[2],

1. Foreign Economic Cooperation Center,
Ministry of Agriculture and Rural Affairs, China;

2. Department of International Cooperation,
Ministry of Agriculture and Rural Affairs, China.

Translated by Guo Wen,
International Agriculture Research Institute,
Yunnan Academy of Agricultural Sciences, China)

6 | Regional Rural Revitalization

LMC is a new type of subregional cooperation platform which was jointly initiated and established by China and the five Mekong countries, aiming to deepen good-neighborly and friendly cooperation, build a Community of Shared Future, and make new contributions to promote South-South cooperation and the implementation of the UN 2030 Agenda for Sustainable Development in Lancang-Mekong subregion. In January 2018, the Chinese government issued *Opinions on the Implementation of the Rural Revitalization Strategy*, which clearly defined the strategic objectives and paths of "Rural Revitalization", insisted on the priority development of agriculture and rural areas, and orderly promoted the construction of Rural Revitalization in accordance with the general requirements of industrial prosperity, ecological livability, rural civilization, effective governance and rich life. Nowadays, Rural Revitalization has not only been practiced in China, but also extended to other countries. Lancang-Mekong basin is rich in agricultural production resources and has a large agricultural population. Agriculture is the basic industry and rural construction is the focus in LMC countries. Based on this common foundation, Chinese government had integrated the concept of Rural Revitalization into the Lancang-Mekong Cooperation framework. China has actively explored cooperation in areas such as exchange platform construction, agricultural technology promotion, livelihood development, capacity training, and poverty reduction demonstration, to promote the

194

revitalization and development of rural areas in the six countries.

6.1 Sharing of the Experience of Rural Revitalization

In order to promote regional rural revitalization, the 6 countries of Lancang-Mekong have established multi-level exchange platforms to promote sharing development experience and tapping the cooperation potential for grassroots organizations in the region.

6.1.1 The LMC Village Head Forums Held to Promote Village Community Exchanges

In order to strengthen exchanges and cooperation among village heads of LMC countries, boost regional rural development and benefit farmers, Chinese government proposed to hold the LMC Village Head Forums and incorporated it into *Five-year Plan of Action on LMC (2018-2022)*. In April 2017, Lancang-Mekong Agricultural Cooperation and China-Cambodia-Myanmar-Lao-Thailand Village Heads Forum was held in Mengla County, Xishuangbanna Dai Autonomous Prefecture, Yunnan Province, China, nearly 100 village heads, enterprises representatives and officials from relevant government departments from these 5 countries attended the forum. During the forum, 11 villages and enterprises at home and abroad signed 8 cooperation agreements, covering vegetable planting, coffee production and processing, rice high-yield demonstration, agricultural technical services, leisure agriculture and other fields.

In April 2018, the second Lancang-Mekong Cooperation Village Heads Forum was held in Mangshi City, Dehong Dai and Jingpo Autonomous Prefecture, Yunnan Province, China, and nearly 200 representatives from the Ministries of Agriculture, provinces and villages (cooperatives) of LMC countries attended the forum. "Cooperation, Innovation, Win-win, and Jointly Promote Rural Revitalization" was the theme of the forum. The participants shared experiences in rural development through thematic reports, exchanges and discussions, bilateral talks, exhibitions and demonstrations, enterprises and villages matchmaking, field study and other form. The forum issued *LMC Village Community Cooperation Mangshi Initiative*, which advocated village and enterprise exchange and cooperation, promoting green production methods, improving the quality of agricultural products, strengthening standard mutual recognition and training, and attaching importance to the development of agricultural industry chain and value chain. On the Forum, the China Village and Community Development Promotion Association proposed the establishment of Village and Community Development Alliance in Lancang-Mekong. Eight cooperation agreements were signed at the exhibition and demonstration matchmaking activity of the forum with a contract value about 120 million CNY.

6. 1. 2 Establishment of the Mechanism of Science and Technology Exchange and Cooperation to Promote Technological Upgrading and Industrial Development

Yunnan Academy of Agricultural Sciences of China has successively led the establishment of a series of cooperation mechanisms and platforms, including ECCAST-GMS, Yunnan Agriculture Oversea Development Technology Innovation Alliance (YAODTIA), Exchange and Cooperation Consortium for Agricultural Science and Technology in China-South Asia (ECCAST-CSA), Innovation Alliance for Agricultural Science and Technology in South & Southeast Asia (IAAST-SSA), aiming to promote agricultural technology exchanges, increase agricultural production and farmer income by helping host countries to select suitable varieties, demonstration and extension. In August 2019, the ECCAST-LMC was officially established. It would build a multi-disciplinary platform for agricultural technology exchanges, such as planting, animal husbandry and fishery, and focus on strengthening cooperation in key diseases and insect pests, animal epidemics and water ecological conservation, and promote the upgrading of agricultural technology and industrial development.

6.2 Poverty Alleviation Demonstration Cooperation Carried Out to Promote Comprehensive and Sustainable Development of Rural Areas

The problem of poverty has always been an important issue of people's livelihood in the Lancang-Mekong subregion, also an issue that the government urgently needs to solve. In recent years, in order to promote the sharing of poverty reduction ideas and experiences between China and East Asian countries, to continuously deepen the exchanges and cooperation in poverty alleviation of China and its neighboring countries, a series of institutionalization cooperation platforms have been established, including the Global Poverty Reduction and Development Forum, ASEAN-China Forum on Social Development and Poverty Reduction, etc. The State Council Leading Group Office of Poverty Alleviation and Development of China led the establishment of the Poverty Alleviation Working Group of LMC, organized and implemented the East Asia Poverty Alleviation Demonstration Cooperation Technology Aid Project with various forms of poverty alleviation cooperation activities, such as ASEAN Poverty Alleviation Forum, Poverty Alleviation Workshop, and ASEAN Village Officials Exchange. The China International Poverty Reduction Center held several training courses on poverty reduction and development with a large number of trainees from the LMC countries. Since 2016,95 officials from Vietnam, Cambodia, Myanmar and Thailand have come to China to participate in the seminar, and the ASEAN + 3 Village Officials Exchange Program has been held for seven consecutive times.

In 2014, Chinese government proposed to implement the "East Asia Poverty Alleviation Cooperation Initiative" with budget 100 million CNY to carry out the rural poverty alleviation promotion plan, and establish the East Asia poverty reduction cooperation demonstration site. According to the project design, the Yunnan International Poverty Alleviation and Development Center, the Guangxi Foreign Capital Poverty Alleviation Projects Management Center and the Sichuan Poverty Alleviation and Immigration Bureau Projects Center respectively undertake the poverty reduction demonstration cooperation technology aid projects in Myanmar, Laos and Cambodia. These aid projects had been implemented in 6 villages in Myanmar, Laos and Cambodia, and the main content included improving the infrastructure and public service facilities in the village, industrial development projects and capacity-building activities, etc. The implementation of all these poverty alleviation demonstration project has effectively improved the production and living conditions of local villagers and enhanced the development vitality of the rural village.

6.2.1 The Cases of Chinese Poverty Reduction Demonstration Cooperation Aid Project in Aye Chan Thar and Min Pyin Villages of Myanmar

Agriculture is the pillar industry of Myanmar, thus the Myanmar government has been committed to improving people's living standards and making great efforts for rural development and poverty alleviation, but many villages are still in poverty. About 70% of Myanmar's population lives in rural areas, and the rural poor account for about 23% of the country's population. In November 2017, China and Myanmar signed an agreement on the implementation of China-aided Pilot Project of Poverty Reduction Cooperation in Myanmar. In February 2018, the project was officially launched, with the construction of roads, water supply, schools, health centers and other infrastructure in two villages—Min Pyin

Village in Lewe Township and Aye Chan Thar Village in Tetgone Township in Nay Pyi Taw, which benefited 7,820 villagers in 1,481 households.

Aye Chan Thar Village is an immigrant village relocated from four villages, with 483 households and 2,274 villagers. There was a lack of farmland and water shortage, and no water conservancy facilities for agricultural irrigation. Most of the houses in the village was very dilapidated, made of wood or bamboo woven materials; only 170 households were electrified accounting for 35% of the total number of households, with a large demand for electricity. Calculated by the poverty standard of 1.25 USD per person per day, the poverty households in the village account for 2/3 of the total number of households, and the incidence of poverty is over 65%. It was a representative poverty-stricken village in the central part of Myanmar. In the rainy season, the roads in the village were very muddy and slippery; the water supply in the village relies on a 25 feet deep well with poor water quality and bitter taste; some peasants built their own large water pools to receive rainwater from the roof for daily use or even drinking. No Safety guarantee of drinking water seriously restricted villagers' production and life.

After the field investigation in Aye Chan Thar Village, the project team decided to take all-round poverty reduction measures within three years. First of all, started infrastructure-based construction activities, including roads and drinking water projects. Considering that there is a lot of rainfall in the area where the village is located, while repairing the roads, the drainage ditches and culverts on both sides of the roads were renovated. A 600-foot deep well was excavated with the pumping station to take water from the ground, meanwhile, the project built clean-water pool and laid the pipe network to each household to solved the problem of water intake for farmers. This project also equipped with transformers and power lines to solve the problem of electricity consumption of the whole village, and realized public lighting in the housing concentration area, key road sections, schools, temples and other places. At the same time of water supply for each household, power supply for each household had been realized. Secondly, the project governed environment and held professional training courses after completed the infrastructure, to help villages develop planting, breeding and other industries. In agricultural cultivation, the project introduced high-quality, high-yield and stable grain crops and improved varieties of cash crops to increase the output. In terms of animal husbandry, the project set village-level livestock breeding and epidemic prevention and control demonstration households, introduced high-quality boars, provided livestock breeders with good meat-quality and fast-growing livestock cubs, constructed standardized pens for 100 livestock households, promoted artificial feed of livestock, and increased sideline income. In addition, the project demonstrated courtyard economy of 150 households to achieve multiple income generation. Combined with the tradition of hand-woven fabrics in Aye Chan Thar village, the project helped the villagers establish textile cooperatives to develop handicraft industry.

There are more than 1,000 households in Min Pyin Village. The road condition in the village was poor, and the road surface was rugged and very bumpy. As in the village of Aye Chan Thar, considering the characteristics of inconvenient transportation and poor drinking water conditions in this village, the expert group of the project formulated a three-year plan. In the first year, the project concentrated on drilling wells for water and repairing roads in village. In the second year, the project mainly built village activity center and power supply. And in the third year, the project built the flood dikes and schools. The implementation of the project also took sustainable development and environmental protection as the objectives of the project, established public service programs for garbage disposal to enhance the environmental awareness of farmers. In April 2019, the project of the Chinese part organized more than 40 villagers' representatives from these two demonstration villages to visit Kan Pyung and Wae Gyi, which are waste treatment demonstration villages in Kyauktan, southern of Yangon City. Activities of field visits and knowledge exchange let the villagers have a more intuitive experience of environmental remediation activities and enhanced environmental awareness; improved the organizational capacity of managers at all levels of the project, and contributed to inspiration and reference for promotion of environmental improvement and waste disposal project in the China-Myanmar project.

6.2.2   The Case of Chinese Poverty Reduction Demonstration Cooperation Aid Project in Kandal Province of Cambodia

On December 21, 2017, the launching ceremony of the China-aided Pilot Project of Poverty Reduction Cooperation in Cambodia was held in Svay Ampear Commune, Kandal Province, Cambodia. The project was planned to take 3 years and implemented in two villages—Chheuteal Phlos Village and Svay Ampear Village, Svay Ampear Commune, Mok Kampoul District, Kandal Province, Cambodia. It was expected that 886 households and more than 3,900 villagers would be benefited directly from the project. Based on the management of local poverty-causing factors and development needs, the project carried out community poverty reduction activities according to local conditions, covering infrastructure, industrial development, technical training and others; rural roads, water supply and other infrastructure construction to improve local safe drinking water and other production and living conditions; rural health rooms, learning centers and other public service facilities establishment to meet the basic requirements of local people; sending experts to provide technical training for villagers to support development of planting, breeding and other industries. The project improved the production and living conditions, enhanced the ability of self-development and explored ways to increase income for farmers of local communities in Cambodia by the government-led and farmer participation model. It provided a demonstration for poverty reduction and improvement of people's livelihood in East Asian countries.

The project built a community activity center with a total area of 400 square meters, which is used as a daily office for village cadres in Svay Ampear Commune, as well as the general public activity place for the entire community, especially as a place for meeting, training or other activities. On the ground floor of the activity center, there are 2 offices, 1 material room, 1 meeting room, 2 lounges and 2 restrooms; on the first floor there are 1 kitchen, 2 restrooms and 1 dining room, which can accommodate 100 people for dining at the same time. On September 5, 2019, the rural drinking water project was officially started in Svay Ampear Commune. The project included the construction of new water source program, water purification program (water plant), water delivery and distribution network program (including household pipe network and water meter) and its ancillary works, and solved the drinking water problem of for 3,840 people in 800 households in two villages of Svay Ampear Commune. In terms of technical training, the training of rural project executors and project villagers' labor skills have been carried out once respectively and enhanced the village development ability in all aspects. For the poor, 100 toilets have been rebuilt, 82 power connections have been completed and 500 cooking ranges and 1,000 firewood saving stoves have been distributed to the villagers. At the same time, the project also helped a poor household to open a small shop, with an average monthly income of 60-120 USD. Although this project is still under construction, it has achieved some phase results and been affirmed by the local government and villagers.

6.2.3 Experience and Enlightenment of the Projects

The China-aided Pilot Projects of Poverty Reduction Cooperation in Myanmar and Cambodia have better achieved the goal of rural poverty reduction and promoting sustainable development through two aspects of cooperation on infrastructure improvement and development capacity-building. On the one hand, according to the actual situation, the projects helped to improve the local infrastructure construction and provide a strong basic guarantee for the later economic development. On the other hand, based on the goal of cultivating ability and realizing sustainable development, the projects established communication and cooperation programs in various fields, set up numerous training platforms, expanded talent training channels to improve talent quality in all aspects, and trained people for rural construction in various countries, enhanced rural self-development ability, and improved the production and living conditions of communities.

In the meantime, China brought the poverty alleviation concept of "Targeted Poverty Alleviation" and "Whole Village Promotion" into Mekong countries through the project implementation. From the feasibility study to the final implementation plan, the projects took into account the actual situation and needs of the poor villages and villagers. During the implementation of the projects, the Chinese investigation teams went to villages and households to made field surveys, drew resource maps and learned about the production season and traditional culture. On program selection, they widely listened to the opinions of the masses, discussed with officials of local poverty alleviation institutions at all levels, held people's representatives meeting, and analyzed the basic situation of the project village and the poverty situation of the farmers with the participation of village managers, group leaders and villager representatives. In the process of projects construction, the implementation group and supervision group were set up at the village level to ensure projects completion on time and with high quality. After the completion of the projects, guided to formulate the village level follow-up management measures. The implementation of the projects pays more attention to comprehensive development, based on the working experience of "Whole Village Promotion" of Targeted Poverty Alleviation in China, comprehensively considering the needs of local farmers, realized the coordinated long-term sustainable development of internal infrastructure, very important livelihood projects and industrial development.

6. 3　Enhance Infrastructure Construction and Improve People's Livelihood to Promote Rural Development

The areas of people's livelihood cover widest range and connect closely with farmers. It is the key to realize rural development and regional poverty reduction. Perfect infrastructure construction is the prerequisite to realize rural leapfrog development. However, due to the rarely weak industrial development, the imperfect infrastructure, and the limited capacity of sustainable infrastructure construction in the Mekong countries, the development speed has been restricted seriously. There is a large gap in infrastructure especially in rural areas, so it needs to speed up to make up for the shortcomings of rural people's livelihood to realize regional rural revitalization, particularly in improving the conditions of rural transportation and logistics facilities, and strengthening the construction of rural water conservancy infrastructure networks. In addition, it is also necessary to pay attention to the protection and conservation of resources in the process of infrastructure construction, with people's livelihood and sustainability as the guide to promote rural construction and development from changing the life style of farmers.

6.3.1 The Cases of Chinese Poverty Reduction Demonstration Cooperation Aid Project in Ban Xor and Xienglom Villages of Laos

In 2017, implementation of aid provision by China for poverty alleviation demonstration cooperation project in Laos determined two target villages of Ban Xor of Sangthong District in Lao Capital Vientiane and Xienglom in northern Luang Prabang Province. There were 17 programs of the aid project, including 9 programs in Ban Xor Village and 8 programs in Xienglom Village, focusing on infrastructure and public facilities such as the bridges, roads in villages, water supply to households, activity centers, clinics, dormitories for teachers and students, solar street lamps, etc. The project construction have improved the production and living conditions of local communities, strengthened the self-development capacity of communities, diversified income-increasing channels for the poor, and have been the models and samples for poverty reduction and improvement of people's livelihood in East Asian countries.

Laos is an agricultural country, and its infrastructure needs to be improved, with lack of railways and expressways, and many places use secondary roads. There are rich agricultural resources and fertile soil, especially the forest coverage and the per capita land occupation are relatively high in the two villages, but the lack of irrigation and other water conservancy facilities, the land utilization rate is low. Furthermore, it is impossible to carry out in-depth agricultural development because of the relative lack of funds and technology. Agricultural production "depends on the weather", and the foundation of rural industrial development is relatively weak. The villagers' motivation for self-change is really insufficient and they know little about what a cooperative is and how to develop it. In order to effectively promote poverty reduction, China and Laos have established a multi-sectoral contact system to provide support from various aspects such as funds and personnel; at the same time, the expert groups of Guangxi Zhuang Autonomous Region strengthened cooperation with Laos, visited target villages and project sites for many times, and reached consensus with Laos on project mode, project planning, implementation plan, organization setting, etc. Guangxi Zhuang Autonomous Region sent expert groups to Laos for three times, respectively in October, December 2016 and May 2017, to visit the project sites with relevant personnel in Laos, carefully determine the location of the project and well prepare for the early stage of the project. Both China and Laos implemented the joint management mode for the project. Foreign Capital Poverty Alleviation Project Management Center in Guangxi Zhuang Autonomous Region cooperated with National Rural Development and Poverty Reduction Committee in Laos to establish a joint project management office at different levels, and sent Chinese experts and technicians to the office to joint organize the implementation and manage the project with Laos. The relevant departments in Laos fully participated in providing management assistance, labor input, land for project implementation, etc., in the construction process of the project. This kind of joint management helped to play a better role in local place after the completion of the project. At the same time, the joint office widely listened to the opinions of the masses on project selection, guided the establishment of the implementation group and supervision group in village, ensured the project completed on time and quality, and also guided the village level to formulate follow-up management measures after the completion of the project.

Drinking water facilities problems are closely related to production and life. The domestic water of Xienglom Village in Luang Prabang County mainly depends on the Nam Khan River flowing by the village, but the villagers can only save money to buy barreled drinking water because of the difficulty of water extraction from Nam Khan River in dry season and the water quality fails to meet the drinking water standard. Moreover, the original water pipe in Xienglom Village has aged and cannot be used. A family needs at least 20 barrels of water per month to meet the demand, equivalent to about 200 CNY, which is not a small expenditure for a poor family in need. In order to solve the problem of difficulty in drinking water, the project team members and local government officials investigated on-the-spot many times and climbed mountains and mountains to find water sources together with the cadres and masses of the project village. Finally, they found clean mountain spring water in Shuangshan Mountain where was 5 kilometers away from the village. Under the principle of villagers' voluntary, Chinese experts and the local government of Laos jointly organized villagers to invest in labor, excavate and backfill the ditches 4,000 meters, lay 13,000 meters of water pipes, and put in more than 5,000 working days, drawing spring water that meets drinking standards from Shuangshan Mountain, which ended the history of local farmers buying barreled water life. The solution of drinking water problems not only promoted the construction of rural infrastructure, but also improved the livelihood environment of farmers, and provided advantage conditions for the next tasks for poverty reduction.

China will provide whatever assistance villagers need most urgently, based on the local condition. Compared with Xienglom Village, the main problem of Ban Xor Village is the construction of transportation facilities. The wooden Ban Xor bridge, as an important traffic road and the main road in the village, has been used for more than ten years, and it has been seriously damaged and dangerous. Under the bridge, there is a river about 20 meters deep and with great hidden danger. In order to eliminate the potential safety hazards, the project team rebuilt the original dangerous bridge with damaged boards into a safe Ban Xor bridge, connecting the residential area and farming area in the village to help the villagers have a convenient life. With the continuous improvement of infrastructure, how to improve livelihood conditions became the next area of concern. Ban Xor Village has a total of more than 2,000 villagers and 3,438 hectares of land, with good natural endowment. However, due to the lack of funds, technology, and backward agricultural infrastructure, a small paddy field for a household only meets the basic needs of life every year, and there are a lot of abandoned land with low production efficiency. In view of the current situation of extensive rice cultivation in the local area, China strived to increase the yield of rice and the income of local farmers by strengthening the construction of water conservancy and irrigation infrastructure and increasing technical training in the form of cooperatives and driven by competent people.

The project also included technical training, industrial development, exchanging and cooperation for the villagers of the two villages based on improving infrastructure. In the first half of 2018, the project completed cultivation and tourism training for 155 farmers, project management personnel training for 35 people, capable training in China for 10 Lao people, and 70 low-income families were supported to carry out cultivation and breeding activities[①]. Based on the foundation of Xienglom Village tourism scenic area and the needs of local residents, the project planning program increased the support for micro processing industry to help them develop family handicraft industry and use tourism resources to drive the sale of special handicrafts and peripheral products. In addition, China and Laos established "Friendship Village" exchange activities, the "Friendship Village" activities between Longsheng and Luang Prabang have been held for 2 times since the implement of the aid project. In 2019, totally 12 representatives from Luang Prabang County officials, village leaders and poor families of Laos "Friendship Village" project visited Guangxi of

---

① Wei Jichuan, 2018. Guangxi Information of Technology Aid Project in Laos of the East Asia Poverty Reduction Cooperation [N]. Guangxi Daily, 05-30.

China, learning the experience and practice of poverty alleviation in Longsheng Ge Autonomous County through symposiums and visiting village cadres, rich leaders and poor farmers.

6.3.2 Experience and Enlightenment of the Projects

Infrastructure construction is currently an important area for the implementation of the Lancang-Mekong poverty reduction cooperation project. The aid project pays more attention to the livelihood projects closely related to local people of the recipient country. The implementation of the project is not only the improvement of the material conditions, but also the improvement of the main body consciousness and sense of responsibility of local villagers, the cultivation and improvement the villagers' management capabilities, the introduction of China's experience and mode of participatory poverty alleviation and industrial poverty alleviation to the local villages, and giving play to the villagers' sense of ownership, the participation in all aspects of project design, planning, implementation, supervision and inspection. The project made full use of local development resources and advantageous industries, met local development demands, the solution of bottlenecks problems, improved the infrastructure most needed for industrial development, while laid the solid foundation, focused on local human resources capacity building, and let the villagers gradually embark on the road of self-reliance and independent development.

6.4 Technology Extension and Industry Development to Promote from Poverty to Prosperity in Rural Areas

The Lancang-Mekong basin has excellent natural conditions, fertile land, and the relatively low labor costs, and excellent endowment of agricultural resources, which is one of the most potential regions in Asia and even in the world, as well as the main production area in the world such as food crops, sugar crops and tropical economic crops. The five Mekong countries are traditional agricultural countries, and agriculture is their pillar industry of economy, with huge development potential. However, due to the lack of technical support and guidance, the potential has not been fully realized. The technology demonstration projects can help farmers grow crops better, improve the quality of crops, and increase the income while obtaining the economic benefits of agricultural industry. With its geographical and technological advantages, China is committed to the demonstration and promotion of agricultural technology in Mekong countries. In view of the local conditions, China has carried out cooperation in various fields to help establish the modern agricultural industrial system, production system and business system, stimulate rural vitality in various countries, and achieve poverty alleviation and prosperity through the development and expansion of rural industries.

6.4.1 The Case of China's Aided Project for Organic Vegetable Planting Zone in Jinhua Village of Laos

The Guangxi Vocational and Technical College of Agriculture took the important task to establish China-Laos Joint Test Station for Good Variety Crops in Jinhua Village, Laos in 2013. And it was entrusted by International Poverty Alleviation Center in China and Foreign Capital Poverty Alleviation Project Management Center in Guangxi to carry out the China-Laos cooperative communities Poverty Reduction Demonstration Projects in 2015, which relied on the China-Laos Joint Test Station for Good Variety Crops in Jinhua Village, Laos. In 2019, China-Laos poverty alleviation cooperation community demonstration project organic vegetable planting area was launched in Jinhua Village. Through cooperation with enterprises, the project had successfully carried out the demonstration of the organic vegetable planting in greenhouse in Jinhua

Village, which greatly increased the income of local farmers.

Jinhua Village is by the side of the Nam Ngum River, a tributary of the Mekong River. The water overflows and the farmland is often flooded in the rainy season. The villagers rely on rice planting once per year for living due to lack of agricultural facilities and technology. Chinese experts found that the vegetable market in Vientiane City and its surrounding areas were in short supply after detailed investigation, and Jinhua Village has the natural advantage of planting vegetables, which can be the direction of future development for Jinhua Village. In 2016, the project assisted the villagers to construct five greenhouses in the village, and handed over to 10 farmers for demonstration, in which Chinese experts and technicians taught practical and advanced planting technology on site. The villagers learned a lot through professional translation. In addition, the project carried out the construction of irrigation equipment, provided technical on planting, contacted vegetable distributors and developed a management mechanism for greenhouse leasing, and helped villages build vegetable bases.

From 2013 to 2018, more than 160 crop varieties had been taken the trial in the test station, and selected 48 good varieties suitable for cultivation and promotion in Laos, including 11 fruit trees, 31 melons and vegetables, 2 rice, 2 corn, 1 peanut and 1 forage. Moreover, 2,833 hectares of crops extension were demonstrated, and more than 1,000 agricultural technicians were trained. At the end of 2013, the expert who took the lead in developing the technique of soilless cultivation of anti-season Hami melon in Guangxi was invited to Jinhua Village to take charge of Hami melon planting. Hami melon was successfully planted in only 3 months, which made the test station as the only Hami melon planting base in Laos. After that, the test station taught Hami melon planting technology to Lao agricultural technicians and growers by holding technical training courses. Besides Hami melon, Chinese experts continuously popularize practical and advanced agricultural technologies such as rice, corn and pitaya planting. At the same time, the test station also accepted 230 graduates from Laos universities to practice in the test station and provided training, recommending 7 agricultural technicians of Laos to study in China at public expense. The test station has become an important platform for agricultural technology promotion in Laos. Jinhua village has developed from an unknown village into a famous vegetable base[①].

6.4.2 Technology Exchange and Industrial Cooperation Projects Cases

In 2018, the LMC Special Fund supported Guizhou Mountain-specific Agricultural Technology Promote the Lancang-Mekong Subregional Poverty Reduction Demonstration, focusing on the cultivation demonstration of Guizhou characteristic pepper varieties, rare edible fungi, red kiwifruit and Dendrobium nobile in-Lancang-Mekong river basin, and the economic benefit evaluation of the promotion of the characteristic agricultural technology of Southwest China in Lancang-Mekong Basin. Since 2014, Guangxi Zhuang Autonomous Region of China established the project of China (Guangxi)-ASEAN Improved Crops Varieties Experimental Station, which introduced more than 300 crop trials varieties to relevant countries, and screened a total of 30 varieties suitable or purified and rejuvenated for local cultivation, with a total demonstration and promotion area of more than 60,000 mu. In addition, the technology exchanges and cooperation projects on prevention and control of cross-border animal epidemics and disease in LMC countries, the joint proliferation and release projects in LMC countries and other projects have played important role in deepening technology exchanges and cooperation in the Subregion,

---

① Jian Wenxiang, 2019. Like-minded and Harmonious, Deeply Attached and Interchange: "Journey of Thousands Miles in ASEAN, View the Silk Road Picturesque Scenery" of Laos [N]. Guangxi Daily, 09-10.

promoting the development of rural industry and increasing farmers' income.

In order to promote the sales and circulation of rural products, cross-border e-commerce related training was also carried out to promote the connection between e-commerce and rural development. In June 2016, the GMS Cross-border E-commerce Cooperation Platform Enterprise Alliance was established in Kunming, Yunnan Province. Enterprises from all countries can register their e-commerce websites on the platform to carry out B2B and B2C E-commerce. In March of 2019, Mekong Institute held the regional modular training of Rural E-commerce Development in LMC countries. Through various training courses, the latest knowledge and skills of rural e-commerce development were taught to participants from all countries to promote the development of local rural e-commerce.

6.4.3 Experience and Enlightenment of the Projects

To promote technology cooperation and industrial development in Lancang-Mekong subregion, the technology demonstration projects paid more attention to the front and back ends of the industrial chain, and emphasized on the production and sales to promote the upgrading and development of technology and products. On the one hand, the project gave full play to the advantages of agricultural resources of all countries in the basin and carried out precise cooperation against the shortcomings of agricultural technology. The high applicability of agricultural technology in Yunnan, Guangxi, Guizhou and other border provinces and regions of China maximized the effect of technology promotion and application in the region. At the same time, in view of the local agricultural production conditions, the projects researched and developed high-quality agricultural products suitable for local area, helped set up local brands of agricultural products, and provided conditions for achieving sustainable development. On the other hand, to promote product upgrading and circulation, the cooperation expanded to product sales, which opened up a new way for agricultural products sales and promoted industrial development and revitalization from multiple perspectives through the matching of village and enterprise and e-commerce platform construction.

(Written by Tang Lixia and Zhang Yike,
College of Humanities and Development Studies,
China Agricultural University;
Translated by Guo Wen,
International Agriculture Research Institute,
Yunnan Academy of Agricultural Sciences, China)

Province and
Country Reports

7 | Agricultural Development and the Progress of Lancang-Mekong Agricultural Cooperation in Yunnan Province of China

7. 1 General Situation of Agricultural Development

7. 1. 1 Overall Development Status and Characteristics

In recent years, with the strong support of the Ministry of Agriculture and Rural Affairs of China, the government of Yunnan province has vigorously promoted agricultural modernization, fully promoted the implementation of the Rural Revitalization Strategy, accelerated the green development of agriculture, and steadily promoted agricultural and rural reform. Under these measures, Yunnan province development has achieved a good beginning in Rural Revitalization, the agricultural and rural modernization has taken solid steps, and the whole provincial agriculture and rural areas have achieved high-quality leapfrog development.

(1) **The income of farmers has reached a new stage.** The Per Capita Disposable Income (PCDI) of rural residents in the province maintained a sustained and rapid growth. In 2018, it exceeded the 10,000 CNY mark for the first time, reaching 10,768 CNY, a year-on-year growth of 9.2%, 0.4 percentage points higher than the national PCDI of rural residents.

(2) **The agricultural production capacity has reached a new level.** In 2018, the Added Value of agriculture, forestry, animal husbandry and fishery in the province reached 255.278 billion CNY, a year-on-year

growth of 6. 3%, ranking the second in China. The grain sown area was 4. 17 million hectares, output was 18. 61 million tons, the comprehensive production capacity had been steadily improved for three consecutive years. The rice and wheat production functional area and the important agricultural product production and protection area were designated 642. 7 thousand hectares, and 162. 6 thousand hectares of high-standard farmland construction was completed. The supply of major agricultural products was stable, and the ratio of agricultural product processing output value to total agricultural output value is increased to 1. 11 : 1. The export value of agricultural products reached 3. 875 billion USD, ranking the first among the western provinces of China for many years, and it continued to maintain the status of the largest category of export commodities in the province.

(3) **The rural condition has been improved greatly.** 65 counties (municipalities) in the province have completed the Rural Construction Planning. The rural residential environment improvement started to implement, the collection and treatment rate of rural domestic waste reached 88. 37%, the treatment rate of rural domestic sewage reached 26%, there were 1,870 newly built (modified) flushing public toilets, and 459. 2 thousand harmless sanitary household toilets were newly built, and the popularization rate of sanitary household toilets reached 72. 92%.

(4) **Poverty alleviation through industrial development has taken new steps.** The way of new type business entities encouraged to help poverty alleviation is clearer, and the "double binding" interest linking mechanism between poor households and professional cooperatives and between professional cooperatives and leading enterprises, is further more improved. There were 33, 000 new type business entities that had established the mechanism of interest connection with the poor households in the province, covered 6. 12 million people, accounting for 89. 3% of the poor. Industrial coverage has continued to expand, and the ability to bring benefits to the poor has improved significantly.

(5) **The green development leads new pattern.** The building of "the Green Food Brand" has created a new engine for the green development of modern agriculture with plateau characteristics. Tea and other 7 advantageous industries' agricultural output value and comprehensive output value increased by 10.7% and 15.5% respectively, realizing the simultaneous growth of quantity and benefit. The first "Top 10 Famous Products" of green food such as "Top 10 Famous Teas" "Top 10 Famous Flowers" "Top 10 Famous Fruits" and "Top 10 Famous Vegetables" were appraised and elected, which were favorite by the masses. The green food "Top 10 Enterprises" and "Top 20 Innovative Enterprises" selected set up benchmarks for Yunnan agricultural enterprises, and has received strong response from all over the country. There were 428 newly certified green foods and 665 organic products. The green prevention and control coverage rate of major crops in the province was 31%, and the usage of chemical fertilizer and pesticide both achieved negative growth. The tasks such as delimitation of livestock and poultry breeding prohibited area have been fully completed. The comprehensive utilization rate of livestock and poultry manure has reached 76%, which was 6% higher than that of the whole country.

(6) **Agricultural products safety and security has been further improved.** The coverage rate of the whole-village promoting mode for animal epidemic disease prevention in the province reached 95.5%, the immune density of highly pathogenic avian influenza, foot-and-mouth disease and small ruminant animal disease reached 100%, and the prevention and control of equine infectious anemia passed the standard assessment and acceptance by the Ministry of Agriculture and Rural Affairs of China. The qualified rate of agricultural products remained at 96.6%, and seven counties included Binchuan, Songming and Qilin District passed the establishment assessment of the second batch of national agricultural product quality and safety counties.

(7) **Rural reform breeds new momentum.** The government made steady progress in special agricultural-related reforms and successfully

completed 13 tasks of agricultural and rural reform. Confirmation of contracted land was 7.32 million hectares, right confirmation contractors 8.872 million, issued certificates 8.559 million, and the certificates issued rate was 96.5%. The reform of rural collective property right system and the share-holding power of the rural collective assets have been accelerated. The social function reform of the agricultural reclamation farms ranked 9th out of 35 reclamation areas in China. The reform design of the agricultural comprehensive administrative law enforcement system has taken shape, and the reform offered "releasing management services" to deal with the relationship between the government and the market, has been deepened.

7.1.2   Agriculture Development Policy

(1) **Defining development direction.** Yunnan will stick to the guidance of Xi Jinping thought on socialism with Chinese characteristics for a new era, the overall goals include finishing building of a moderately prosperous society in all respects, the lead of the new development concepts of innovation, coordination, greenness, openness, and sharing to vigorously promote agricultural and rural modernization, fully promote the implementation of the rural revitalization strategy and accelerate agriculture green development, steadily push forward the reform of agriculture and rural affairs and build pattern of agricultural all-round opening to the outside world.

(2) **Issuing a series of relevant policies.** In recent years, Yunnan Province has successively issued a series of policy documents, such as "Opinions on Speeding up the Modernization of Plateau Characteristics Agriculture and Realizing the Goal of a Moderately Prosperous Society in all Respects" "Opinions of the General Office of the People's Government of Yunnan Province on Cultivating and Strengthening of Small Agricultural Giants" "Implementation Opinions of the Yunnan Provincial Committee of the Communist Party of China & Yunnan Provincial People's Government

on Speeding up the Construction of Chinese Radiation Center Facing South Asia and Southeast Asia" "Opinions of the Yunnan Provincial People's Government on 22 Measures for Promoting the Economy Sustainable, Healthy and Rapid development" "Encouraging Investment Measures for Cultivating Leading Enterprises of Green Food Industry" "Implementation Opinions on Promoting Green Development of Yun-Tea Industry" "Guiding Opinions of Yunnan Provincial People's Government on Establishing 'One County, One Industry' Demonstration County and Accelerating the Building of World-Class 'Green Food Brand'". These documents focus on 8 dominant and characteristic industries and make "Big Industry, New Platform, New Entities" as development idea, to create a world-class "Green Food Brand", expand and deepen the agricultural opening up.

(3) **Implementing relevant measures.** Yunnan will adhere to the general policy of giving priority to agricultural and rural development, the overall goal of realization of agricultural and rural modernization, the general starting point of the implementation of rural revitalization strategy, the main line of the structural reform of the agricultural supply side, to promote the reform and development of agriculture and rural affairs, and accelerate the construction of the radiation center facing South Asia and Southeast Asia, and practically promote agricultural foreign cooperation.

7.2 Lancang-Mekong Agricultural Cooperation

7.2.1 Cooperation Progress

(1) **Overall planning agricultural foreign cooperation with top-level design as the core.** Since the first LMC Leaders' meeting, Yunnan Province has successively issued implementation opinions on foreign cooperation in agriculture, compiled the plan of foreign cooperation in agriculture, clarified the guidance, basic principles, objectives, tasks and policy measures Yunnan's agricultural foreign cooperation, and established the joint conference mechanism

of Yunnan agricultural foreign cooperation, which provided basis of directivity, guideline and decision-making for Yunnan agriculture to participate in Lancang-Mekong agricultural cooperation.

(2) **Promoting mutual benefit and trust with cooperation mechanism construction.** The provincial and municipal levels governments have signed a series of cooperation agreements with the relevant LMC countries, reached a lot of consensus on jointly carrying out comprehensive agricultural development, established the Exchange and Cooperation Consortium for Agricultural Science and Technology in Greater Mekong Subregion and the Southeast Asia Protective Agricultural Cooperation Network, which has effectively promoted the development of agricultural cooperation between Yunnan and LMC countries in a healthy, efficient and sustainable direction.

(3) **Focusing on enterprise investment and promoting industrial cooperation.** Driven by the Belt and Road Initiative, Yunnan strengthened agricultural supply-side structural reform and the *Sanya Declaration* (the first Lancang-Mekong Cooperation Leaders' Meeting), more and more agricultural enterprises have participated in Lancang-Mekong agricultural cooperation. In 2018, there were 144 enterprises investment in agriculture overseas in Yunnan Province, a year-on-year increase of 13.39%; 164 agricultural enterprises invested and established overseas, a year-on-year increase of 19.71%; the cumulative value of investment in agriculture overseas reached 1.15 billion USD, a year-on-year growth of 39.14%; the new investment amount was 192.694 million USD, a year-on-year growth of 12.10%; the total value of assets of enterprises investment overseas was 2.06 billion USD, a year-on-year increase of 117.54%. Among these enterprises, there were 68 in Laos, 70 in Myanmar, 10 in Thailand, 5 in Vietnam and 5 in Cambodia, accounting for more than 96% of the total number of enterprises investment in agricultural overseas in the province, employing 43.7 thousand foreign personnel with the total salary of the

foreign employees was 106 million USD, and paying taxes to the host country 9.539,3 million USD.

(4) **Promoting technical cooperation with overseas agricultural science and technology demonstration parks as bridges.** Yunnan cooperated with Cambodia, Laos, and Myanmar successively to build 4 agricultural science and technology demonstration parks, and actively carried out improved varieties planting demonstration, comprehensive practical agriculture supporting technology extension, agricultural technicians training, etc. While actively carrying out agricultural technical assistance, the frontier prefectures, municipalities and counties also further promoted agricultural technology testing and demonstration, and constantly expanded the agricultural effect of radiation center. Under the mechanism of the Exchange and Cooperation Consortium for Agricultural Science and Technology in Greater Mekong Subregion, agricultural scientific research institutions exchanged 264 crops varieties, extended and demonstrated 38 suitable varieties, the demonstration area was over 6,667 hectares, and trained more than 10,000 scientific and technological personnel and farmers from relevant countries. In addition, the China-Myanmar Joint Agricultural Technology Training Center established by Yunnan Agricultural Vocational and Technical College also trained 72 technical personnel and more than 2,000 farmers for Myanmar, contributing to improve the level of agricultural science and technology in LMC countries.

(5) **Promoting the sharing of high-quality agricultural products with the matching of production and marketing as the starting point.** First, based on the rich and diverse resource advantages of the plateau, the government will vigorously build the "Green Food Brand" in Yunnan Province, continue to build the agricultural product quality and safety demonstration zones, and constantly develop famous and special agricultural products. By the end of 2018, it successively built 10 agricultural product quality and safety demonstration zones at all levels, with a total area of 96.3 thousand

hectares, including 1 national level demonstration zone (Mengzi City) and 1 provincial level demonstration zone (Luxi County). Second, aimed at the domestic and foreign markets such as LMC countries, and regularly organize innovative, professional and industrial types exhibitions, including agricultural Expo, agricultural Fair, Tea Expo and the "Internet ＋" modern agriculture innovation and entrepreneurship for new technology and new farmers Expo. , Yunnan vegetable production and marketing matching conference. Third, local government will fully explore domestic and foreign markets by actively holding products introduction exhibitions in Southeast Asia, West Asia, the Middle East, Europe, Hong Kong, Macao and Taiwan. According to the statistics, the agricultural products export value in the province reached 3.875 billion USD in 2018, and of which the LMC countries accounted for more than 50%, ranking the first among the western provinces of China for many years, and continued to maintain the status of the largest category of export commodities in the province. The products have been exported to more than 110 countries and regions, and the main productions included vegetables, potatoes, fruits, coffee, tea, animals and products, flowers, and so on.

(6) Building a security barrier with joint prevention and control of animal and plant epidemic disease as an opportunity. In 2018, first, the pilot project for the regional management of cross-border animal epidemic disease in China, Laos and Myanmar was implemented, with a cumulative investment of more than 500 million CNY. At present, the integrated pilot projects of slaughterhouse in Ruili City, Dehong Dai and Jingpo Autonomous Prefecture has been put into trial operation, and in Jinghong City, Xishuangbanna Dai Autonomous Prefecture is progressing in an orderly manner. Second, the project of Cross-Border Prevention and Control of Animal Epidemic Disease Technology Exchange and Cooperation among Countries in Lancang-Mekong Subregion had been successfully completed. Through epidemic disease monitoring and transmission risk research, mastered the main cross-border animal epidemic disease transmission risks, Yunnan proposed the solutions and suggestions, provided scientific basis for formulating cross-border animal epidemic disease prevention and control countermeasure and animal product trade policies in LMC countries. Third, we jointly carried out 3,500 cases Etiology monitoring with Laos, Vietnam and Myanmar. Totally 5 sessions of international veterinary technical training courses were held in Kunming, Pu'er, Xishuangbanna and Dehong, training more than 210 veterinary technical personnel from Laos, Myanmar and Vietnam, and more than 250 overseas farmers, agricultural enterprise personnel and government agency officials. Fourth, it further completed the follow-up work of locust eradication in 5 provinces of Laos, included Luang Prabang, Phongsalu and Oudomsay.

(7) **Bringing benefit to the grassroots farmers with forums as the platform.** Yunnan government actively implemented the initiatives at the Lancang-Mekong Cooperation Leadership Conference, cooperated with the Ministry of Agriculture and Rural Affairs of China to organize and held two sessions of the LMC Village Headers Forums in 2017 and 2018, with a total of 291 participants, issued LMC *Village Community Cooperation Mangshi Initiative*, and signed 11 investment cooperation agreements between village-village, village-enterprise and enterprise-enterprise, and the total amount of contracts between villages and enterprises and foreign parties was more than 150 million CNY. The forum provided exchange and cooperation platform of village cooperation, rural construction and agricultural and rural development for the village leaders of the five countries.

7. 2. 2　Experience and Practice

(1) **An agricultural cooperation mechanism was established.** Provincial Level: the Department of Agriculture and Rural Affairs of Yunnan Province has successively signed memorandums of understanding on agricultural cooperation with Bangladesh, Sri Lanka and other countries;

the provincial agricultural scientific research institute has signed agricultural science and technology cooperation agreements with Cambodia, Laos, Thailand, Vietnam, Myanmar and other countries, and established Exchange and Cooperation Consortium for Agricultural Science and Technology in Greater Mekong Subregion. Prefecture and City Level: reached the co-construction consensus with neighboring countries respectively. Dehong and other seven border prefectures and cities of Yunnan Province had successively carried out the construction of cross-border economic cooperation zones with Myanmar, Laos and Vietnam. The people's governments of Lincang and other border prefectures and cities of Yunnan Province have signed a memorandum of agricultural cooperation was with the government of Myanmar and the two sides would jointly carry out comprehensive agricultural development.

(2) **The joint conference system of agricultural foreign cooperation was established.** To study and analyze the situation and development trend of agricultural foreign cooperation in Yunnan Province, Yunnan formulated the objectives, tasks, development strategies, work plans and guidance, and coordinated all the relevant organizations and departments in Yunnan Province to study and propose policy recommendations, to determine and urge the implementation of measures for agricultural foreign cooperation, and coordinate to solve problems and difficulties encountered in cooperation.

(3) **An all-round cooperation pattern of agriculture was built.** Gave full play to Yunnan's location and technological advantages, focused on the LMC countries, improved the agricultural cooperation mechanism and implemented series of agricultural cooperation projects, guided overseas investment in agriculture, promoted trade in agricultural products and scientific and technological cooperation, formed a comprehensive, wide-ranging and multi-level agricultural cooperation pattern of government as the guide, enterprise as the main body, technology as the support.

(4) **The cross border agricultural cooperation was deepened.** Proactive

service and integration into the Belt and Road Initiative, focusing on building a world-class "Green Food Brand", strived to promote the development model of "Big Industry＋New Entities＋New Platform" and the development of the whole industrial chain of "Scientific Research＋Planting and Feeding＋Processing＋Circulation", encouraging enterprises in the province to deepen cross-border agricultural cooperation with LMC countries in planting, animal husbandry and fishery in order to achieve the mutual benefit and common development.

7. 3　Future Cooperation

7. 3. 1　General Idea

Yunnan will incorporate proactive service and integration into the Belt and Road Initiative, closely centered on the creation of a new highland for economic cooperation in the Greater Mekong Subregion, and based on the general requirements of the radiation center facing to South Asia and Southeast Asia. It will take the new development concept of innovation, coordination, green, opening and sharing as the guidance, strengthening the structural reform of the agricultural supply side, and enhancing the comprehensive competitiveness of the plateau characteristic agriculture and expanding the development space as the general goal, focusing on fostering agricultural opening enterprises and opening market system, strengthen scientific and technological support and government leading. Furthermore, it will promote "Five Action" situation of agricultural foreign cooperation featuring "Enterprise Initiative, Market Pulling, Science and Technology Driving, Prevention and Control Linkage, and Government Pushing", to make the plateau characteristic agriculture be the leading industry for Yunnan Province to serve and integrate into the Belt and Road Initiative. Furthermore, it is going to improve mechanisms, optimize distribution, deepen cooperation, and strive to advance the development of Lancang-Mekong agricultural cooperation.

7. 3. 2　Cooperation Objectives

By 2020，strive to significantly improve the world popularity of Yunnan plateau characteristic agricultural products and strive to cultivate a number of opening agricultural enterprises with certain sales revenue, international competitiveness and technological advantages. Preliminarily establish opening market system with the regional international agricultural products trading center, logistics center, futures trading market and agricultural machinery production base. Expand agricultural foreign investment annual scale to more than 150 million USD. Further improve the multi-level agricultural science and technology cooperation system, with accelerating to export of advantageous agricultural technology of Yunnan Province，widely spread the advantageous crop varieties abroad. Have a sound joint prevention and control of animal and plant epidemic diseases system. Basically form export-oriented modern agricultural industry system with plateau characteristics and the scale and quality of agricultural foreign cooperation reach a new level.

By 2022, Yunnan will support large-scale multinational agricultural-related enterprises to carry out foreign cooperation，and form a cluster of agricultural open enterprises led by large enterprises and followed by small and medium-sized enterprises，significantly enhance the comprehensive competitiveness of plateau characteristics agriculture of Yunnan Province. All kinds of bases will be installed in South Asia，Southeast Asia，Southwest and the Yangtze River economic belt of China，including regional agricultural products trading center, logistics center, futures trading market and agricultural machinery production base，significantly enhance the resource allocation ability of the opened-market system of plateau characteristics agricultural products. Overall complete joint prevention and control system of animal and plant epidemic disease at the border areas，initially construct cross-border agricultural industrial economic belt. The development of Yunnan Province agriculture "going global" becomes an important force to enhance friendship between China and neighboring countries.

7.3.3 Cooperation Tasks

(1) **Optimizing industry layout and clarifying general idea of agricultural foreign cooperation.** The combination of near and far will be highlighted in layout, with different emphasis. "Near" should be oriented to border countries and regions, and support enterprises to go overseas mainly by capital and technology; "Far" should be targeted at countries of the Middle East, Europe, North America, and support enterprises to go overseas with products, and achieve mutual benefit.

(2) **Fostering agricultural cooperation main bodies and building an opening enterprises echelon.** A group of leading agricultural enterprises will be created with good comprehensive benefits and strong driving force, encourage opening enterprises cooperation between provincial and the "national team" agricultural enterprises to set up an alliance of agricultural enterprises going overseas and improve the opening-up level of Yunnan's agricultural industry.

(3) **Building an open market system and enhancing regional market influence.** Establish international agricultural product trading hubs which radiate both at home and aboard, such as important agricultural products trading centers and logistics centers, encourage enterprises in Yunnan Province to set up agricultural products processing and trading parks in the border area. Strengthen the construction of cross-border e-commerce platform and marketing system for agricultural products with regional characteristics.

(4) **Building a cross-border industrial economic belt and fostering industrial development momentum.** Strengthen cooperation in animal and plant germplasm resources, advantageous animal and plant varieties, and

agricultural products processing, warehousing and distribution, encourage Yunnan agricultural enterprises to establish bases overseas for the production, processing, storage and transportation of agricultural products, and promote foreign cooperation in agricultural materials, machinery and equipment.

(5) **Deepening exchange and cooperation of agricultural science and technology and occupying industrial technology highlands.** Establish multi-level platforms for agricultural science and technology exchange, and strengthen the training of overseas agricultural production technicians and farmers. Strengthen the cooperation of agricultural information science and technology to promote the docking of technical standards in key links.

(6) **Strengthening prevention and control of animal and plant epidemic disease and ensuring agricultural public safety.** Promote establishment of the cross-border joint prevention and control system for animal and plant epidemic diseases and the pilot work for regionalization of cross-border animal epidemic disease prevention and control to ensure agricultural public safety within the region.

(7) **Enhancing talent cultivation and reserving agriculture foreign cooperation talents group.** Cultivate a group of internationally-comprehensive talents who understand agriculture, foreign languages and good at management, and actively participate in special training courses organized by the Ministry of Agriculture and Rural Affairs of China to improve the practical work ability of officials in agricultural foreign affairs and economic departments.

(Written by Hu Xinmei and Liu Qingsheng,

Department of Agriculture and Rural Affairs,

Yunnan Province, China;

Translated by Li Lu,

International Agriculture Research Institute,

Yunnan Academy of Agricultural Sciences,

Yunnan Province, China)

8 | Agricultural Development and the Progress of Lancang-Mekong Agricultural Cooperation in Guangxi Zhuang Autonomous Region of China

8.1   Overview of Agricultural Development

Guangxi (Guangxi Zhuang Autonomous Region, China) has superior natural conditions and is rich in resources such as climate, light, water, soil, heat, etc. In recent years, Guangxi has cultivated and strengthened large number of agricultural advantageous industrial belts and industrial clusters with obvious regional characteristics, high industrial agglomeration, and outstanding comparative benefits around the advantages of resources and ecological characteristics.

The total output of major agricultural products has continued to increase, ranking the forefront of the country. Grain production has been developing steadily for many years, maintaining about 15 billion kilograms. The total output of sugarcane and silk cocoons has been growing continuously, keeping the first place in China for many years, accounting for more than 60% and 50% of the total national output respectively. The output of vegetables reached 30.73 million tons, which makes Guangxi to be the most important base of "Transporting the Vegetables from South to North" and the largest autumn and winter vegetable production base in China. The production of agaricus bisporus reached three consecutive championships, and the production of russula (red vertebro bacterium) accounts for more than 80% of the country. Guangxi is the largest province (region) in cassava cultivation and the second largest production area of Chinese medicinal herbs. The fields of garden fruits are 1.38 million hectare, with an output more than 17.9 million tons in 2018, achieving a leap from the second for years to the first in China, among which the outputs of citrus, persimmon, mango, dragon fruit and passion fruit continue to maintain the first. The output and quality of tea have been continuously improved. The first early spring tea brand in Guangxi is well-known in the world. Wuzhou Liubao Tea is exported to Southeast Asia through the the ancient "Tea Boat Road" and the Maritime Silk Road. Jasmine tea production accounts for more than 80% of the whole country and 60% of the world. The total output of pork, beef, sheep and poultry in the whole region is 4.184 million tons, and the output of aquatic products is 3.3 million tons, both ranking among the top ten in the country. The total output of prawn and tilapia ranked second and third in the country respectively.

In 2018, the added value of the primary industry was 311.442 billion CNY, an increase of 5.6% over 2017, the fastest growth year since 2013, which increased by 5.6% during the year, and it is the fastest growing year since 2013. The per capita disposable income growth rate of rural residents is 12,435 CNY, ranking second in the country.

8.2 Agricultural International Cooperation

(1) **Agricultural investment and intelligence introduction steady progress.** Guangxi actively strives for policy and projects support, attracts more foreign investments in agriculture, builds agricultural cooperation platforms and directly introduces a number of agricultural enterprises and projects to develop in Guangxi. In 2018, Guangxi introduced 415 new domestic agricultural projects with the contracted value 62.15 billion CNY,

up 15.7% year on year. Guangxi actively organized and implemented loan projects from international financial organization. By the end of 2018, 7 agricultural foreign investment projects have been implemented and the total investment is 2.882 billion CNY, of which about 177 million USD of foreign capital was utilized. While introducing foreign funds, Guangxi attaches importance to the work of introducing agricultural technology and intelligence. It has implemented a large number of agricultural technology projects such as the improvement of the supply chain of Siraitia grosvenorii raw materials, the introduction, breeding and demonstration promotion of new citrus varieties, and it held special activities of introducing agricultural intelligence such as "foreign experts visiting Guangxi", which effectively promotes the development of agricultural industry in Guangxi.

(2) **Gradual boost in agricultural products trade.** Guangxi strongly supports the construction of advantageous agricultural product export bases and export agricultural product quality and safety demonstration zones, establishes international trade platforms through various channels, recommends enterprises to register with foreign countries, and continuously enhances the competitiveness of Guangxi agricultural products in the international market. All these measures have effectively promoted the development of export trade of Guangxi agricultural products. In 2018, the total import-export volume of agricultural products in Guangxi reached 7.533 billion USD, including exports 2.105 billion USD, a year-on-year increase of 5.11%.

In Guangxi, there are more than 130 export destinations and more than 500 types of agricultural products, mainly including live pigs, vegetables, aquatic products, tea, fruits, seeds, Chinese medicinal herbs, feed, bamboo, wood and grass products, etc. Among them, the export of cultured tilapia products ranks third in China.

At present, there are 20 quality and safety demonstration zones of export food and agricultural products, with a cumulative output value of about 3. 63 billion USD and foreign exchange earnings of about 2. 16 billion USD.

(3) Continuous deepening of agricultural science and technology exchange. The fields and scope of Guangxi agricultural science and technology international exchange and cooperation are becoming increasingly extensive, covering genetic breeding, agricultural biotechnology, integrated control of crop diseases and insect pests, prevention and control of diseases of livestock and poultry, agricultural information technology and product processing, etc.

Guangxi has implemented numbers of projects such as aid construction of Ethiopia agricultural demonstration center, Cambodia agricultural promotion center technical cooperation, China (Guangxi)-ASEAN crops excellent varieties experimental station, Brunei deep sea cage cultivation, etc. It has started with technology demonstration and promotion to attract local enterprises in Guangxi to develop cooperation and gradually extending industrial chains such as post-production processing, intensive processing, logistics storage and trading. Effects are quite significant.

At the same time, Guangxi has established the International Association of Professionals in Sugar and Integrated Technologies (IAPSIT), the Guangxi-Taiwan Agricultural Development and Technology Exchange Association, and the China-ASEAN Agricultural Science and Technology Innovation Alliance, and actively carried out agricultural science and technology exchanges and cooperation with relevant countries and regions by holding seminars and training courses, establishing demonstration bases and joint laboratories, dispatching experts, etc.

(4) Agricultural overseas investment accelerates. Agricultural overseas investment of Guangxi mainly concentrated in the countries along the Belt and Road, including Vietnam, Cambodia, Myanmar, Laos and other ASEAN countries. Among the 45 recorded agricultural overseas investment projects, 34 projects are distributed in ASEAN countries, accounting for 75. 6%. These projects covered the fields of planting, processing and trade of agricultural and sideline products, and animal husbandry, etc. The planting projects account for about the half, followed by projects of processing and trade of agricultural and sideline products which account for about 25%. By the end of 2018, there are 102 "going global" agricultural enterprises, with an agreed investment amount of 3. 14 billion USD, ranking fourth in terms of investment flow in China. In 2018, the new investment amount of "going global" agricultural enterprises ranked 7th in China. Private enterprises have become the main force of Guangxi "going global" agriculture, investment projects account for 97. 3% of all agricultural overseas investments.

8. 3   Lancang-Mekong Agricultural Cooperation

8. 3. 1   Cooperation Progress

Lancang-Mekong cooperation is a new type of sub-regional cooperation mechanism jointly established by China, Cambodia, Thailand, Laos, Myanmar, and Vietnam along the Lancang River and Mekong River. It is a significant part of the Belt and Road Initiative and China-ASEAN cooperation. In recent years, Guangxi has actively taken advantage of its location, resources, and platforms, actively participated in Lancang-Mekong agricultural exchanges and cooperation, and achieved good results.

(1) **Guangxi and ASEAN countries bilateral agricultural science and technology exchanges and cooperation have been continuously improved with the construction of "two stations"—China (Guangxi)-ASEAN crops excellent varieties experimental station and ASEAN crops excellent varieties Guangxi experimental station—as the starting point.** Since 2014, a total of 36 million CNY has been allocated from the budget of the department at the same level of the autonomous region for the construction of China

(Guangxi)-ASEAN crops excellent varieties experimental station projects in Laos, Vietnam, Cambodia, Myanmar and other LMC countries. At present, three experimental station projects in Laos, Vietnam and Cambodia have been completed and passed the acceptance tests. More than 750 new varieties of vegetables and rice from China have been tested, and nearly 150 suitable varieties were selected in ASEAN countries by the station. The demonstration area was 27.8 thousand hectares, and the accumulated demonstration and promotion areas of excellent crops varieties were over 333 thousand hectares. These crops varieties introduced from China have shown their advantages of high yield, high quality and good benefit with the application of advanced matching technologies and management models. Especially in terms of yield and benefit, the yield of the crop varieties introduced by the experimental station increased generally 20%-50% than the local varieties, the income increased more than 20%. Through the experimental station, more than 8,700 local agricultural administrative department staff, technicians, farmers and agricultural college students have been trained.

In order to realize the two-way exchange and cooperation of agricultural science and technology, Guangxi has also built two ASEAN crop excellent varieties experimental stations, providing a platform for the exhibition and exchange of ASEAN countries' improved varieties into the Chinese market. Meanwhile, the 2019 China (Guangxi)-ASEAN New Vegetable Varieties Expo was successfully held, in which there were more than 1,000 vegetable varieties, including 44 varieties from Vietnam, Thailand, Cambodia, and Myanmar.

The construction of the two experimental stations projects has aroused the attention of different parties. The leaders of the country where the project is located, the Ministry of Agriculture and Rural Affairs and Guangxi Autonomous Region have visited the experimental stations and extended full affirmation in Vietnam and Cambodia.

At the same time, Guangxi organized Guangxi Wanchuan Seed Industry Co., Ltd., Guangxi Hengbaofeng Agricultural Development Co., Ltd. and other enterprises to undertake the project implementation of the Lancang-Mekong Cooperation Special Fund (LMCSF)—the construction of experimental demonstration project of rice green yield-increasing technology, to carry out the introduction and demonstration of new rice varieties in Cambodia, Myanmar, Laos and Vietnam, to establish a test demonstration base of rice green yield-increasing technology, to optimize the rice green yield-increasing technology in local area, to carry out the test of rice field integrated planting and breeding model. All these measures have effectively promoted bilateral agricultural science and technology cooperation with good results.

For example, the new technology of rice mechanical hole direct seeding was used in the Cambodian project to reduce the amount of seed consumption per unit area, improve the performance of ventilation and light transmission in the field, effectively reduce the degree of disease and insect damage, and effectively reduce the pests, and reduce the pesticide consumption by 30%, with the yield increased 25.9% and added income 2,392.5 CNY per hectare than the original. Through centralized strong seedling cultivation, direct seeding and seedling throwing, projects in Myanmar realized 3 labor force reduced per hectare on average, and the yield increased by 10.2% and benefits increased by 3,150 CNY per hectare through the vibration frequency insecticidal lamp and yellow board used in the field and through unified management and control of diseases and pests and reduced the amount of pesticide application in Myanmar.

Through technologies such as centralized seedling, machine transplanting, water and gas balance, "three-control" cultivation, precision fertilization, returning straw to the field, and integrated control of major pests and diseases have been assembled and promoted, rice standardized production technology established, projects in Laos realized rice yield increased by

47.4% and the income increased by 1,800 CNY per hectare after the field test of experts. According to field measurement of the technical experts organized by the Advanced Technology Application Center of the Department of Science and Technology in Bac Giang Province, projects in Vietnam realized rice yield increased by 10.3% and the economic benefit increased by 1,680 CNY per hectare through rice direct seeding cultivation test and demonstration.

In addition, Guangxi also supports colleges and universities and scientific research institutes to take advantage of their technologies, organize high-level exchanges of agricultural talents, and participate in the plan of 100 ASEAN talent young scientists come into China and work in Guangxi. Platforms on of China-ASEAN Agricultural Training Center and China (Guangxi)-ASEAN crops excellent varieties experimental station, Guangxi focused on technical and managerial personnel training for ASEAN countries. During the period of "12th Five-Year Plan", it held more than 60 seminars and training courses and served more than 3,000 trainees from Vietnam, Laos, Cambodia, and Myanmar.

(2) Guangxi and ASEAN countries bilateral agricultural investment cooperation has been continuously improved with the construction of "two zones" (Overseas Agricultural Cooperation Demonstration Zone and Domestic Agricultural Opening-up Cooperation Experimental Zone) as the focus. At the beginning of 2018, Guangxi launched the construction of two provincial zones pilot projects of China (Guangxi)-Vietnam Agricultural Cooperation Demonstration Zone, China (Guangxi)-Cambodia Agricultural Cooperation Demonstration Zone and Pingxiang Agricultural Opening-up and Cooperation Experimental Zone, and built an internal and external linked and two-way driving agricultural industry cooperation platform. Among them, Pingxiang Experimental Zone combined with the construction of cross-border labor cooperation pilot area, border trade national inspection pilot area and border financial comprehensive reform pilot area, promoted the relevant policies to be tested first, strengthened to support for agricultural opening-up in terms of labor supply, trade customs clearance and investment convenience.

At present, the Pingxiang Agricultural Opening-up and Cooperation Experimental Zone has introduced 9 enterprises including Yanjin Shop Food Co., Ltd., Zengtai Agriculture and Animal Husbandry Co., Ltd., and Wanchuan Seed Co., Ltd.. and 2 foreign-related enterprises. Cambodian demonstration zone has completed the investment of 120 million CNY, and built initially an ecological circular agricultural industrial park integrating rice new varieties research and development, production and processing, planting and breeding, with the total output of rice more than 10 thousand tons and the output value more than US $2 million. Through the China (Guangxi)-Cambodia Agricultural Cooperation Demonstration Zone platform services, many companies and institutions such as Phnom Penh Wanbao Agricultural International Investment Co., Ltd., Shenzhen Nuopuxin Co., Ltd., and Guangxi Academy of Fishery Sciences have been introduced into the zone or signed an entry agreement to cooperate in the development of agricultural processing, aquatic research, technology promotion and other services.

China (Guangxi)-Vietnam Agricultural Cooperation Demonstration Zone introduced Vietnam Central Seed Co., Ltd. to settle, cooperate to establish the crops research center. At the same time, Anhui Tongcheng City Yahui Printing Co., Ltd. reached the development intention of entering the zone. By undertaking the implementation of the China (Guangxi)-Vietnam Agricultural Cooperation Demonstration Zone Project, Guangxi Wanchuan Seed Industry Co., Ltd. has signed cooperation agreement with Vietnam Central Seed Co., Ltd., and established long-term cooperative relationship with Vietnam Central Fruit and Vegetable Corporation and seed companies in Lang Son, Tuyen Quang, and Cao Bang Province. The company exports and sells about

2,000 tons seeds of rice, vegetables and other seeds to Vietnam every year, with the export value more than 60 million CNY, becoming an enterprise with the largest volume domestic seed export to ASEAN countries, and one of the first top 100 agricultural foreign cooperation companies in China.

In 2018, the promotion of the construction of the "two zones" of Guangxi was affirmed by the Ministry of Agriculture and Rural Affairs of China and recommended to other provinces as a model. Driven by the "two zones" platform, a group of private enterprises and research institutes of Guangxi have joined forces to "going global", enhancing the innovation capability of agricultural science and technology and the ability of resisting risks in "going global".

(3) **Highlight industrial security and highlight cross-border cooperation.** Guangxi has always attached great importance to border agricultural cooperation. Since 2008, Guangxi has established a Director joint meeting system with the Department of Agriculture and Rural Development of Quang Ninh, Lang Son, and Cao Bang Province of Vietnam, and held 4 joint meetings, resolved some major important cooperation problems together.

The cooperation memorandum on prevention and control of cross-border animal and plant diseases has been signed with the departments of plant protection and veterinary branch of Quang Ninh and Lang Son, border province of Vietnam. Under the framework of the memorandum, the Technical Support for the Construction of China-Vietnam Border Major Animal Disease Prevention and Control Test Station, China Guangxi-Vietnam Quang Ninh Plant Diseases and Pests Prevention and Control projects have been organized and implemented, donated insect detection and reporting lights to the border provinces of Vietnam, aided construction of major animal epidemic disease prevention and control test stations (diagnostic laboratories), actively promoted the cooperation in animal and plant diseases and insect pests prevention and control with Quang Ninh, Lang Son, Cao Bang and other border provinces in Vietnam, improved the ability and level of prevention and control of animal and plant diseases and insect pests in Vietnam, and provided a scientific basis for China to do well in monitoring, early warning and prevention and control of animal and plant diseases and insect pests.

8.3.2 Difficulties and Problems

(1) **The sustainability of policies and project support is insufficient.** Compared with Yunnan Province, Guangxi has fewer policies and projects supported at the national level in carrying out Lancang-Mekong agricultural cooperation. In the past three years, it was only approved in 2017 to undertake the project of the construction of experimental demonstration of rice green yield-increasing technology supported by the Lancang-Mekong Cooperation Special Fund (LMCSF). In addition, the economic development of Guangxi is relatively backward, and the projects funds that can be arranged to support foreign cooperation in agriculture are relatively small and constantly declining. Projects and policies support lack stability and sustainability.

(2) **The mechanism of jointly promoting Lancang-Mekong agricultural cooperation has not yet been formed.** Although Guangxi has established a inter departments joint meeting system for agriculture cooperation with some border provinces of Vietnam, due to the lack of evaluation, incentive and restraint mechanism for each member, it is currently not possible to integrate resources in finance, taxation, insurance, customs clearance, business and other aspects. Additionally, the policies, projects, platforms and other resources of relevant departments are relatively scattered, and it is difficult to form a joint support force.

(3) **The international cooperation ability of enterprises needs to be improved.** There are some problems in agriculture development in

Guangxi, such as industry large but not strong, large but not excellent, with small-scale, high cost and poor management, and weak innovation ability of agricultural science and technology, etc. For enterprises, the main participants of agricultural international cooperation still have some problems including low level, partner countries concentration, single cooperation mode and low autonomy. All these problems lead to the weak competitiveness of Guangxi agriculture in the international market, the lack of brand effect, the lack of advantages for enterprises in integrating global resources through direct investment.

At present, there were 97 "going global" enterprises in Guangxi, which are active in international cooperation. However, most of them are private enterprises, which are generally small in scale and lack the ability to warn, control, and prevent risks in advance. And there are also some problems which restrict these enterprises development: weak ability to explore the international market, lack of transnational management talents and compound talents, and most of the investment fields concentrated in the elementary part, and still focus on the domestic market.

(4) The level and ability of agricultural product export trade need to be improved. Presently, the agricultural products trade between Guangxi and LMC countries are still mainly in the form of small-scale border trading and mutual market trading. Furthermore, most trade of agricultural products is the transit trade of "buy in and sell out" at low-level, fewer high-level cooperation such as intensive processing of agricultural products and services. Meanwhile, the agricultural trade market of Guangxi is concentrated on Vietnam, lack of market diversification.

8. 4　Future Cooperation Prospect

8. 4. 1　General Idea

Guangxi is a unique province (region) in China that has both land border and sea passage with ASEAN countries, playing an important strategic role in the exchanges and cooperation between China and ASEAN as well as the Lancang-Mekong subregion. Next, Guangxi will strengthen practical exchanges and cooperation with Lancang-Mekong countries in agricultural science and technology, two-way investment, agricultural product trade and capacity building.

8.4.2　Key Tasks

(1) **Exploring and innovating agricultural cooperation mechanism policies.** Guangxi should highlight market needs and enterprises dominant position, under the guidance of the country's foreign cooperation strategy, innovate and improve Guangxi's foreign cooperation system, formulate Guangxi agricultural foreign cooperation special work plans, and arrange a number of major cooperation projects and set up cooperation platforms in the Lancang-Mekong subregion. Actively promote the Belt and Road agricultural cooperation, explore first try first policy relevant to cross-border agricultural cooperation in the China (Guangxi) Pilot Free Trade Zone.

(2) **Expanding the market in LMC countries to help export trade of agricultural products.** Implementing promote agricultural product export with special characteristic of Guangxi plan, build a number of agricultural product export production bases, continue to hold economic and trade activities such as China-ASEAN Agricultural International Cooperation Exhibition, China (Guangxi)-ASEAN Agricultural Products Trade Matchmaking Conference, Guangxi Agricultural "Silk Road Trip", build regional agricultural products trade cooperation platforms. Support Guangxi agricultural export enterprises and industry associations to carry out international marketing activities such as international advertising promotion and product introduction and promotion.

(3) **Accelerating the construction of "two zones" to boost the two-way**

agriculture cooperation of "going global" and "bringing in". It will adhere to the principle of enterprise lead and market-oriented operation, support enterprises to build a number of overseas agricultural cooperation demonstration zones of rice, fruit and vegetable, animal husbandry, fishery and other key industries in LMC countries, highlight the leading role of demonstration, and drive domestic agricultural enterprises to go abroad jointly. Meanwhile, it will build some of agricultural opening-up cooperation pilot zones in the border areas of Guangxi, introduce and absorb advanced agricultural experience, technologies, and patterns from the LMC countries, establish service platforms of agricultural international cooperation, and develop a number of multinational agricultural enterprise groups with international competitiveness.

(4) Focusing on the weak links of the industry and strengthening the introduction of agricultural investment and intelligence. Guangxi will give full play to the location, resources, environment and market advantages, increase the use of foreign investment in agriculture, promote "Bagui Action" —encourage cooperation and exchanges between Fortune 500 companies and the local top 50 enterprises, actively undertake international agricultural aid projects, and strive for bilateral and multi-lateral preferential loans and non-reimbursable aid projects and help to upgrade agricultural industry of Guangxi. In view of the weak links in agricultural development of Guangxi and the problems urgently needed to be solved in agricultural production, by increasing the introduction of advanced industries, varieties, technologies, talents and management experience, strengthen agricultural intelligence introduction cooperation, and contribute to poverty alleviation and rural revitalization in Guangxi.

8.4.3 Projects Plan

(1) Construction of crops excellent varieties experimental station in Lancang-Mekong subregion. This kind of projects will be implemented by

"going global" enterprises of Guangxi in different LMC countries, to carry out the introduction, testing, demonstration and promotion of new crop varieties, research and demonstrate of advanced production technologies and pest and disease joint prevent and control technologies, collection and utilization of germplasm resources, personnel exchange and training, etc.

(2) **Construction of China (Guangxi)-ASEAN agricultural cooperation demonstration zone.** Guangxi will implement a series of overseas agricultural cooperation demonstration zone projects, strengthen infrastructure construction in the demonstration zones, establish overseas agricultural support service mechanisms and quality safety standard management system, demonstrate excellent varieties introduced from China. It is going to give full play to the leading and service role of the demonstration zones, attract domestic and foreign enterprises enter for cooperation and development, and establish agricultural industry chains serving bilateral agricultural exchanges and cooperation in local countries.

(3) **Holding China-ASEAN Agricultural International Cooperation Exhibition and Agricultural International Cooperation Forum.** During the period of China-ASEAN, Guangxi will continue to hold China-ASEAN agricultural international cooperation exhibition and China-ASEAN agricultural international cooperation forum series activities in Nanning, Guangxi. Inviting domestic companies from different province (autonomous regions and municipalities) of China and the agricultural departments of the LMC countries to attend and participate in the Exhibition, focusing on showing of famous agricultural products from different countries and regions, and bilateral and multi-lateral cooperation projects. Inviting officials, experts, scholars and business representatives from ASEAN countries, including Lancang-Mekong subregion, to attend the forum to exchange on agricultural science and technology, investment, trade and personnel.

(4) **Testing and demonstration of rice green yield-increasing technology**

in Lancang-Mekong subregion. "Going global" enterprises of Guangxi will carry out new rice varieties introduction and demonstrations, improved rice green yield-increasing technology, testing rice field planting and breeding integrated mode, personnel training, etc.

(5) Organizing ASEAN training course on standardized production of animal husbandry. It will establish the platform of China-ASEAN agricultural training center, hold a training course on standardized production of animal husbandry in Nanning by Guangxi Agricultural Vocational College, and help improve the level of professional work of animal husbandry practitioners from LMC countries.

(Written by Wei Qingfang and Chen Jiqun,

Department of Agriculture and Rural Affairs,

Guangxi Zhuang Autonomous Region, China;

Translated by Mo Nan,

International Agriculture Research Institute,

Yunnan Academy of Agricultural Sciences, China)

9 | Agricultural Development and the Progress of Lancang-Mekong Agricultural Cooperation in Hainan Province of China

9.1 Overview of Agricultural Development

Agriculture is the basic and advantageous industry of Hainan. With its superior tropical agricultural natural resources, Hainan has been given the development mission of becoming a "National Tropical Modern Agriculture Base"[①]. Hainan is committed to the establishment of "one center, two zones, and three bases", including the National Tropical Agricultural Science Center, Qionghai Agricultural Opening-up and Cooperation Pilot Zone, Agriculture Green Development Pioneer Zone, and the National Off-season Breeding Scientific Research Base, and the Global Animal and Plant Germplasm Resource Introduction and Transfer Base.

In 2018, the total output value of agriculture, forestry, animal husbandry and fishery of Hainan was 153. 573 billion CNY, an increase of

---

① On April 13, 2018, General Secretary Xi Jinping delivered an important speech at a conference celebrating the 30th anniversary of the establishment of the Special Economic Zone of Hainan Province, stating: "Hainan is the only tropical province in China. It is necessary to implement the strategy of rural revitalization, give play to the climate advantages of tropical regions, strengthen and improve the tropical and highly efficient agriculture, build national tropical modern agricultural bases, and further promote the brand of tropical agricultural products in Hainan. "

3.15% over the previous year. Among them, the agricultural output value was 72.951 billion CNY, increased 3.12% over the previous year; the forestry output value was 11.044 billion CNY, with an increase of 2.53% over the previous year; the animal husbandry output value was 24.532 billion CNY, with an increased of 0.11% over the previous year; the fishery output value was 38.744 billion CNY, an increase of 3.94% over the previous year. The output value of agriculture, forestry, animal husbandry and fishery major and auxiliary activities was 6.302 billion CNY, an increase of 12.70% over the previous year. The output value of three categories of vegetables and horticultural crops, fruits, nuts, beverages and spices crops, as well as seawater products all exceeded 30 billion CNY respectively, accounting for 19.76%, 19.89%, and 22.70% of the total output value of agriculture, forestry, animal husbandry and fishery respectively. Vegetables, fruits, and seafood have become the main forces driving agricultural output value growth of Hainan, reflecting Hainan's advantages of unique tropical agricultural climate resources and marine resources.

As of the end of 2018, the total power of Hainan's agricultural machinery was 5.603,0 million kilowatts, an increase of 0.6% over 2017; the total number of agricultural tractors was 87,500, decreased by 2.0%, and the number of agricultural transport vehicles was 35,300, a decrease of 4.1%. In the whole year, the amount of chemical fertilizer applied (pure) was 475,400 tons, down by 7.4%; and the effective irrigation area of farmland was 185,000 hectares, dropped by 4.6%.

9.2 International Agricultural Cooperation

9.2.1 Import and Export Trading of Agricultural Products

In recent years, the import and export volume of Hainan's agricultural products has been relatively stable, with some decline and an absolute trade surplus of agricultural products. In 2018, in terms of agricultural products exports, the total value of Hainan's agricultural products exports reached 3. 348 billion USD, a decrease of 6. 27% over 2017, and agricultural product exports accounted for 11. 24% of total merchandise exports. Exported agricultural products were mainly aquatic products such as frozen fish and frozen fish fillets. The other types of products, especially Hainan tropical fruits and vegetables which had advantages of natural resource, of the value of exports was quite low due to the limit by fresh-keeping technology and transportation time. The structure of agricultural products exports was single. In terms of agricultural products imports, the total value of agricultural products imports was 1. 451 billion USD, which dropped by 5. 65% compared to 2017. The value of agricultural products imports accounted for 2. 64% of the total imports of all commodities, indicating a high self-sufficiency rate of agricultural products of Hainan. The types of imported agricultural products include frozen fish, fruits, grains, and the most imported agricultural products are fresh and dried fruits and nuts.

9. 2. 2　Foreign Investment in Agriculture

Hainan actively attracted foreign investment, and issued policies such as *Implementation Opinions on Expanding Opening-up and Actively Utilizing Foreign Investment*, *Guidelines for Approval and Archival Filing of Foreign Investment Projects* and other policies. On September 6th, 2018, the American Anchor Center for Certification and Department of Agricultural and Rural Affairs of Hainan Province signed a contract to carry out cooperation in the fields of agricultural standardization system construction, research and development of tropical fruit preservation technology, improvement of deep processing value chain, and production and marketing platform docking[1]. Furthermore, Department of Agriculture and Rural Affairs of Hainan Province has also attracted 2 agricultural projects with the preferential policies of the Free Trade Zone, including Perfection Fresh Australia (Hainan Free Trade Zone) Agricultural Development Co., Ltd.'s, which settles its Chinese headquarters in Haikou and Hainan-Australia Tropical Ecological Agriculture Demonstration Base[2].

In 2018, Hainan signed a total of 18 investment projects in agriculture, forestry, animal husbandry and fisheries with foreign investors, accounting for 10.78% of the total projects signed in all industries. Foreign investment in agriculture, forestry, animal husbandry and fishery contracts amounted to 71.41 million USD, accounting for only 1.39% of the all foreign investment in all industries. The actual used foreign investment in agriculture, forestry, animal husbandry and fishery reached 5.58 million USD, accounting for only 0.75% of the all actual used foreign investment in all industries[3].

9.2.3 Key Construction Projects for Agricultural Opening-up

The Ministry of Agriculture and Rural Affairs issued *Implementation Plan for the Guiding Opinions of the Central Committee of the Communist Party of China and the State Council on Supporting Comprehensive Deepening of Hainan's Reform and Opening-up* in 2018, in which focused on supporting the construction of "one center, two zones, and

① Wang Xinwu, 2018. 26 Internationally Renowned Companies Signed a Strategic Cooperation Framework Agreement with Hainan Province. Foreign-funded Companies are Optimistic about Hainan. Accelerate Cooperation in Multiple Fields of Agriculture and Logistics [J]. Strategic Emerging Industries of China (37), 65.
② Fu Renyi, 2018. Provincial Department of Agriculture and Rural Affairs Promotes Agricultural Supply-side Structural Reform. Making Hainan's Agriculture Stronger, Rural Areas more Beautiful, Farmers Richer [N]. Hainan Daily, 12-29.
③ Committee of Haina Statistical Yearbook, 2019. Hainan Statistical Yearbook 2019 [M]. Beijing: China Statistical Press.

three bases" the agriculture-related project in the overall plan of Hainan Free Trade Zone. In accordance with *Notice on the Construction Plan of the "Two Agricultural Foreign Cooperation Zones"* issued by the Ministry of Agriculture and Rural Affairs, Hainan has promoted the construction of the "two zones" of agricultural foreign cooperation, which is the National (Qionghai) Agricultural Opening-up and Cooperation Pilot Zone and China-Cambodia Tropical Ecological Agriculture Demonstration Zone.

In terms of promoting the construction of the National (Qionghai) Agricultural Opening-up and Cooperation Pilot Zone, Hainan is establishing the Global Animal and Plant Germplasm Resource Introduction and Transfer Base, and the National Off-season Breeding Scientific Research Base, as well as an international trade center for seed industries and Nanfan science and technology city, developing seed trade facing to the Belt and Road countries. At the same time, in order to attract internationally renowned seed industry companies to start seed trade such as setting up regional headquarters in Hainan, Hainan will also improve port facilitation, inspection and quarantine levels, expand bonded storage and other functions.

In terms of promoting the construction of China-Cambodia Tropical Ecological Agriculture Demonstration Zone, taking Hainan Dingyi Oasis Ecological Agriculture Co., Ltd. as the main body of construction, it is planned to invest 14.2 billion CNY in accordance with the idea of "one zone, multiple gardens and N bases". The project is planned to take 10 years (2017 – 2026) to be constructed in three phases. The first phase is the construction period of the industrial demonstration garden (2017 – 2020), the planned investment is about 1.8 billion CNY. The second phase is the construction period of the industrial garden (full industrial chains) (2021 – 2024), the planned investment is about 11.4 billion CNY. The third phase is the construction period of the whole demonstration zone's agricultural tourism (2025 – 2026), the planned investment is 1 billion CNY[①].

9.3 Lancang-Mekong Agricultural Cooperation

9.3.1 Cooperation Progress

(1) Participation in the co-construction of agricultural cooperation mechanism. The first Lancang-Mekong cooperation leaders' meeting was held in Sanya, Hainan Province, which indicated the necessity for Hainan to participate in Lancang-Mekong agricultural cooperation. Taking advantage of the platform of Boao Forum for Asia, Hainan took the initiative to participate in building a community of common destiny of LMC countries, and carried out agricultural technology exchanges and capacity building cooperation with LMC countries. Hainan has also taken advantage of its tourism culture to promote cooperation and development of international agriculture by deepening the establishment of a mutually beneficial and win-win mechanism with the LMC countries. Hainan hosted Sanya Forum of Lancang-Mekong Tourist Cities Cooperation in 2016 and 2018. The forum not only promoted pragmatic cooperation of communication mechanisms, tourism projects between Sanya and tourist cities in the LMC countries, but also discussed how to promote the

---

① "One area, multiple gardens, and N bases" refers to: One area: Cambodia-China Tropical Ecological Agriculture Demonstration Zone. Multi-gardens: Cambodia-China Banana Industry Demonstration Garden; Cambodia-China Pepper Industry Demonstration Garden; Cambodia-China Tropical Fruit Industry Demonstration Garden; Cambodia-China Rubber Industry Demonstration Garden; Cambodia-China Cassava Industry Demonstration Garden; Cambodia-China Livestock and Poultry Breeding Industry Demonstration Garden; Cambodia-China Agricultural Science and Technology Demonstration Garden; Cold Chain Logistics Garden, etc. N Bases: Banana planting base, pepper planting base, aromatic coconut planting base, cashew nut planting base, mango planting base, durian planting base, grapefruit planting base, germplasm resource breeding base, beef cattle breeding base, pig breeding base, sow breeding Base, poultry breeding base, agricultural product processing base, etc. China Council for the Promotion of International Trade, 2020. Introduction of Cambodia-China Tropical Ecological Agriculture Demonstration Zone [EB/OL]. [12-22]. https://oip.ccpit.org/ent/parks-introduces/47.

common development of agriculture, economy and trade with tourism culture driving.

(2) Promotion of construction of China-Cambodia Tropical Ecological Agriculture Demonstration Zone. Hainan and LMC countries have good agricultural cooperation foundations. Among them, agricultural cooperation with Cambodia has achieved the most significant results. As early as 2010, Hainan has established friendly provincial relations with Cambodia's Kampong Cham Province, and the two sides have actively carried out cooperation in several fields such as agricultural product trade and investment in agricultural projects. After China-Cambodia Tropical Ecological Agriculture Demonstration Zone was identified as China's first batch of overseas agricultural demonstration zones for foreign cooperation, Hainan promoted the construction of China-Cambodia Tropical Ecological Agriculture Demonstration Zone in phases with the idea of "one zone, multiple gardens and N bases". According to the statistics from the Department of Agriculture and Rural Affairs of Hainan Province, by the end of September 2019, many bases have been established in Kratie Province of Cambodia, including 5,000 mu of banana core demonstration base, 500 mu of pepper core demonstration base, 1,000 mu of cassava core demonstration base, 2,000 mu of rubber core demonstration base, 500 mu durian core demonstration base and 10,000 mu aromatic coconut core demonstration base. Meanwhile, Hainan also cooperated with China-Cambodia Hongtai Agricultural Technology Development Co., Ltd. to build Cambodian agricultural product processing, warehousing and logistics centers, and established one-stop service platform for Cambodian agricultural and sideline products export.

(3) Strengthening agricultural science and technology exchange. Besides the construction of agricultural industrial gardens, Hainan has also strengthened exchange of agricultural science and technology with LMC countries. In July 2017, Department of Agriculture and Rural

Affairs of Hainan Province and Chinese Academy of Tropical Agricultural Sciences signed a tripartite strategic cooperation agreement with the Royal University of Agriculture in Phnom Penh, Cambodia. According to the agreement, the three parties will jointly establish Tropical Agricultural Technology Training Center, Tissue Culture Seedling Center, Organic Fertilizer Research and Development Center and Tropical Crops Research Center, and will jointly carry out scientific research and development of new varieties on tropical crops such as rubber, cassava, banana and pepper. During the signing ceremony of the China Hainan-Cambodia project, there were 10 major cooperation projects signed, including 3 academy-university cooperation projects and 7 economic and trade projects, and the total contracted amount reached 250 million USD.

In May 2018, the 2018 China (Hainan)-Cambodian Tropical Agricultural Technology Training Course sponsored by Chinese Academy of Tropical Sciences and Department of Agriculture and Rural Affairs of Hainan Province was held in Haikou City. Twenty-three trainees from the Ministry of Agriculture, Forestry and Fisheries of Cambodia, Agriculture Department of Kampong Cham, Cambodia, Royal Cambodian Agricultural University and Chinese-funded agricultural enterprises in Cambodia participated in a 22-day intensive training. In October 2018, International Seminar and Training Course on the Protection of New Plant Varieties in LMC Countries was held in Danzhou, Hainan province, and 23 representatives who were engaged in variety protection and variety management from five Mekong countries and China participated in the training. In November 2018, the opening ceremony of the tropical agricultural economic management seminar for officials of Ministry of Agriculture, Forestry and Fisheries of Cambodia was held at Hainan University. The management officials from the Ministry of Agriculture, Forestry and Fisheries of Cambodia and its three subordinate agricultural universities attended the training on the theme of "China-Cambodia

Agricultural Trade and Policy". In November 2018, Department of Agriculture and Rural Affairs of Hainan Province and the Royal Cambodian Agricultural University held 2018 (China) Hainan-Cambodian Tropical Agricultural Technology Training Course (Second Phase) in Phnom Penh, Cambodia. More than 70 trainees from Ministry of Agriculture, Forestry and Fisheries of Cambodia, Cambodian Royal University of Agriculture, Chinese-funded enterprises in Cambodia participated in the training. Through the above-mentioned agricultural technology training activities, the communication and exchanges between Hainan and the LMC countries were strengthened, laying a solid foundation for further promoting Lancang Mekong agricultural cooperation.

9. 3. 2　Achievements and Experience

(1) **Cooperation promotion by taking advantage of policies trend.** The Lancang-Mekong cooperation mechanism is an important part of the Belt and Road Initiative. Since China launched the Belt and Road Initiative, Hainan has been playing an important role as the "Maritime Silk Road", and it has continuously deepened its cooperation and exchanges with Southeast Asian countries in economic, trade and cultural exchanges. With the significant opportunity and broad space for Lancang-Mekong cooperation, Hainan has actively promoted Lancang-Mekong agricultural cooperation and continued to explore effective ways on the base of the original international cooperation. Furthermore, Hainan also used a series of investment preferential policies such as special economic zones, international tourist islands and duty-free shopping, and the opening of low-altitude aviation rights to attract investors at home and abroad, consolidate the development of basic industries such as agriculture, and create more favorable conditions for international agricultural cooperation.

(2) **Cooperation promotion by taking advantage of platforms.** Taking advantage of the regional influence and home-field diplomacy of Boao

Forum, Hainan promote high-level visits and pragmatic cooperation in agriculture sector among LMC countries. Additionally, Hainan organized and planned many activities on modern agricultural technology exchanges, international agricultural research seminars, featured agricultural product introduction, and agricultural cultural dissemination, etc., which has enriched the agricultural exchange platforms and expanded the channels of agricultural cooperation among Hainan and LMC countries.

(3) **Cooperation promotion by taking advantage of industries.** Hainan has good industrial development advantages in international tourism and tropical agriculture. Hainan has carried out " one-tour, multi-stop " Lancang-Mekong cities tourism cooperation with world-renowned tourist destinations such as Siem Reap of Cambodia, Luang Prabang of Laos, Phuket of Thailand, and Halong Bay of Vietnam, not only achieved a win-win development of tourism among the Lancang-Mekong cities, but also effectively promoted the cooperation and development of local specialty agricultural products, leisure agriculture and other fields. In addition, Hainan has exported technology and cooperated with Cambodia in the cultivation of bananas, peppers, rubber, durians and other tropical crops with its own technological advantages in tropical agricultural production. The construction of China-Cambodia Tropical Ecological Agriculture Demonstration Zone has achieved initial results.

9.3.3　Difficulties and Problems

(1) **The situation of agricultural comprehensive cooperation has not yet been formed.** At present, the agricultural cooperation between Hainan and LMC countries is mostly reflected in the cooperation with Cambodia and Thailand. The agricultural cooperation with Laos, Myanmar and Vietnam is still relatively shallow and needs to be further deepened. In recent years, the agricultural cooperation between Hainan and Cambodia, which relied on the construction of the China-Cambodia Tropical Ecological

Agriculture Demonstration Zone, have become closer and achieved good results. The agricultural cooperation between Hainan and Thailand benefited from the "early harvest program" and the "China-Thailand Zero Tariff Fruit and Vegetable Agreement" formulated by the two countries in the early stage, and the trade cooperation on vegetables and fruits went smoothly. The agricultural cooperation mainly reflected in the natural rubber industry with Laos, and the tropical fruit industry with Myanmar, less cooperation in other agricultural fields.

(2) **Cooperation platform functions and project layout need to be improved.** Most of the existing Lancang-Mekong agricultural cooperation platforms in Hainan mainly carried out agricultural science and technology training and exchange. Most of the Lancang-Mekong agricultural cooperation promoted through the platform were technical aid and demonstration and extension projects. The platform function and cooperation mode were relatively single. In terms of the layout of cooperation projects were often limited to a certain crop or a certain country, and have not formed obvious agglomeration advantage and regional synergy. In the design of cooperative projects, the lack of measures to fully reflect the interests of the partners or to form a dual/multi-party sustainable development has led to problems such as low enthusiasm of foreign investors to participate, cooperation projects are focused on the construction whereas pay less attention to the management, and weak sustainable of operation.

(3) **Enterprises ability to "go to the five Mekong countries" needs to be improved.** Presently, Hainan and the five Mekong countries' agricultural investment and project construction are still driven by the government, and there are relatively few market-oriented non-governmental spontaneous cooperation behaviors. The ability of Hainan's agricultural enterprises of "going global" need to be improved, especially in terms of overseas geopolitical risk identification, legal risk management in host country,

and respond to price fluctuations in the international market for agricultural products. In order to help more Hainan enterprises to enter the market of LMC countries, the relevant government departments and agricultural scientific research institutions need to strengthen the support and service capabilities.

9. 4　Future Cooperation

9. 4. 1　General Idea

In the future agricultural cooperation with LMC countries, Hainan should give full play to the location advantages of the "Maritime Silk Road", the platform advantage of Boao Forum for Asia, the industrial advantages of tropical agriculture and international tourism, and seize the development opportunities of exploring and building the free trade pilot zone and a free trade port with Chinese characteristics, to promote the practical cooperation with LMC countries in such fields as agricultural policy exchange, agricultural technological innovation, personnel training, tropical crops breeding and cultivation, improved varieties demonstration and extension, and further enhance Hainan's participation and importance.

9. 4. 2　Key Tasks

(1) **Explore a new situation in Lancang-Mekong agricultural cooperation.** Hainan should seize the opportunity to construct the free trade pilot zone, actively attract foreign investment in agricultural-related projects, and focus on introducing investment projects that will promote the deep processing of agricultural products and adjustment of the industrial structure in Hainan, avoid blind construction. And it is going to expand agricultural products trade with the five Mekong countries step by step, focus on developing import and export trade of agricultural product that is highly complementary to the LMC countries, and avoid homogeneous

competition. Accelerate the construction of Qionghai Agricultural Opening-up and Cooperation Pilot Zone and Agriculture Green Development Pioneer Zone, and explore a new situation of all-around, wide-ranging, and multi-level pragmatic cooperation.

(2) **Improve the construction of agricultural cooperation platform system.** Compared with Yunnan, Guangxi and other provinces, Hainan's most prominent advantage is the platform. It will make full use of the platforms of Boao Forum for Asia, The 21st Century Maritime Silk Road Islands Economic Cooperation Forum, the Island Tourism Policy Forum to build a more comprehensive agricultural cooperation and exchange platform system based on the actual development of Hainan's agriculture, meets the needs of multilateral agricultural development, timely sharing information, and continuously improve platform functions.

(3) **Strengthen scientific and technological support for enterprises "going global".** Hainan will rely on the scientific research advantages of the Chinese Academy of Tropical Agricultural Sciences, promote tropical agricultural scientific and technological innovation, cooperative research, transfer and transformation of industrial technology by docking with Hainan's leading agricultural companies and relevant chambers of commerce in the LMC countries, organizing and implementing scientific and technological cooperation projects, cultivating and transmitting agricultural scientific and technological talents for enterprises. Provide powerful technological support for Hainan's enterprises to go abroad and enter the markets of LMC countries.

9.4.3 Projects Plan

(1) **Create an international cooperation and exchange platform for seed breeding industry in Hainan.** Rely on the hybrid rice seeds and high-quality conventional rice and vegetable seeds selected by the national off-season breeding base in Hainan (known as the Nanfan breeding base), go abroad

to promote planting in the Lancang-Mekong subregion, and deepen the agricultural practical cooperation among Hainan and LMC countries. On this basis, the Nanfan breeding base will be established as an important technology research and development and exchange platform for China's modern seed industry and international modern seed industry, and to realize the functions of agricultural resource information technology exchange, achievement transformation, and seeds trade.

(2) **Build diplomatic service platforms for international agricultural cooperation.** Hainan will establish a platform for agricultural foreign exchange and diplomatic service in conjunction with Boao Forum for Asia, and elevate the strategic position of Hainan in developing tropical agriculture in conjunction with the China-Africa Cooperative Agriculture Conference. It will promote Hainan's agriculture to participate in international cooperation on a larger scale, in a wider fields and at a higher level, enhance the international competitiveness of Hainan's agriculture, and further promote Hainan to develop more pragmatic and efficient agricultural cooperation with Lancang Mekong countries.

(3) **Accelerate the construction of China-Cambodia Tropical Ecological Agriculture Demonstration Zone.** At present, the construction of the China-Cambodia Tropical Ecological Agriculture Demonstration Zone has completed the first phase tasks of the industrial demonstration garden, including bananas, peppers, cassava and rubber core demonstration bases establishment. The next step is to explore the establishment of industrial standards in line with the actual situation in Cambodia, construct the development model of industrial gardens with the entire production chain of "production-processing-sales". To form overseas industrial agglomeration effects and driving effects by establishing the demonstration zone, and jointly create a new agricultural cooperation development model of "environmental protection+ecological agriculture".

(4) **Develop the construction of tropical agricultural industry cooperation**

demonstration zone in LMC countries. Under the framework of Lancang Mekong agricultural cooperation, Hainan will develop the construction of tropical agricultural industry demonstration zones in Cambodia, Laos, Myanmar, Thailand, and Vietnam in stages and steps, relying on the successful experience of the China-Cambodia Tropical Ecological Agriculture Demonstration Zone, supported by the Chinese Academy of Tropical Agricultural Sciences and other institutions, and the main body of "going global" enterprises. In order to lay a solid public opinion foundation and provide necessary talents for the establishment of Lancang-Mekong tropical agricultural industry cooperation demonstration zone, it will organize regular agricultural talents exchange and trainings, building mutual understanding among the agricultural officials, expertise, scholars, entrepreneurs, farmers, and news media in LMC countries.

(Written by Liu Yi, Zhang Hongliang and Xue Jingjie,
Department of Agriculture and Rural Affairs,
Hainan Province, China;
Translated by Liu Zhenhuan,
International Agriculture Research Institute,
Yunnan Academy of Agricultural Sciences, China)

10 | Agricultural Development and the Progress of Lancang-Mekong Agricultural Cooperation in Cambodia

10. 1 Overview of Agricultural Development

10. 1. 1 Resources and Development

(1) Resources and main agricultural products. Cambodia is located in Indochina Peninsula, bordering the Gulf of Thailand, between Thailand, Vietnam and Laos. It is rich in aquatic resources, the coast along the Gulf of Thailand is about 460 kilometers, the Mekong river runs through Cambodia from north to south. With land area is 181,000 square kilometers, forest area 98,000 square kilometers and coverage rate of 55. 7%, the natural conditions for the development of planting and aquaculture are superior. The total agricultural land area is 54,600 square kilometers, accounting for 30. 9% of the total land area. Among them, the arable land area is 38,000 square kilometers, permanent crop land area is 1, 600 square kilometers and permanent pasture land area is 15, 000 square kilometers. Rural people are 12. 601 million, making up about 80. 17% of 15. 718 million of the country's total population[①]. Cambodia has a tropical monsoon climate with high temperature and rainfall. Its

---

① The ASEAN Secretariat, 2018. ASEAN Statistical Year Book [M]. The ASEAN Secretariat [2020-12-22]. www. asean. org.

climate is dominated by the annual monsoon cycle with its alternating wet
(May through October) and dry (November through next April)
seasons. Based on the traditional farming style, Cambodian agricultural
planting is almost in wet season and the planting area, and in dry season
the output is about one tenth of that in rainy season.

Rice, maize and cassava are the main crop in Cambodia. For the
importance of rice, Cambodian government takes it as the priority development
crop. The rice planting area covers about 77.63% of the total arable land,
along the shores of the Mekong River, Tonle Sap River and Bassac River
are the main producing area. Maize is the second crop, which was mainly
distributed in the east plateau and near Phnom Penh[1]. Furthermore,
economic crops, such as rubber, vegetables, cashew, tropical fruit,
soybean, sesame, groundnut, sugarcane, tobacco, sisal and so on are
distributed in Cambodia. From the data published by FAO (Table 10 - 1),
the top 10 crops with harvested area and yield in 2018 are as follow:

Table 10 - 1 The Yield and Planting Area of Major Crops in Cambodia in 2018

Serial number	Variety of crops	Area harvested (hectare)	Yield (ton)	Yield per unit area (kg/hectare)
1	Rice, paddy	3,071,696	10,892,000	3,545.9
2	Cassava	481,679	12,805,875	26,585.9
3	Maize	242,237	1,232,000	5,085.9
4	Rubber, natural	226,028	220,100	973.8
5	Soybeans	105,000	170,000	1,619.0
6	Vegetables, fresh nes	103,768	665,497	6,413.3
7	Beans, dry	68,448	88,070	1,286.7
8	Sesame seed	40,000	30,000	750.0
9	Banana	30,699	142,890	4,654.5
10	Sugar cane	28,770	640,000	22,245.4

Source: http://www.fao.org/faostat/en/#data.

---

[1] Institute of Yunnan Science, Institute of Agricultural Economics and Information, YAAS,
2006. Research on Agricultural Cooperation of Yunnan and ASEAN [M]. Kunming: Yunnan Science
and Technology Press: 190.

Fishery is an important part of Cambodia's agriculture, accounting for about a quarter of Cambodia's gross output value of agriculture. Almost 90% total fishery production comes from the freshwater area of the Tonle Sap lake and along the Mekong river. According to the statistics of FAO and Ministry of Fisheries of Cambodia, as the largest lake in Indochina Peninsula, Tonle Sap lake has the most abundant freshwater fishery resources in the world with the fourth largest total catch. Marine fisheries account for a relatively small proportion of Cambodian fisheries, mainly concentrated on the east coast of the Gulf of Thailand. In 2018, Cambodian natural and raising aquatic products is up to 910,000 tons, including freshwater aquatic 535,000 tons, marine fisheries 121,000 tons and raising products 254,000 tons. Total processing products of fresh water and marine aquatic is 84,000 tons, and exporting marine fisheries is 14,000 tons[①].

Animal husbandry is still dominated by small-scale production and relatively low proportion in Cambodian agricultural. Poultry, cattle and pig are the main livestock (Table 10 - 2).

Table 10 - 2　Basic Situation of Cambodian Animal Husbandry in 2018

Serial number	Name of the livestock and poultry	Breeding quantity (head)
1	Chicken	13,200,000
2	Duck	8,897,000
3	Cow (including buffalo and cattle)	3,483,060
4	Pig	2,107,659
5	Horse	30,629

Source: http://www.fao.org/faostat/en/#data.

(2) Current status of agricultural development. For a long time, agriculture has dominated Cambodia's national economy. However, with

---

① Wang Xiangshe, 2019. Remarkable Achievements in Cambodia's Fishery Administration Construction in 2018 [J]. World Tropical Agriculture Information (4): 28.

the development of modernization, Cambodian industry and service industry have grown rapidly, and its economic structure is transforming from agricultural oriented to service and industry. Although the agricultural scale is still steadily expanding year by year, the growth rate is relatively slow and lagging. As shown in Figure 10-1, from 2000 to 2010, Cambodian agricultural added value grew at an average annual rate of about 6% but significantly slowly after 2010, and the average annual growth rate of agricultural added value was less than 1% from 2010 to 2018. At the same time, the proportion of agricultural in national economy was decreasing year by year. According to the statistics from the World Bank, Cambodian agriculture added value in GDP dropped from 36% at the beginning of this century to 22% in 2018, while the industrial added value in GDP rose from 22% to 32% in the same period. In the composition of the agriculture to GDP contribution in 2018, crops still accounted for over a half (58.1%) of the total, husbandry accounted 11.2%, aquaculture accounted for 24% and forestry for 6.7%.

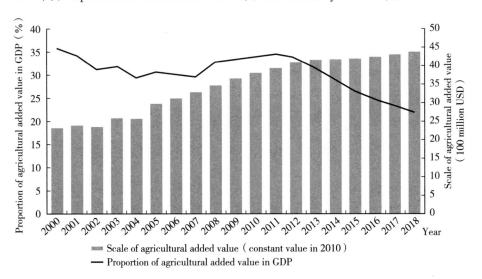

Figure 10 - 1　The Change Trend of Agricultural Added Value in Cambodia from 2000 to 2018
Source: https://data.worldbank.org.cn.

10. 1. 2 Import and Export Trade of Agricultural Products

Cambodia has established trade relationship with most countries in the world. The scale of agricultural trade has increased year by year, from 3. 66 million tons in 2013 to 5. 13 million tons in 2017, an average annual increase of 7%[①]. Rice is the most important export commodity, followed by rubber and cassava. Other major agricultural products exported include corn, pepper, and tropical fruits. According to the statistics of the Ministry of Agriculture Forestry and Fisheries of Cambodia, the export volume of rice was increased from 378,900 tons in 2013 to 635,700 tons in 2017. In 2018, the export volume of rice was 626,200 tons, of which 170,200 tons were exported to China, accounting for 27.17%, ranking the first for four consecutive years. The other 4 countries which were the top 5 rice export countries were France (86,100 tons), Malaysia (40,900 tons), Gabon (33,100 tons) and the Netherlands (26,700 tons)[②]. The export volume of rubber (mainly natural rubber dry plates) was increased from less than 100,000 tons in 2013 to 217,500 tons in 2018. The export volume of cassava (mainly including dry cassava plates, fresh cassava and cassava flour) also increased, about 2 million tons in 2018, are mainly exported to Vietnam, China, Netherlands, Czech Republic, Canada, Italy and India[③].

According to the statistics of ASEAN database, Cambodian top 10 agricultural products export trade partners in 2018 (ranked by the amount of export trade) were shown in Table 10 - 3. The total agricultural

---

① This report was compiled according to the reports of participants from Cambodia on 2019 Mekong-Lancang River agricultural materials cooperation summit meeting and Economic and Trade Fair.

② Shi Dengfeng, 2019. China Becomes the Continuously Biggest Rice Inporting Country from Cambodia for Four Years [EB/OL]. (01 - 14) [2020-12-22]. https://finance. sina. com. cn/money/future/agri/2019-01-14/doc-ihqfskcn7046005. shtml.

③ Wang Xiangshe, 2019. General Situation of Agriculture in Cambodia and a Brief Introduction of Recent Agriculture Public Opinions [J]. World Tropical Agriculture Information (9): 8-9.

products export amount of these 10 countries took 79.86% of the Cambodian total agricultural products. Agricultural products exported to China accounted for 29.86% of the total exports of agricultural products, and export trade countries are highly concentrated. In terms of the types of agricultural products exported, the export amount of grain was the largest, reaching 411 million USD; sugar and sugar food were smaller than grain and ranked at the second, reaching 82.28 million USD; the other agricultural products with a large exported amount included flour milling industrial products, vegetable oils and animal fats and their decomposition products, edible vegetables and tubers, coffee, tea and spices, edible fruits and nuts, cereal flour and confectionery and dessert, oil-bearing seeds, nuts and fruits, medicinal plants, cocoa and cocoa products, etc.

Table 10 - 3   Top 10 Countries of Cambodian Agricultural Products Exported in 2018

Serial number	Exported countries	Export value (USD)
1	China	188,713,246
2	Vietnam	97,744,810
3	France	56,540,056
4	Malaysia	53,356,374
5	Gabon	29,372,328
6	Netherlands	25,895,616
7	Italy	15,961,551
8	Belgium	13,686,457
9	Germany	11,890,607
10	Poland	11,608,400

Note: Based on the 2 digits' code of HS, the data of goods trade (IMTS) was sorted out by selected data from HS (01-20).

Source: https://data.aseanstats.org.

Table 10 - 4 shows Cambodian top 10 agricultural products imported trade partners (ranked by the amount of import trade) in 2018. The total agricultural products imported amount from these 10 countries accounted for 75. 70% of the Cambodian total amount import of agricultural products. The agricultural products imported from Thailand accounted for 23. 22% of the total agricultural products imported, import trade countries are highly concentrated also. In terms of the types of agricultural products imported, grain, cereal flour and confectionery and dessert were the largest mount imported commodities, the amount was 135 million USD; malt, starch, inulin, wheat bran and other flour milling industrial products' imported amount were ranked at the second, their imported amounts were reached 70. 57 million USD; the other agricultural products with a large imported amount included sugar and its products, milk, eggs, natural honey, animal fats and their decomposition products, grains, meat and other aquatic invertebrate products, live animals, vegetables and tubes, fruits, etc.

Table 10 – 4　Top 10 Countries of Cambodian Agricultural Products Imported in 2018

Serial number	Imported countries	Import amount (USD)
1	Thailand	95,542,207
2	Malaysia	50,658,158
3	Vietnam	43,036,952
4	China	31,962,039
5	Australia	20,481,895
6	Singapore	18,910,532
7	Denmark	14,706,052
8	United States	12,441,654
9	Argentina	12,143,931
10	France	11,514,040

Note: Based on the 2 digits' code of HS, the data of goods trade (IMTS) was sorted out by selected data from HS (01-20).

Source: https://data. aseanstats. org.

10. 2　Agricultural Investment Policy

10. 2. 1　Macro Policy

The government of Cambodia has attached great importance to the development of agriculture as a priority area, strengthened the depth and diversification of agricultural production through investment and full use of domestic resources to promote economic development, create employment opportunities, and increase farmers' income; meanwhile, the government also encouraged private investments and created a good environment for privately-operated participated in development projects. They preferentially developed the border and remote rural areas, the necessary infrastructures, to make further improvement on people's living standards and local economy.

The "Four Corner Strategy" implemented by Cambodia is the blueprint for Cambodian economic development. The Strategy is a five-year plan and issued in 2018, and the core content of which is "to reduce the poverty rate of Cambodia to less than 10% and continue to ensure 7% the annual growth rate of national economy". The strategy emphasizes: firstly, agricultural production should be improved; secondly, private economy and increasing employment will be developed; thirdly, infrastructure will be restored and rebuilt; fourth, personnel will be trained and human resources developed. The detail plans of "improving agricultural production" include: improving productivity and maintaining agricultural diversification and commercialization; promoting animal husbandry, fishery and aquaculture; carrying out land reform and mine clearance; reforming forestry and promoting sustainable development of national resources. Through the above measures, the growth rate of agriculture is expected to increase about 5% per year.

10. 2. 2 Legal System Related on Agriculture

Investment Law of the kingdom of Cambodia is applicable to agricultural investment. It is applicable to all Cambodians and foreigners engaged in investment activities in Cambodia. The investors, whether natural or legal, are subject to the law.

Laws and regulations related to agricultural materials in Cambodia include: Land Law of the Kingdom of Cambodia, Forest Law of the Kingdom of Cambodia, Water Resources Management Law, Administrative Regulations on Water Pollution Management, Chemical Fertilizer and Pesticide Management Law, etc. Laws and regulations related to agricultural production and operation include: Business Administration and Business Registration Law, Commercial Contract Law, Commercial Enterprises Law, etc. Protection system related to agricultural include: Environmental Protection and Resource Management Law, Environmental Impact Assessment Process Implementation Act, etc. Cambodia has always pursued an open free market economic policy, and economic activities are highly liberalized. 28 countries (regions) in the world, such as the European Union, the United States and Japan, have granted Cambodia GSP treatment. Cambodian competition and price policies are comparatively opening, so there is almost no government monopoly; in addition, the government does not directly interfere with the commercial goods or services price, nor does it conduct price control.

10. 2. 3 Market Access and Agricultural Products Trad System

(1) Legal and policy system of foreign investment management in agriculture

- Access system for foreign investors Cambodia's foreign investment policy is relatively free, and foreign investment is treated in the same way as domestic investment. It is emphasized that all

investors, regardless of nationality and race, are equal before the law.

- Land system and policy related to agriculture   According to the Constitution of the Kingdom of Cambodia, foreign natural or legal persons are not allowed to own the land of the Kingdom of Cambodia. Land Law of the Kingdom of Cambodia is applicable to agricultural land management, according to the law, " it is permitted to lease land to domestic and foreign enterprises or individuals in the form of franchise to engage in agricultural production. " In accordance with the provisions of order No. 146 of the Cambodian government on land for franchise, Economic Land Concessions (ELC) refers to the establishment of a way to grant the state's private land through franchise rights for agricultural production or industrial agricultural development, which includes grain cultivation, industrial planting, animal husbandry and aquaculture, plant cultivation, agricultural processing industry and related facilities, some or all of the above industries. Franchised land can be approved to domestic and foreign enterprises or individuals in different ways, but it requires: maximum area is not more than 10,000 hectares; the approved land can only be the state for private use; the maximum period is 99 years.

- Investment system and policy in agriculture   The Cambodian government has always encouraged foreign capital direct investment in the development of agriculture and agricultural processing industry, and its investment preferences mainly include exemption from entire or part customs duties and taxes.

- Foreign exchange management system and policy   According to the Foreign Exchange Law of Cambodia approved in 1993, Cambodia does not implement foreign exchange control, the exchange rate is regulated by the market, and the US dollar can be freely circulated.

Both remittance and transfer payment can be done through registered financial institutions in Cambodia. Most transactions in Cambodia are denominated in US dollars, and remittances are only subject to withholding taxes. Foreign investors may remit foreign exchange to overseas for the purpose of paying off debts related to investment activities and returning investment income and surplus assets, etc.

- Legal system and policy of agriculture related labor   The Investment Law of the Kingdom of Cambodia stipulates that the principle of freedom of hiring labor is that investors in Cambodia have the right to freely choose and employ Cambodian or foreign employees in accordance with relevant provisions of the Kingdom of Cambodia Labor Law and the Kingdom of Cambodia Immigration Law.

(2) **Trade system of agricultural materials and products.** Laws and regulations related to trade in Cambodia include: Customs Duties on Import and Export Commodities Management Act, Decree on Issuance of Certificate of Origin of Clothing, Commercial Invoice and Export License, Regulations on the Implementation of the Management of the Commodities Inspection before Shipment, Accession to the World Trade Organization Law, Sub-Decree on Risk Management, Regulation on the Establishment of the Risk Management Office of the Customs and Revenue Administration, Law on the Trade Activities of Commercial Companies, etc.

Cambodia foreign trade treated the system of GSP. In most cases, Cambodian imported commodities do not need a license, but some products can only be exported after obtaining special export authorization or permission from relevant government departments. The trade and circulation of mahogany is banned by Cambodian government order. General export goods, except for 5 categories of products such as natural rubber, gemstone, semi-finished or finished wood, seafood and sand, do not need to pay customs duties. Goods are subject to import tax upon entry into Cambodia, except those exempted from taxation under the Investment Law or other special regulations. Import tariff mainly consists of four kinds of exchange rates: 7%, 15%, 35% and 50%. Under the common effective tariff system of ASEAN Free Trade Agreement, products imported from other ASEAN member countries and fitted the rules of origin can enjoy lower tariff rates.

10. 3 Progress and Results of Lancang-Mekong Agricultural Cooperation

10. 3. 1 Main Progress

（1） **Participation in exchange activities of the Lancang-Mekong mechanism.** Cambodia and China were the co-chairs of the second Lancang-Mekong Cooperation Leaders' Meeting held in Phnom Penh, the capital of Cambodia, on January 10, 2018. On January 11, 2018, Chinese Premier Li Keqiang held talks with Cambodian Prime Minister Hun Sen in Phnom Penh. After the meeting, *Joint Communique between the Government of the People's Republic of China and the Government of the Kingdom of Cambodia* （hereinafter referred to as the "Communique"）was issued. The communique showed that China would strengthen cooperation with Cambodia in agriculture and other key areas, "Vigorously promote agricultural cooperation, joint work to formulate the development plan of Cambodian modern agriculture, construct agricultural cooperation demonstration zone and agricultural products deep processing zone, so as to promote the development of Cambodian agricultural products processing, warehousing and logistics, and the extension of agricultural industry chain." Leaders of China and Cambodia witnessed the signing of 19 cooperation documents, including *Memorandum of Understanding on the Joint Prepare the Development Plan of Cambodian Modern Agriculture*, *Memorandum of Understanding on Cooperation in Rice Research*, *Agreement* *on the Construction of a Precious Tree Species Breeding Center in Cambodia.*

(2) Implementation status of agricultural projects supported by Lancang-Mekong Cooperation Special Fund (LMCSF)[①]. The first 16 projects of the Special Funds of Lancang-Mekong Cooperation for Cambodia were signed in December 2017, including 3 agricultural related projects with a total budget of 1. 5 million USD. At present, the first 3 agricultural related projects are implementing on schedule. The progressing statements and current results are as follows:

An Effective Regional Strategy for Combatting Illegal, Unreported and Unregistered (IUU) Fishing in the Mekong Countries for Sustainable Fisheries Management in the Mekong Region will be promoted, whose budget is 500,000 USD. At present, the second revised draft of *Assessment Report on Current Illegal, Unreported and Unregistered Fishing Fisheries, Gaps and Best Practices in Lancang-Mekong Subregion* was finished; the second draft of *Effective Regional Strategy of Crack Down Illegal, Unreported and Unregistered Fishing in Lancang-Mekong Subregion* was modified; the materials of the Independent Electoral Commission was drawn up to raise awareness of illegal fishing and the capacity-building of effective regional strategic practices; the implementation recommendations of the plan of Lancang-Mekong subregion strategy and action was laid down.

The budget of Forest Restoration and Promotion of Sustainable Forest Use in Southeast Asia is 500,000 USD. In July 2018, the Minister of Agriculture, Forestry and Fisheries of Cambodia (MAFF) held a meeting with Siem Reap Forestry Bureau, delivered project equipment and patrol equipment, and held the first technical meeting with Thailand and Vietnam. In December 2018, Cambodia sent a group of Forestry Bureau officials to visit Thailand, focused on investigate Lad Krathing Forest

---

① According to the reports of participants from Cambodia on the Second Meeting of the Lancang-Mekong Cooperation (LMC) Joint Working Group on Agriculture in 2019.

plantation and the tree species source area, Ra Yong Botanical Garden and forestry, and the effective experience of the Nern Phra community forestry based on non-wood forest products; 2 nursery garden demonstration sites were established to cultivate a variety of local tree species, a field trial plot system (FTPS) was established at the same time to compare the field performance of local fast-growing tree species, to test the effect of fertilization on field characters, evaluate the effect of afforestation, the restoration of wildlife habitat and food chain, and the safety of wildlife seed diffusion.

Sustainable Land Management will addressing Land Degradation and Improving Local Livelihoods, and the budget is 500,000 USD. A series of measures have been taken to prevent and control land degradation, such as rational use of water resources, etc. At present, the project progressing is going smooth and well.

The second batch of Cambodian 19 projects of the Lancang-Mekong Cooperation Special Fund were assigned in February, 2019, included 2 agricultural related projects, and these 2 projects' total budget is 670,000 USD. They were: Capacity Development for Sustainable Forest Management in Lancang-Mekong Economies, of which the budget is 500,000 USD; Community Fisheries Co-management: Capacity Building and Sharing experiences and lesson learnt among Mekong Region Member Countries, of which the budget is 170,000 USD. At present, these projects are in the stage of organizational planning, will be carried out implementation soon.

Some challenges were occurred during implementing the Lancang-Mekong Cooperation Special Fund. In agricultural production, the challenges are the relatively low level of productivity and product quality, the high costs of production, the fierce market competition, the weak technical level and management ability, the insufficient scientific research investment and the low level of agricultural industrialization; in agricultural products trade, the problems include the weak procurement system (mainly based on the market of neighboring countries), imperfect price and commercial contract system, and the most of the importing countries' trade barriers "agreements on the implementation of sanitary and phytosanitary measures"; in terms of supporting environment, the insufficient level of infrastructure construction and modernization supported for agricultural development, imperfect logistics system and insufficient law enforcement efforts to combat forest and fishery crimes.

(3) Agricultural cooperation with other LMC countries

① Agricultural cooperation with China

Among the cooperation with other five Lancang-Mekong Cooperation countries, Cambodia has the closest agricultural cooperation with China. China has been an important trade partner of Cambodia for a long time, and there is still a huge development space for agricultural products trade between the two countries. Cambodian agricultural trade with China had been a trade deficit in a long-term, since 2014, Cambodia has expanded its export of agricultural products to China, and then the agricultural products trade of Cambodia to China has been changed from deficit to surplus, and the export volume has expanded rapidly year by year. In 2018, the agricultural products export volume of Cambodia to China was 199 million USD, and the import volume of Cambodia from China was 57 million USD, resulted trade surplus and the volume was 142 million USD. From the types of agricultural products imported and exported, the main agricultural products Cambodia exported to China (including Hong Kong and Taiwan) was rice, accounting for 42.73% of the total export of agricultural products; other agricultural products with large export volume included cassava, starch, centrifugal crude sugar and other commodities; the agricultural products with large import volume included cigarettes, distilled alcohol and other commodities[1]. In agricultural investment,

---

[1] Data source: http://www.fao.org/faostat/en/#data.

there were about 40 Chinese agricultural investment enterprises in Cambodia till the end of 2017, mainly investing in rice, maize and other cereal crops, as well as natural rubber, sweet potato, oil palm and other economic crops[①].

On June 27, 2018, on the first "the Belt and Road" Agricultural Food Industry and Trade Summit Forum, Veng Sakhon, the Minister of Agriculture, Forestry and Fisheries of Cambodia (MAFF), called on Chinese large scales of investment companies to increase investments in Cambodia, including increasing the investment in processing industry of agriculture and agricultural food, expanding Cambodian agricultural products market, and enhancing bilateral cooperation. On October 18, 2018, Premier Minister of China Li Keqiang met with Prime Minister of Cambodia Hun Sen in Brussels, and Li Keqiang pointed out that China and

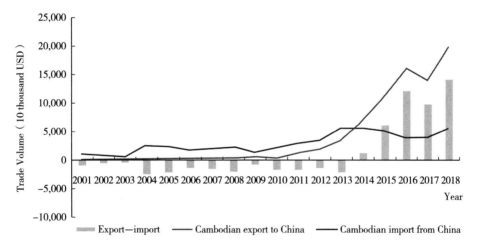

Figure 10 - 2   The Development of Bilateral Agricultural Products Trade
between Cambodia and China from 2001 to 2018
Source: https://comtrade.un.org.

---

① Department of International Cooperation, Ministry of Agriculture and Rural Areas, Foreign Economic Cooperation Center, Ministry of Agriculture and Rural Areas, 2018. Analysis Report on Chinese Foreign Investment and Cooperation in Agriculture [M]. Beijing: China Agriculture Press: 26.

Cambodia should expand the scale of bilateral trade. Moreover, China would continue to import Cambodian advantageous agricultural products, encourage Chinese powerful enterprises to invest and start businesses in Cambodia, and better achieve mutual benefits and win-win results.

In August 2018, Cambodia and China assigned *Protocol of Phytosanitary Requirements for the Export of Bananas from Cambodia to China*, opening the door for Cambodian banana to enter the Chinese market. The signing of the agreement marked the completion of the Cambodian banana for Chinese quarantine admittance, Cambodian banana became the first fruit variety exported to China. In the past, Cambodian banana must be exported to Vietnam first if it wanted enter to Chinese market. In May 2019, the first 100 tons of Cambodian banana exported to China successfully arrived. Cambodia has unique advantages in banana planting, where the area is rarely affected by typhoon, that the light and heat conditions are suitable for banana growth round the year, and that especially the incidence of Wilt in Cambodia is almost zero. With the expansion of Cambodian banana planting area, Cambodia will be expected to become the largest banana exporter to China in the future.

② Agricultural cooperation with Thailand

Cambodian has a close relationship with Thailand in agricultural products trade. The main agricultural products of Cambodia exported to Thailand are maize, cassava, beans, etc. , while the main products Cambodia imported from Thailand are agricultural machinery, food, etc. In recent years, for Cambodian stable politics, rapid growth economic, abundant agricultural resources and labor force, many Thailand companies, businessmen and investors are investing in Cambodia. In 2015, DIPI company of Cambodia and Ubon Bio Ethanol (UBE) Company of Thailand signed a cooperation agreement on unlimited supply of cassava. According to the agreement, UBE company of Thailand will purchase Cambodian cassava in unlimited quantity and guarantee a stable price for cassava[①]. In 2017, Cambodian AMRU Rice Company and Thailand Thai Starch Company signed a Memorandum of Understanding (MOU). According to the plan, Cambodian AMRU Rice Company would supply 8,000 tons organic cassava to Thailand Thai Starch Company in 2018, and it is expected to grow to 20,000-40,000 tons organic cassava in 2020[②]. Cambodian companies supplied cassava to Thailand could resist the competitions from neighboring countries' cassava products and improved the economic income of cassava farmers.

In addition to the agricultural products trade, Cambodia and Thailand also strengthened the infrastructure connectivity construction and policies communications and exchanges, jointly promoting agricultural cooperation between the two sides. In May 2019, Cambodia and Thailand signed an agreement on the Construction of Stung Bot Port, and Thailand provided 800 million Thai baht (26 million USD) loan for Cambodia. Through the loan, Cambodia started a project which included the construction of the Stenborg Port on the border between Cambodia and Thailand and the infrastructure connected to Cambodia Highway No. 5. This project could relieve the problem of long-term freight transportation of agricultural products and help to expand the scale of trade between Cambodia and Thailand[③]. In July 2019, a delegation of Cambodian was lead by Phan Chanthol, governor of Pailin Province, visited Chonburi Province, Thailand. The leaders of Cambodia and Thailand reached a consensus on cooperation in increasing exports of agricultural products, promoting trade

---

① Anonymity, 2015. Cambodian and Thailand Companies Signed an Agreement on Unlimited Supply of Cassava [J]. World Tropical Agriculture Information (12): 17-18.

② Chen Benzong, 2017. Cambodian and Thailand Companies Cooperation, Promote Organic Cassava Export [N/OL]. Cambodian China Daily, 11-23 [2020-12-22]. http://www. ccpit. org/Contents/Channel_4117/2017/1123/918941/content_918941. htm.

③ Yan Xin, 2019. Cambodia and Thailand Signed the Agreement on Construction of Stenborg Port [N/OL]. Khmer Daily, 05-24 [2020-12-22]. http://www. sohu. com/a/316303557_99978839.

between the two provinces and combating cross-border crimes[1].

③ Agriculture cooperation with Vietnam

Cambodia is one of the near and potential important markets for the export of agriculture, forestry and aquatic products of Vietnam, which accounts for a high proportion of the total trade volume between Cambodia and Vietnam. Vietnam used to be the first-class investment source country in the agricultural field of Cambodia, with close agricultural cooperation between the two sides. In December 2017, Cambodia government reached a cooperation agreement with the Cashew Association of Vietnam using Cambodian 500,000 hectares land to develop cashew cultivation on a large scale. Vietnam provided Cambodia with the funds needed to purchase 1,000,000 cashew saplings from 2018 to 2022; in addition, Vietnam and Cambodian Cashew Nuts Research and Development Working Group were established, and the Cashew Association of Vietnam and the cashew companies provided the technologies and saplings for Cambodian and purchase the fruit nuts[2]. In July 2019, the Cambodia-Vietnam Trade and Investment Promotion Forum was held, and enterprises of these two countries exchanged specific issues on tariffs, customs procedures, investment preferences, etc. Cambodia and Vietnam hoped to further promote bilateral investment in agricultural, import and export trade by a series of preferential policies.

④ Agricultural cooperation with Myanmar and Laos

Cambodia, Myanmar and Laos are all traditional agricultural countries, and they are similar and complementary in natural resource endowments and

---

① Anonymity, 2019. Deepening the Friendly and Cooperative Relations between Cambodia and Thailand. Pan Zhantuo, Governor of Pailin Province Visited Thailand [N/OL]. Chinese Businessmen media, 07-28 [2020-12-22]. https://www. sohu. com/a/329895652_413350.

② Business Office of Consulate General in Ho Chi Minh City, 2017. Vietnam and Cambodia Joint Develop Large Scale of Cashew Planting [N/OL]. Vietnam Economic Times, 12-08 [2020-12-22]. http://hochiminh. mofcom. gov. cn/article/jmxw/201712/20171202682738. shtml.

agricultural development conditions. However, at the stage of now, there are relatively few agricultural cooperation and exchanges among these three countries, so there is still a large space for their development. In February 2017, representatives of Laos Mekong River Commission and Cambodia Mekong River Commission held a meeting in Siem Reap, Cambodia, to discuss the joint fisheries management plan, which aims to rebuild inland fishery resources of Mekong River and Sekong River Basin. The two countries would manage five species of long-distance migration fish in the above rivers by the joint plan. According to *Khmer Daily*, the trade volume between Cambodia and Myanmar in 2018 is 10 million USD, which was not yet in line with the economic potential of the two countries. The two countries should continue to deepen economic cooperation and further develop agricultural cooperation[①].

10. 3. 2　Results and Experience

(1) Actively participating in Lancang-Mekong cooperation to endeavour project financial support. Cambodia has taken full advantage of its resource endowment in crop cultivation (such as rice) and aquaculture, vigorously guided international funds to invest in agricultural sector, undertaken a number of agricultural investment cooperation projects, actively sought support from the Lancang-Mekong Cooperation Special Fund, and become the country with the most approval projects by the Fund for two consecutive years. So far, Cambodia has gained 35 projects from the Lancang-Mekong Cooperation Special Fund, with a total budget of 14.96 million USD, covering agriculture, tourism, telecommunications, education, cultural exchange and other fields. Among the 35 projects, Cambodia has gained 5 agricultural related projects with a total budget of 2.17 million

---

① Anonymity, 2019. Cambodia-Myanmar Bilateral Trade Volume Was only US $ 10 million in 2018, and Cooperation should Continue to Deepen [N/OL]. Khmer Daily, 09-11 [2020-12-22]. http://www.sohu.com/a/340217341_120133562.

USD. Prak Sokhonn, Deputy Prime Minister, Minister of Foreign Affairs and International Cooperation of Cambodia, believed that these projects reflect the needs of LMC countries. "To enhance air connectivity in the Lancang-Mekong subregion, promote agricultural development, and solve problems such as land degradation, sustainable forest utilization and sustainable management of fisheries in the Mekong region will bring real benefits to the countries of the region. "[1]

（2）**Promoting exchanges among LMC countries in co-management fisheries and sustainable management forest.** Cambodia advocated practical cooperation in the field of agriculture, and effectively promote the exchanges and interactions in fisheries, forestry and other fields among LMC countries with the project. By assessing the problems, gaps and best practices of the current illegal, unreported and unregistered fishing in Lancang-Mekong basin, develop effective regional strategies to combat the above illegal fishing activities, enhance the consensus of the countries on solving the problems. Through holding technical meetings with Thailand and Vietnam and the investigating of major forest plantations and tree source areas in Thailand and other activities, enhanced the experience exchange, sharing tree resource, cooperative forestry development, and sustainable forest management among Cambodia, Thailand and Vietnam were enhanced.

（3）**Deepening agricultural cooperation with China and Thailand.** China and Thailand have relatively strong agricultural investment capacity, scientific and technological level, and relatively high degree of agricultural modernization among the LMC countries. Cambodia focused on strengthening agricultural cooperation with China and Thailand by introducing agricultural investment and absorbing advanced agricultural production technology and

---

① Zhao Yipu, Zheng Meichen, 2019. Mekong-Lancang Cooperation Injects New Impetus into Cambodian Development [N]. The People's Daily, 02-23 (3).

management experience, to transform traditional agriculture and then to consolidate its agricultural basic position. The friendly and cooperative relations between Cambodia and China have been developing since establishment of diplomatic relations in 1958, created a good environment for the development of agricultural cooperation for them. Under the Lancang-Mekong Cooperation Mechanism, between the two countries not only agricultural products trade have been expanded, and the remarkable achievements in agricultural investment, zone construction, policy consensus and other aspects of cooperation have been made as well. Between Cambodia and Thailand, the great breakthroughs in the supply of cassava and other major agricultural products, bilateral trade, logistics exchange of agricultural products, and policy mutual trust and exchange areas have also been made.

(Written by Li Xinwei and GuoWen, Translated by Guo Wen,
International Agriculture Research Institute,
Yunnan Academy of Agricultural Sciences, China)

11 | Agricultural Development and the Progress Lancang-Mekong Agricultural Cooperation in Laos

11. 1   Overview of Agricultural Development

11. 1. 1   Resources and Development

(1) **Resources and main agricultural products.** Laos is located in the middle of Indochina Peninsula. It is a landlocked country with a land area of 236,800 square kilometers. The terrain is high in the north and low in the south. About 80% of the area is composed of hills and mountains. The territory is mostly covered by forests, and the forest land area accounts for about 70%. Laos has a tropical and subtropical monsoon climate, with rainy season from May to October and dry season from November to April. The average annual rainfall is 1,834 mm and the average annual temperature is about 26℃. With 90 percent of its territory in the Mekong River basin, it is rich in water resources. The agricultural area is 23,690 square kilometers, of which 16,940 square kilometers are cultivated. In 2018, the total population was 7.061,5 million, of which the rural population was 4.589,7 million, accounting for about 65 percent of the total population of the country[①].

According to the statistics of the Food and Agriculture Organization in

---

① Data sources: http://www.fao.org/faostat/en/#data; https://data.worldbank.org.cn.

2018，the main crops planted in Laos are shown in Table 11 - 1.

Table 11 - 1　The Yield and Planting Area of Major Crops in Laos in 2018

Serial number	Variety of crops	Area Harvested (hectare)	Yield (ton)	Yield per unit area (kg/hectare)
1	Rice，paddy	848,174	3,584,700	4,226.4
2	Vegetables，fresh nes	170,840	1,460,530	8,549.1
3	Maize	165,620	981,680	5,927.3
4	Roots and tubers nes	115,915	2,956,867	25,508.9
5	Coffee，green	82,980	154,435	1,861.1
6	Cassava	71,010	2,279,030	32,094.5
7	Sugar cane	30,555	1,834,525	60,040.1
8	Bananas	23,120	970,985	41,997.6
9	Groundnuts，with shell	19,995	48,885	2,444.9
10	Sesame seed	13,035	16,235	1,245.5

Note：Based on the 2 digits' code of HS，the data of goods trade (IMTS) was sorted out by selected data from HS (01 - 20).

Source：http://www.fao.org/faostat/en/#data.

Laos is rich in animal husbandry and grassland resources，with a total area of 15,000 square kilometers，and almost all farmers raise livestock and poultry. At present，there are 1,370 livestock farms in Laos，in which water buffalo are mainly used for ploughing，cattle are mainly used for meat processing，horses，donkeys and mules are mainly used for pack-carrying，and other livestock and poultry are used for food and market trading. In recent years，animal husbandry in Laos has developed rapidly and is moving forward from traditional breeding to modern breeding，but the current breeding technology is still relatively backward[1]. From the breeding quantity of the livestock and poultry，more pigs，cow，sheep，

①　Kong Zhijian，Cun Jiali，2017. Analysis on the Development Status and Prospect of Animal Husbandry and Fishery in Laos [J]. Southeast Asian and South Asian Studies (4)：64-69.

chickens and ducks were raised in Laos (Table 11 - 2).

Table 11 - 2　Basic Situation of Lao Animal Husbandry in 2018

Serial number	Name of the livestock and poultry	Breeding quantity (head)
1	Pig	3,824,663
2	Cow (including buffalo and cattle)	3,240,947
3	Goat	616,325
4	Horse	32,410
5	Chicken	39,218,000
6	Duck	3,575,000

Source: http://www.fao.org/faostat/en/#data.

In terms of aquatic products, Laos is rich in water resources, and the inland waters cover an area of about 6,000 square kilometers. Fisheries are mainly distributed along the Mekong River and its 14 tributaries[1]. Aquatic products are one of the important food consumed by the Lao people. The main fishery species are tilapia, grass carp, baler fish, and Indian wild carp. According to statistics, there were 765 protective ponds and 199 aquaculture bases in Laos, and private breeding bases have developed rapidly. In general, the production and consumption of aquatic products in Laos are increasing year by year, but it lacks high-quality fish fry and advanced breeding technology, and most of the fry and feed need to be imported from Thailand[2].

(2) Current status of Agricultural Development. In 2018, the added value of agriculture in Laos was 2.847 billion USD (current price), up 4.3% year-on-year and accounting for 15.7% of GDP. The agricultural

---

[1]　Kong Zhijian, Cun Jiali, 2017. Analysis on the Development Status and Prospect of Animal Husbandry and Fishery in Laos [J]. Southeast Asian and South Asian Studies (4): 64-69.

[2]　Tang Zhanyang, Guo Zhongbao, Liang Junneng, 2019. Investigation and Analysis on the Current Situation of Fishery Breeding in Laos [J]. Science to Breed Fish, 355 (3): 90-91.

added value of Laos (according to the statistics of the constant value in 2010) showed a trend of gradual increase from 2000 to 2018, with an average annual growth rate of 3.17% (Figure 11 - 1). The proportion of agricultural added value in GDP decreased year by year, with the average annual decline rate of 4.14%.

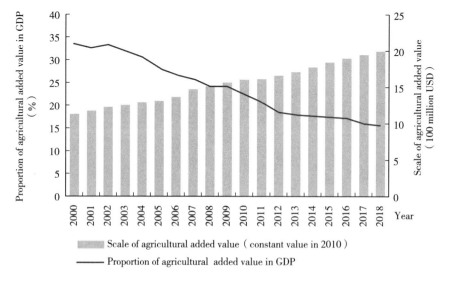

Figure 11 - 1   The Change Trend of Agricultural Added Value in Laos from 2000 to 2018
Source: https://data.worldbank.org.cn.

11.1.2   Import and Export Trade of Agricultural Products

In view of the particularity of agricultural products logistics and transportation, the main partners of Laos in agricultural trade are Thailand, Vietnam and China, accounting for 90% of their total foreign trade. Among them, Thailand and Vietnam share similar culture and customs with Laos, have long land borders, and have significant cultural advantages, which have profoundly affected the development of Laos' agricultural trade. From 2010 to 2016, the trade of agricultural products in Laos made outstanding achievements with a high overall growth rate, but with large fluctuations and lack of stability[①]. In 2017, agriculture accounted for 13. 3 percent of imports, up 0. 2 percentage points compared to 2016. It accounted for 28. 9 percent of exports, up 1. 4 percentage points compared to 2016[②].

According to the statistical analysis of ASEAN database data, in 2018 Laos total agricultural imports was about 322 million USD and total exported about 653 million USD, and the trade surplus of agricultural products was about 332 million USD. Overall, the trade volume of agricultural products in Laos was small.

The top 10 agricultural products export trade partners (ranked by the amount of export trade) of Laos in 2018 are Vietnam, Thailand, China, Japan, Belgium, Germany, Spain, United States, Netherlands and Cambodia (Table 11 - 3). Vietnam is the largest agricultural products export country in Laos. The largest agricultural exports by category were "fruit and nuts", with an export value of 170 million USD, followed by "vegetables and certain roots and tubers" with 110 million USD. The third place was for "coffee, tea, mate and spices", 100 million USD. In addition, "sugars and sugar confectionery", "cereals", "animals" exports were also large.

Table 11 - 3　Top 10 Countries of Lao Agricultural Products Exported in 2018

Serial number	Exported countries	Export value (USD)
1	Vietnam	50,803,567
2	Thailand	41,632,164
3	China	36,031,825

---

① Zheng Guofu, 2018. Characteristics and Prospects of Agricultural Trade in Laos [J]. Agricultural Outlook, 151 (4): 70-73.
② The ASEAN Secretariat, 2018. ASEAN Statistical Year Book [M]. The ASEAN Secretariat [2020-12-22]. www. asean. org.

(cont.)

Serial number	Exported countries	Export value (USD)
4	Japan	3,083,004
5	Belgium	1,814,491
6	Germany	749,896
7	Spain	382,580
8	United States	341,822
9	India	325,067
10	Cambodia	253,550

Note: Based on the 2 digits' code of HS, the data of goods trade (IMTS) was sorted out by selected data from HS (01 - 20).

Source: https://data. aseanstats. org.

The top 10 agricultural products import trade partners (ranked by the amount of import trade) of Laos in 2017 were Thailand, Vietnam, China, United States, India, Japan, Germany, Australia, Malaysia and Russian Federation (Table 11 - 4). The agricultural products imported by Laos from the ten countries account for 99.2% of its total agricultural products imports, with a significantly higher national concentration. Among them, the agricultural products imported from Thailand account for about 81% of the total import volume, significantly more than the number of other importing countries. In terms of import categories, the largest import value of agricultural products was "animals", with an import value 98.867 million USD, followed by "sugars and sugar confectionery" with 51.533 million USD. The third is "fruit and nuts", with 34.652 million USD. The import values of "products of the milling industry", "meat and edible meat offal", "preparations of cereals, flour, starch or milk" and "vegetables and certain roots and tubers" were also high.

Table 11 - 4　Top 10 Countries of Lao Agricultural Products Imported in 2018

Serial number	Imported countries	Import value（USD）
1	Thailand	261,303,622
2	Vietnam	27,086,030
3	China	20,525,818
4	United States	4,683,623
5	India	1,498,957
6	Japan	1,256,375
7	Germany	990,397
8	Australia	719,057
9	Malaysia	543,823
10	Russian Federation	441,307

Note：Based on the 2 digits' code of HS，the data of goods trade（IMTS）was sorted out by selected data from HS（01 - 20）.

Source：https：//data. aseanstats. org.

11. 2　Agricultural Investment Policy

11. 2. 1　Macro Policy

Laos is a traditional agricultural country，with agricultural production accounting for one third of Laos' national economy，and the overall agricultural productivity is relatively low. Since the establishment of the Lao People's Democratic Republic，the Lao People's Revolutionary Party and the Lao government have paid special attention to agricultural development. The government encourages cooperation with foreign enterprises. In February 2015，the Ministry of Agriculture and Forestry of Laos issued *Laos Agriculture Development Strategy 2025 and 2030 Vision*，which proposed to apply new agricultural technologies，integrate with market mechanism，promote the development of agriculture in the direction of clean and efficient, and move towards industrialization, modernization and international integration by 2030. Total investment in the agricultural and forestry sectors will reach 18.7 trillion LAK (23.375 billion USD) by 2025, of which private investment in domestic and foreign direct investment was 160 trillion LAK (about 20 billion USD), accounting for 85.56% of total investment (with an annual increase of 25%), domestic investment for 30% and foreign direct investment for 70%.

11. 2. 2　Legal System Related on Agriculture

The Lao government encourages foreign companies and individuals to invest in all sectors. The Investment Promotion Act was promulgated in 2009, and the Regulations on the Implementation of the Investment Promotion Act were promulgated in April 2011. The legal system of foreign investment in Laos is a complete legal system including a series of laws and regulations represented by the Investment Promotion Act, which expands the scope of concession for investors and maximizes the investment efficiency in Laos. By improving policies, planning and implementation mechanism, credit policies, tax exemption or reduction policies to attract foreign investment to agriculture and rural infrastructure, agricultural products processing, human resources training and market development, public service, etc., so as to improve domestic food and nutrition security, build sustainable products and the conditions of natural resources, enhance the ability of resistance to natural and other disaster risk.

The existing laws in the field of agriculture in Laos include: Constitution, Investment Promotion Act, Land Law, Agriculture Law, Contract and Tort Liability Law, Enterprise Law, Tax Law, Value Added Tax Law, Environmental Protection Laws, Customs Law, Wildlife and Aquatic Resources Law, Fisheries Law and Economic Dispute Resolution Law and other basic laws.

11. 2. 3   Market Access and Agricultural Products Trad System

(1) Legal and policy system of foreign investment management in agriculture

- Access system for foreign investors   The Investment Promotion Act sets up an access system for foreign investors, stipulating that foreign investors can invest through domestic or foreign sole investment, domestic and foreign joint ventures or contractual joint ventures. It requires foreigners to register general operating companies with a total capital of at least 1 billion LAK. Agricultural enterprises shall, within 90 working days after obtaining the enterprise registration certificate, contribute to complete 40% of the initial registered capital and make up within one year. If franchising is involved, a Special Purpose Company (SPC) should be set up with sign a franchise agreement with the government. The Investment Promotion Act and the List of Enterprises with Reservations for Lao Citizens, clearly provides the types of industries controlled exclusively by the government, the occupations reserved for Lao citizens, and the fields in which foreign citizens and legal persons cannot invest.

- Agricultural land system and policy   The Land Law stipulates that Laos implements public land ownership, and the law prohibits the purchase and sale land ownership. The transaction in the real estate market is only the transaction of land use rights. The state has the right to possess, use, profit from and dispose of all land in Laos. Foreigners and stateless persons who need to use land in Laos can only lease the land that has been granted the right to use from the Lao government and citizens and other organizations, with the approval of the local government authorities. Foreign-funded enterprises can lease land to operate in Laos, and the lease term shall not exceed 50 years, depending on the project, industry, scale and characteristics of the foreign investment, but it may be renewed as the government decides.

- Agricultural investment system and policy For foreign investment in grain products processing enterprises, the registered capital shall not be less than 1 billion LAK (about 800,000 CNY), and the proportion of foreign equity shall not be less than 20%. For projects related to agro-forestry, agro-forestry and handicrafts processing, the registered capital of the enterprise should be 2.1 million CNY or more. The Lao government has preferential tax policies for key industries. Depending on the remoteness of the investment area and the different conditions of economic and social infrastructure, investors can get 10 years, 15 years of tax exemption, on this basis, such as investment in clean, pollution-free agriculture, traditional characteristic handicraft processing industry can get another 4 years or 3 years of tax exemption. Special economic zones, industrial zones, border trade zones and special economic zones shall be governed by the special laws and regulations of each region.

- Foreign exchange management system and policy The Lao Foreign Exchange Management Law stipulates that the national bank of Laos pursues a loose monetary policy and implements foreign exchange control. The central bank supervises foreign exchange circulation in accordance with the law, and individuals or enterprises should use LAK within the territory of Laos. Loans and projects from foreign sources are subject to approval and permission, and exemptions under any laws or regulations usually require approval by Congress or the Standing Committee of the Parliament (for laws and enforcement ACTS) or the Prime Minister (for ordinary ACTS). The project sponsor must set up a limited liability company in Laos to host the project, and foreign entities are not allowed to have direct ownership of the project. Loans to foreign shareholders are subject to approval by the Lao People's Bank (BOL). Any registered capital (equity) is limited to registered capital injected through the Lao banking system (capital introduction certificate is required). The "Regulations on the Administration of Foreign Exchange and Precious Metals" stipulates that investors are not allowed to make loans to commercial banks in Laos until the registered capital has been paid in. The investors repatriating profits outside Laos requires prior approval from the national bank of Laos.

- Labor legal system and policy concerning agriculture   The current Lao People's Democratic Republic Labor Law adopted in 2013 is divided into 17 parts: general rules, labor skills training and development, promoting employment, labor protection, labor contract, female and child Labour, salary and wages, labor occupational safety and health, mobile labor, labor funds, labor information registration, banned terms, labor dispute settlement mechanism, tripartite organizations, labor management and supervision, rewards and punishment policy and Supplementary articles. There are regulations on the proportion of hiring foreign employees and handling of employment procedures.

(2) **Trade system of agricultural materials and products.** Laos was the last ASEAN country to join the World Trade Organization. In 2013, Laos obtained full membership and was granted exemption from import tariffs and other trade preferences by the European Union, the United States, and Japan. Its products can generally enter markets around the world at lower tariff rates.

Import and export matters in Laos are governed by the Customs Law and the Customs Bureau under the Ministry of Finance is the main law enforcement agency. Different commodities have different regulations in Laos' trade management. Laos has different regulations on different commodities in terms of trade management. Only companies registered in Laos can be permitted to import and export goods. Before importing or exporting goods, the company may need to apply for an import and export license. Laos adopts the commodity coordination system, and imports and some exports are subject to customs duties. In addition, all imports are subject to VAT, while exports are exempt from VAT. Laos' trade-related laws and regulations also include the Laos Contract and Tort Liability Law, Laos Fruit and Vegetable Quality Management Standards, Livestock and Product Technical Management Specifications, and Product Standard Law, etc.

11.3 Progress and Results of Lancang-Mekong Agricultural Cooperation

11.3.1 Main Progress

(1) **Participation in exchange activities of the Lancang-Mekong mechanism**[①]. Since the Lancang-Mekong Cooperation was formally established in 2016, Laos has actively participated in the co-construction of the mechanism and a series of exchange activities to promote agricultural cooperation among the six countries under the "3 + 5" cooperation framework. In addition to the consensus on agricultural cooperation under the top-level meetings mechanism such as the leaders' meeting and the foreign ministers' meetings, Laos has also participated in many exchange activities such as seminars, training and mutual visits in the field of agriculture under the framework of the Lancang-Mekong Cooperation

---

① According to the reports of participants from Laos on the Second Meeting of the Lancang-Mekong Cooperation (LMC) Joint Working Group on Agriculture in 2019.

(Table 11 - 5). In terms of international visits, for example, a delegation from the Global Center for Mekong Studies (GCMS) of Laos visited China in February 2019, during which the Lao delegation had in-depth exchanges with Chinese experts and scholars on such topics as Laos-China agricultural cooperation, water resources cooperation and how to construct the Lancang-Mekong river economic development belt.

Table 11 - 5 Participating in Seminars and Training Activities in Recent Years of Laos

Serial number	Activities	Date
1	Seminar on the Planning of Modern Agricultural Industrial Park and the Application of Agricultural Information Science	July 2018
2	Training Course on Scaled Raising of Livestock and Planting Technique of Feed Crop in Tropical Agriculture	August 2018
3	Training Course on One Village, One Product of Sustainable Development for Modern Agriculture	September 2018
4	Seminar on Plant Variety Protection for LMC Countries	October 2018
5	Workshop (the First Lancang-Mekong Water Resources Cooperation Forum) on Water Partnership for Sustainable Development (Kunming)	November 2018
6	Workshop on Lancang-Mekong Cooperation Special Fund (Beijing)	November 2018
7	Training on 2019 Lancang-Mekong Training Class on Modern Practical Agricultural Technology and Poverty Reduction Experiences	June 2019
8	Training on Coordination LMC	May 2019
9	Training Course on Modern Agricultural Technical Personnel in Laos and Training Course for Hybrid Rice Technical Personnel in Laos	September 2019
10	2019 Lancang-Mekong Agricultural Resources Cooperation Summit and Economic and Trade Fair	October 2019

(2) Implementation status of agricultural projects supported by Lancang-Mekong Cooperation Special Fund (LMCSF)[①]. In 2018, Laos

---

① According to the reports of participants from Laos on the Second Meeting of the Lancang-Mekong Cooperation (LMC) Joint Working Group on Agriculture in 2019.

applied for 8 agricultural projects to the LMCSF, of which three projects were approved and implemented, including "Capacity Building on Sharing and Technical Exchanges of Rural Development and Poverty Reduction under Lancang-Mekong Cooperation", "Joint Research Programme on the Impact of Community Driven Development Approach on Rural Development of CLMV plus China", "Regional Seminar on Poverty Reduction Through Community Driven Development Approach". In 2019, Laos submitted 15 agriculture-related projects to the LMCSF, focusing on rural development, poverty reduction, rural finance and agricultural cooperation.

(3) Agricultural cooperation with other LMC countries

① Agricultural cooperation with China

Agriculture is a key area of cooperation between Laos and China, and it is showing rapid development momentum, which has created a situation in which aids and investment, zone development projects and individual investment projects promote each other and develop together. In 2000, Laos and China signed *Memorandum of Understanding on Agricultural Cooperation* in Vientiane, marking the development of bilateral cooperation in the field of agriculture. In 2001, the two countries signed *Summary of Agricultural Cooperation* in Yunnan, further strengthening cooperation.

In recent years, China has provided Laos with gratuitous aids in many aspects of agriculture, including the introduction of varieties, agricultural technical training and the provision of agricultural equipment. For example, the "Laos-China Agricultural Technology Demonstration Center" undertaken by Yunnan enterprise and supported by the Yunnan Academy of Agricultural Sciences.

In terms of agricultural science and technology exchange, the two sides have carried out frequent exchange and cooperation in promoting the development of agricultural science and technology. One of the more widely used models is to set up research institutions, agricultural parks, agricultural bases and other cooperation platforms in Laos, sign cooperation agreements and further carry out agricultural science and technology cooperation on this basis. For example, Yunnan Province and Laos Louang Namtha Province signed *Framework Cooperation Agreement between the Agricultural and Rural Bureau of Xishuangbanna Dai Autonomous Prefecture of Yunnan Province and Department of Agriculture and Forestry of Louang Namtha Province*, established the Crops Joint Breeding Center, the Tropical and Subtropical Hybrid Maize Engineering Research Center, the Low Latitude Plateau Hybrid Corn Industrialization Engineering Research Center in Laos Louang Namtha Province, and carried out the new varieties of corn test, demonstration, production test, tropical pomelo technical guidance and technical exchange, etc. At the China-ASEAN Technology Fair in 2014, Guangxi Subtropical Crops Research Institute and the Lao National Agricultural and Forestry Research Institute signed an agreement on cooperation in agricultural science and technology to jointly develop a demonstration base for tropical agricultural science and technology in Saravan Province, Laos. Besides, cooperative research was strengthened in tropical fruit technology, including genetics, biotechnology, breeding, planting and post-harvest technologies. In addition, the Laos-China Chongqing Comprehensive Agricultural Park was jointly established by Chongqing Foreign Trade and Economic Commission and the Department of Agriculture and Forestry of Vientiane of Laos, Trial Planting Base of New Fruits and Vegetables of China was jointly established by Guangxi Zhuang Autonomous Region and Champasak Province, Agricultural Science and Technology Demonstration Park was jointly established by Yunnan Province and Oudomoxay Province, Agricultural and Forestry Demonstration Base and Agro-forestry Testing-Scientific Research Center was jointly established by Henan Changjiu Agricultural Technology Co., Ltd. and Lao National University, etc.

In recent years, agricultural investment cooperation between Laos and

China has gradually increased, mainly investing in rubber, traditional Chinese medicine, cassava, rice, sugar cane, eucalyptus and pig breeding. By the end of 2017, there were about 80 Chinese enterprises investing in agriculture in Laos[1]. For example, Yunnan Changshengda Co., Ltd., Chongqing Energy Investment Import & Export Co., Ltd., and Phongsali Province of Laos signed a cooperation agreement on the development of coffee base in 2016 on the base of the previous cooperation. The project reduced poppy cultivation and poverty by creating employment and promote local farmers' income generation[2]. Hunan Xuanye (Laos) Co., Ltd. invested in rice cultivation in Laos and gained access to the Chinese market in 2015. Yunnan State Farms Group Yunxiang Company has developed the rubber planting and processing industry in northern Laos. By 2018, it has 21 production bases totaling 130,000 mu of rubber forest in four provinces in northern Laos, driving the development of 500,000 mu of rubber forest, and it has built four rubber processing plants with an annual output of 100,000 tons.

The Action Plan on Building a China-Laos Community of Common Destiny clearly states that it is necessary to vigorously strengthen the people's livelihood and poverty reduction cooperation, and promote Laos to get rid of underdevelopment situation as soon as possible. China and Laos have taken a series of effective measures in their cooperation on poverty reduction. For example, a poverty reduction demonstration project was implemented in one village in Vientiane and one in Luang Prabang, involving 16 subprojects covering infrastructure, public services

---

① Department of International Cooperation, Foreign Economic Cooperation Center, Ministry of Agriculture and Rural Affairs, 2018. Analysis Report on China's Agricultural Outbound Investment Cooperation (2018) [M]. Beijing: China Agriculture Press.

② Anonymity, 2019. Yunnan Enterprise will Build Asia's Largest Coffee Base in Laos [N/OL]. Kunming Daily, 07-28 [2020-12-22]. http://news.eastday.com/eastday/13news/auto/news/world/20160728/u7ai5876667.html.

and farmers' livelihoods. Laos Vientiane City Jinhua Village Industry Demonstration Projects of Poverty Reduction implemented by the Guangxi Foreign Investment Project Management Center, has successfully launched a greenhouse organic vegetable planting demonstration in Jinhua Village through cooperation with enterprises. The completed I phase of the project has increased farmers' annual income by between 10,000 and 20,000 CNY, greatly increased the income of local farmers, and played a good driving role. In December 2016, the East Asia Poverty Reduction Cooperation Demonstration Project was Launched in Vientiane, Laos, which improved the production and living conditions of villagers in the project area and increased the development vitality of villages.

② Agricultural cooperation with Cambodia

Agricultural cooperation between Laos and Cambodia is detailed in the Cambodian chapter of this book (10.3.1).

③ Agricultural cooperation with Myanmar

In 2008, Myanmar cooperated with Laos to implement a small-scale inland fish farming program, which was funded by Japan for three years. The two countries have also maintained cooperation in cross-border rubber cultivation. Laos and Myanmar have little cooperation and exchanges in the field of agriculture, and there will be greater development space for cooperation between the two countries in the future.

④ Agricultural cooperation with Thailand

Thailand is one of the major trading countries of agricultural products in Laos and the largest importer of agricultural products in Laos. In 2017, 87.5% of agricultural products in Laos came from Thailand. The main agricultural products include sugar, grains, farmed animals and fruits. In March 2013, Laos and Thailand signed a memorandum of understanding on agricultural cooperation, under which Thailand will plant sweet corn, sesame, chestnut, castor bean, soybean, peanut, mung bean, cassava, eucalyptus and feed corn in Laos. The signing of the memorandum of cooperation provides Thailand with more convenience in importing agricultural products from Laos[1].

⑤ Agricultural Cooperation with Vietnam

Laos-Vietnam has established diplomatic relations for 55 years. In recent years, both sides have made good progress in agricultural investment, cooperation exchange at the government and enterprise levels. In February 2019, leaders of Laos and Vietnam signed 9 cooperation agreements, including *Memorandum of Transfer by the Government of Laos and Vietnam on the Construction of the Agricultural Technology Center in Houaphanh Province*. In June 2019, the ministries of planning and investment of Laos and Vietnam held an exchange meeting in Vientiane, and signed a cooperation agreement between the two ministries from 2019 to 2021. At the meeting, Nguyen Chi Dung, Minister of Planning and Investment of Vietnam, proposed that the two countries should focus on promoting agriculture and tourism in the future.

Vietnam is the largest exporter of agricultural products in Laos. Laos mainly exports sugar, coffee, grains and fruits to Vietnam, and the Vietnamese market occupies an important position in the foreign trade of agricultural products of Laos. Agricultural investment cooperation between the two countries has also increased in recent years. For example, Dao-Heuang Group, the largest corporate group in Laos, signed a cooperation agreement with Vietnam Blue Star Distribution Co., Ltd. to distribute Vietnamese coffee products[2]. The provincial government of Champasak in Laos has signed a cooperation agreement with the Vietnam Coffee Corporation to grow coffee on the Boloven Plateau, which not only promotes investment cooperation between Vietnam and Laos, but also

---

① Anonymity, 2013. Thailand and Laos Sign Memorandum on Agricultural Cooperation [J]. World Tropical Agriculture Information (3): 12.

② Gu Xiaoling, 2014. Vietnam Signs New Trade Deal with Laos' Company [J]. World Tropical Agriculture Information (5): 20-21.

provides employment opportunities for thousands of local workers and helps southern Laos accelerate its poverty reduction and enrichment program[①].

11. 3. 2 Results and Experience

(1) **Actively participating in Lancang-Mekong agricultural cooperation.** In June 2019, the Lao Ministry of Agriculture and Forestry participated in the second meeting of the Lancang-Mekong cooperation joint working group on agriculture, held in Cambodia, exchanged views with other LMC countries on major issues of promoting the rapid development of Lancang-Mekong agricultural cooperation, reached a series of consensus and expressed willingness to hold the third meeting of the Lancang-Mekong joint working group on agriculture in 2020. In January 2018, the Lao Ministry of Agriculture and Forestry officially nominated the leader and members of the agricultural joint working group. It laid a solid foundation for the establishment and improvement of the Lancang-Mekong cooperation mechanism and the implementation of *Three-Year Action Plan for MLC Agricultural Cooperation* (2020 – 2022).

(2) **Orderly promoting the application and implementation of LMCSF projects.** Laos has applied for 23 agricultural projects to the LMCSF, including 8 in 2018 and 15 in 2019. The number of agricultural projects approved by Laos increased in 2019, nearly doubling the number of applications in 2018, covering a wider range and increasing attention to rural finance, services and business models.

(3) **Deepening agricultural cooperation with LMC countries.** Laos is the only landlocked country in Southeast Asia. In terms of import and export volume, Laos has the lowest foreign trade volume among the six

---

① Anonymity, 2013. Vietnam and Laos Cooperate to Develop Coffee Production and Export [J]. World Tropical Agriculture Information (11): 26-27.

LMC countries and has little advantage in price. However, with the deepening of Laos' opening up to the outside world, the trade volume of agricultural products has been increasing year by year and the foreign trade has been continuously strengthened. Since the first special economic zone was established in 2002, Laos now has developed 12 special economic zones, with about 351 companies and a total investment of 1. 6 billion USD. The Lao government actively attracts investment and strives to improve the investment environment of the existing special economic zones and economic zones. These special economic zones and economic zones have generated revenue for the government and created jobs for the Lao people[1]. In addition, since the establishment of the MLC mechanism, Laos has gradually deepened its exchanges and cooperation with other MLC countries, and agricultural products trade, agricultural technology and rural development have been improved.

(Written by Rui Yanlan and Guo Wen,

Translated by Guo Wen,

International Agriculture Research Institute,

Yunnan Academy of Agricultural Sciences, China)

---

[1] Yang Zhuojuan, 2018. Laos' Role in Lancang-Mekong Cooperation [J]. Asia-pacific Security and Maritime Studies (2): 100-110.

12 Agricultural Development and the Progress of Lancang-Mekong Agricultural Cooperation in Myanmar[①]

12.1 Overview of Agricultural Development

12.1.1 Resources and Development

(1) **Resources and main agricultural products.** Myanmar is located in the western part of Indochina Peninsula, connected with China, Laos, Thailand, Bangladesh and India, bordering on the Bay of Bengal and Andaman Sea, and facing the international golden waterway "Malacca Strait" to the south. The land area is 676,552 square kilometers and arable land of more than 180,000 square kilometers. Currently, only 120,600 square kilometers of land is used for crop cultivation. Myanmar has a tropical monsoon climate with little change in temperature throughout the year. Most areas are located in the south of the Tropic of Cancer, with an annual average temperature of 27°C. The rainfall is abundant, with 500-1,000 mm in inland dry areas, and 3,000-5,000 mm in mountainous and coastal rainy areas.

Rice, beans and sesame are the three major crops in Myanmar. Rice is the most important and largest export crop in Myanmar. The Ayeyarwaddy River Delta, the Sittaung River Valley, and the Irrawaddy

---

① Supported by the Ministry of Agriculture, Livestock and Irrigation of Myanmar.

River Basin in Sagaing Region are the main rice producing areas. In addition, rubber is also the main crop. Theninthayi State, Mon State, Kayin State, Ayeyarwaddy Region, Yangon Region, Rakhine State and Bago Region are major rubber producing areas. According to the data of the FAO, the top ten crops harvested in Myanmar in 2018 were shown in Table 12 - 1.

Table 12 - 1   The Yield and Planting Area of Major Crops in Myanmar in 2018

Serial number	Variety of crops	Area harvested (hectare)	Yield (ton)	Yield per unit area (kg/hectare)
1	Rice, paddy	7,149,311	27,573,589	3,856.8
2	Beans, dry	3,165,311	5,592,419	1,766.8
3	Sesame seed	1,491,788	715,437	479.6
4	Groundnuts, with shell	1,057,482	1 562,428	1,477.5
5	Maize	519,227	1,984,136	3,821.3
6	Pigeon peas	444,450	358,545	806.7
7	Fruit, fresh nes	402,021	1,433,845	3,566.6
8	Chick peas	382,578	534,602	1,397.4
9	Rubber, natural	329,702	275,487	835.6
10	Vegetables, fresh nes	286,948	3,798,803	13,238.6

Source: Ministry of Agriculture, Livestock and Irrigation of Myanmar.

Husbandry occupies a very important proportion of agriculture and is dominated by family feeding in Myanmar. The main livestock raised in 2018 were chicken, duck, cattle, pig, sheep and horse (Table 12 - 2). Among them, the annual chicken and duck breeding volume reached more than 300 million, and Myanmar also vigorously developed cattle and sheep breeding in recent years.

Myanmar has more than 2,230 kilometers of coastline, 486,000 square kilometers of exclusive economic zone for fishing waters and 8.1 million square kilometers of inland waters. The main fisheries are: aquaculture, leasing fisheries, open fisheries and marine fisheries, of which marine fishery production accounts for more than half of Myanmar's overall fishery production, and aquaculture accounts for about one fifth[①].

Table 12 - 2　Basic Situation of Myanmar Animal Husbandry in 2018

Serial number	Name of the livestock and poultry	Breeding quantity (head)
1	Chicken	361,243,000
2	Duck	28,407,000
3	Cattle	21,786,000
4	Pig	19,779,000
5	Goat	11,051,000
6	Horse	96,811

Source: Ministry of Agriculture, Livestock and Irrigation of Myanmar.

(2) Current status of agricultural development. Myanmar has gradually become one of the fastest economy growing countries in Asia, with GDP growth reaching 8.4% in 2016 and 5.9% in 2017, becoming one of the most attractive countries for foreign investment[②]. The Myanmar government attaches great importance to agricultural development. Agriculture is the leading force in the development of the national economy. Agriculture-based industries play an important role in the country. About 70% of the domestic population is directly or indirectly engaged in agricultural production. Although the scale of agriculture is expanding, the development of agriculture in Myanmar is relatively slow. According to the World Bank statistics, the average annual growth rate of Myanmar's agricultural value added from 2000 to 2009 was 11%, but the

---

① Miao Miao, Chen Jun, Liu Huang, et al, 2019. Potential Analysis and Development Strategy of Fishery Cooperation between China and Myanmar by the view of the Belt and Road Initiative [J]. Tropical Agriculture Science (8): 104 - 110.

② Yang Derong, Zeng Zhiwei, Zhou Long, 2018. Analysis of Agricultural Development in Myanmar [J]. Marketing Industry, 504. (22): 3943.

growth rate from 2010 to 2018 slowing down was just 2%. The proportion of agricultural added value in Myanmar's GDP continued to decline, from 58% in 2000 to 22% in 2017 and back to 25% in 2018 (Figure 12 - 1).

In order to promote the development of agricultural economy and improve the environment and conditions of agricultural production, Myanmar government and agricultural departments issued a series of agricultural development policies in recent years, to encourage the development of private enterprises, seek international cooperation and find technical support.

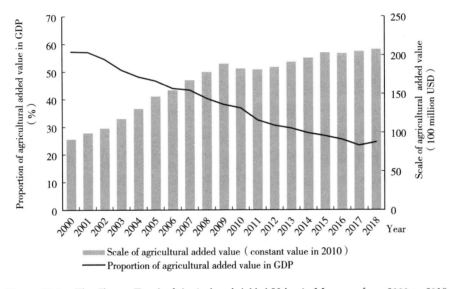

Figure 12-1　The Change Trend of Agricultural Added Value in Myanmar from 2000 to 2018

Source: https://data. worldbank. org. cn.

12. 1. 2　Import and Export Trade of Agricultural Products

From 2018 to 2019, Myanmar's total foreign trade volume reached 29. 211 billion USD. Among them, the export was 14. 047 billion USD and the import was 15. 164 billion USD. The export of agricultural products is 2. 815 billion USD, livestock products 329 million USD, aquatic products 642 million USD and forest products 143 million USD[①].

Myanmar's biggest export crop is rice, and it is the fifth largest rice exporter in the world. It exported 1.7 million tons in 2016 – 2017, and nearly 3.6 million tons in 2017 – 2018, with reached a record. From 2018 to 2019, Myanmar has exported more than 2 million tons of rice (including broken rice), earning over 570 million USD. Among them, China and other neighboring countries accounted for 32.89%, EU countries accounted for 21.03%, African countries accounted for 26.04%, and other countries accounted for 20.04%[②]. Beans are the second largest export commodity of Myanmar, with a total export volume of 1.32 million tons and an export volume of 887 million USD from 2017 to 2018. Sesame is the third largest export crop, mainly exported to Japan, South Korea and China. In addition to the above crops, Myanmar rubber is also one of the important export crops, with 90% of the total export of rubber destined for China.

Myanmar's top 10 agricultural products export trade partners are shown in Table 12 – 3. The total value of agricultural exports to the ten countries accounted for 87.87% of the total agricultural exports.

The top 10 agricultural products import trade partners are shown in Table 12 – 4. Myanmar imports 1.735 billion USD of agricultural products from the ten countries, accounting for 93.50% of the total. The agricultural products with the largest import volume are: sugar and confectionery, animal and vegetable fats and their decomposed products, cereals, grain flour, cakes and snacks; malt, starch, inulin, wheat

---

① Anonymity, 2019. Myanmar's Imports and Exports Fell in the First 10 Months Compared with the Same Period Last Year [N/OL]. (Myanmar) Mirror, 08-21 [2020-12-22]. http://www.sohu.com/a/335661078_99924424.

② Myanmar Rice Association, 2019. Export of Rice (including Broken Rice) in Myanmar in 2019 [N/OL]. Light of Myanmar, 08-06 [2020-12-22]. https://finance.sina.com.cn/money/future/agri/2019-08-08/doc-ihytcerm9383243.shtml.

bran and other industrial products. Other import products are dairy products, eggs, natural honey, edible vegetables, roots, edible fruits, nuts, grains and so on.

Table 12 - 3   Top 10 Countries of Myanmar Agricultural Products Exported in 2018

Serial number	Exported countries	Export value (USD)
1	China	2,790,725,328
2	India	410,236,263
3	Thailand	324,190,432
4	Singapore	130,320,587
5	Belgium	80,973,069
6	Bangladesh	75,856,597
7	Côte d'Ivoire	59,523,649
8	Guinea	56,781,175
9	Japan	54,845,794
10	Malaysia	47,201,066

Note: Based on the 2 digits' code of HS, the data of goods trade (IMTS) was sorted out by selected data from HS (01 - 20).

Source: https://data. aseanstats. org.

Table 12 - 4   Top 10 Countries of Myanmar Agricultural Products Imported in 2018

Serial number	Imported countries	Import value (USD)
1	Indonesia	558,712,745
2	Thailand	460,450,204
3	India	204,106,381
4	Malaysia	140,818,218
5	Australia	101,686,303
6	China	86,353,902
7	Pakistan	72,874,817
8	Singapore	50,743,060
9	New Zealand	33,367,021
10	Viet Nam	26,854,816

Note: Based on the 2 digits' code of HS, the data of goods trade (IMTS) was sorted out by selected data from HS (01 - 20).

Source: https://data. aseanstats. org.

12. 2   Agricultural Investment Policy

12. 2. 1   Macro Policy

In order to achieve the goal of transforming Myanmar's traditional agricultural economy into a productive and sustainable agricultural economy, the Myanmar government encourages the public and foreign enterprises to invest in agriculture, puts agriculture and related services, agricultural products value-added industry at the top ten priority investments, and lists animal husbandry and aquaculture as the second of the top ten priority investments. At the same time, as agricultural production materials, such as chemical fertilizers and agricultural machinery, etc., heavily rely on imports, the Myanmar government encourages investment in alternative manufacturing industries, such as encouraging the construction of chemical fertilizer factories and agricultural machinery factories, etc. As for forestry, although it is not among the top ten priority investments, the Myanmar government has adopted investment laws to include forest plantation and protection and other forest-related businesses into the scope of encouraged investment. The Myanmar government has made great efforts to improve the investment environment, by actively attracting foreign investment and promulgating an investment law to protect the rights and interests of investors under the requirements of macro agricultural policies. In order to improve work efficiency, the Investment Committee has been re-established to complete the examination and approval of foreign capital investment in a short period of time in a quick one-stop service mode. In addition, the exchange rate system has been adjusted to stabilize the exchange rate and reduce the foreign exchange risk of investors.

12. 2. 2   Legal System Related on Agriculture

Myanmar has a far-reaching common law tradition. At present, only the

Myanmar Ministry of Agriculture, Livestock and Irrigation has promulgated 24 laws and 155 regulations, mainly including: Seed Law, Freshwater Culture Law, Fishery Culture Law, Animal Health and Development Law, Veterinary Law and other agricultural laws and regulations.

The laws and regulations related to agricultural materials in Myanmar include: Farmland Law; Vacant, Fallow, and Virgin Lands Management Law; Special Economic Zone Law; Investment Law; Aquaculture Law; Freshwater Fisheries Law; Seawater Fisheries Law; Seed Law; Pesticide Law; Fertilizer Law, etc. The laws and regulations related to production and operation include Company Law, Partnership Law, Special Company Law and State-owned Economic Enterprise Law, etc. The laws and regulations related to the circulation of agricultural products include Commodity sales law, etc. Agriculture-related protection systems include Environmental Protection Law, Detailed Rules for the Implementation of Environmental Protection Law, and standards related to environmental protection, etc.

12. 2. 3   Market Access and Agricultural Trade System

(1) **Legal and policy system of foreign investment management in agriculture**

- Access system for foreign investors   The investment-restricted industries released in April 2017 are divided into four categories: those that are only allowed to be operated by the state, those that are prohibited from being operated by foreign investors, those that can only be operated by joint ventures with local enterprises, and those that can only be operated with the approval of relevant departments. 12 industries prohibited from foreign investment include: Freshwater fishery and related services, establishment of animal import and export quarantine stations (animal husbandry and veterinary departments are responsible for animal inspection and licensing), pet care, forest production in forest areas and natural forest areas managed by the government, small supermarkets and convenience stores (covering an area of less than 929 square meters), etc. There are a total of 22 industries that can only be operated by foreign companies in joint ventures with local enterprises, agriculture-related fields include: construction of fishery docks and fishery markets, fishery-related investigation activities, veterinary clinics, agricultural cultivation, sales and export, some foods production and processing, etc. There are 10 categories of industries that must be approved by relevant departments, of which 18 types are required to be approved by the Ministry of Agriculture, Livestock and Irrigation. It involves many fields such as planting, breeding, fishery, pesticide and fertilizer, etc. A total of 15 types of investments have been approved by the Ministry of Natural Resources and Environmental Protection, including agricultural forest land, timber, transgenic organisms and living organisms, pearl cultivation, etc. And the investment involving import and export should also conform to the relevant policies of the Ministry of Commerce.

- System and policy for the sale and lease of agricultural land and houses   According to Myanmar laws, foreigners and foreign investors cannot acquire ownership of Myanmar land, but they can use the land through leases. According to the Myanmar Investment Law, investors can lease land and buildings with the Myanmar government, enterprises and individuals. Investors in special economic zones can use the land and buildings for 75 years by leasing, while investors can use the land and buildings outside the special economic zones for 70 years by leasing.

- Financing system and policy in agriculture-related fields   There are very limited ways of financing in Myanmar. Small and medium-sized enterprises and most foreign-funded enterprises in Myanmar rarely obtain loans from Myanmar banks. Myanmar enterprises usually obtain loans through private usury, and most foreign-funded enterprises get loans from overseas financial institutions or parent companies, etc. According to the Foreign Exchange Management Law, all domestic and foreign-funded companies that have registered with the Myanmar Investment Commission and the Bureau of Investment and Corporate Affairs, can only borrow money from foreign banks or financial institutions after obtaining the prior examination and approval of the Myanmar Central Bank.

- Foreign exchange management system and policy Myanmar has not yet completely lifted its foreign exchange control, but with the opening-up, the freedom of foreign exchange in and out of Myanmar has increased compared with previous years, and foreign enterprises can remit US dollars into Myanmar through banks. According to the Foreign Exchange Management Law, foreigners or foreign-funded companies can open foreign exchange accounts with the authorization of relevant departments. Foreign investors may remit funds related to investment that meet the relevant regulations out of the country.

- Legal system and policy of agriculture related labor Myanmar has a sound legal system, and the trade unions have strong legal awareness. Myanmar's Labor Law pays special attention to the protection of labor rights and interests. The Myanmar Special Economic Zone Law (2014) and its implementing rules also stipulate that the proportion of Myanmar employees employed in the first year shall not be less than 25%, in the second year not less than 50%, and in the third year not less than 75%. However, it is stipulated that investors may not be restricted by the employment ratio with the approval of the Administrative Committee. In

Myanmar, all employers must sign labor contracts with employees and insure employees in accordance with laws and regulations. In addition, the employer shall pay the corresponding severance to the employee for his dismissal.

(2) **Trade system of agricultural materials and products.** The current laws and regulations related to trade management include: Relevant Provisions of the Ministry of Trade of Myanmar on Importers and Exporters Must Obey and Understand (1989); the Myanmar Import and Export Law (2012); the Provisions of the Union of Myanmar on Border Trade (1991); the Implementation Detailed Rules of Import and Export Trade of the Union of Myanmar (1992); Amendment Act of the Union of Myanmar on Import and Export Trade (1992); the Tariff Law and the latest regulatory documents of Myanmar's Ministry of Commerce, etc.

12.3 Progress and Results of Lancang-Mekong Agricultural Cooperation

12.3.1 Main Progress

(1) **Participating in exchange activities of the Lancang-Mekong cooperation mechanism.** Myanmar has actively participated in various exchanges under the LMC mechanism, including leaders' meetings, foreign ministers' meetings, senior officials' meetings, the agriculture joint working group meetings, as well as various agricultural forums and training activities. In 2019, led by the Ministry of Commerce and the Poverty Alleviation Office of the State Council of China, the China International Poverty Alleviation Center organized relevant experts to go to Myanmar to select suitable villages, and carried out agricultural poverty reduction demonstration cooperation projects by teaching greenhouse organic vegetables and organic rice planting technology. It launched an agricultural poverty reduction demonstration cooperation project. In March 2019, the "Lancang-Mekong Week" was held in Naypyitaw, the

capital of Myanmar, and the awareness of Lancang-Mekong cooperation was further enhanced in Myanmar.

(2) **Implementation status of agricultural projects supported by Lancang-Mekong Cooperation Special Fund (LMCSF)**[①]. On November 28, 2017, Myanmar and China signed the first batch of 10 projects supported by LMCSF with a budget of 2.4 million USD, including five agricultural projects with a total budget of 1.092,9 million USD. The implementation period is 2018 – 2020. These special fund projects involve the improvement of coffee quality, agricultural product processing technology training, etc. At present, the special fund projects are being implemented smoothly. The highest use of project funds has been completed 78.21%, with an average of 37%. This batch of projects covers many areas in Myanmar, mainly for farmers in the selected areas to carry out discussion and exchange information meetings, processing and other infrastructure construction, technical training and establishment demonstration bases. Through the batch of special fund projects, the transformation of Myanmar's fruit and vegetable products from small-scale private markets to large-scale international import and export trades has been promoted, and it has also innovated the operation mode of international cooperation in agriculture, promoted the development of agriculture, and raised the level of agricultural technology in Myanmar.

On January 23, 2019, representatives of China and Myanmar signed the agreement on the second batch of Myanmar projects of LMCSF in Naypyitaw. China will provide support to Myanmar for 19 small and medium-sized projects involving agriculture, education and other fields, including 7 agricultural projects with a budget about 3.28 million USD. Compared with the first batch of LMCSF projects, this batch of projects

---

① According to the reports of participants from Myanmar on the Second Meeting of the Lancang-Mekong Cooperation (LMC) Joint Working Group on Agriculture in 2019.

involves a wider scope, more radiation regions, and deeper levels of cooperation. This batch of cooperation projects will target at the sericulture, rubber, high-quality germplasm resource collection demonstration, and fishery and animal husbandry cooperation. Myanmar has received all the budget in May 2019, and currently 7 agricultural special fund cooperation projects are going on smoothly. These projects aim at strengthening the cooperation between Myanmar and China and other LMC countries, increasing the infrastructure needed for Myanmar to establish a biotechnology laboratory, providing high-quality germplasm resources, establishing research and development centers, improving the quality of Myanmar's agricultural products, carrying out agricultural technology training, boosting the level of agricultural product processing technology, effectively preventing and controlling the spread of animal and plant diseases, and strengthening the use of network informationization.

(3) Agricultural cooperation with other LMC countries

① Agricultural cooperation with China

China is Myanmar's largest trading partner and source of investment. The total amount of agricultural trade between the two countries in 2015 was 355 million USD; compared with 72 million USD in 2006, the growth rate in ten years was 393.06%[①]. Rice is the main trade crop, according to the Myanmar Rice Union (MRF), MRF and COFCO (China Oil & Foodstuffs Corporation) have reached an agreement, and Myanmar will export 100,000 tons rice to China in 2019. Beans are the second largest crop in China's demand on Myanmar. From 2018 to 2019, Myanmar exported more than 470,000 tons of mung beans to foreign countries, with more than 340 million USD (about 515.1 billion MMK), of which China accounted for more than 100,000 tons and accounts for 21%. In 2017, the General Administration of Customs of China and Ministry of Agriculture, Livestock and Irrigation of

---

① Data Source: https://archives.un.org.

Myanmar effectively cooperated to remove barriers of market access for six kinds agricultural products, including flue-cured tobacco, apples and pears, and successfully promoted the export to Myanmar of three kinds of flowers, namely rose, lily and carnation in 2018. In September 2019, the governments of China and Myanmar signed a protocol on plant inspection and quarantine for the export of Myanmar rice and corn to China, which solved the access problem of Myanmar rice and corn export to China. At present, the competent authorities of China and Myanmar are actively promoting the inspection and quarantine of some Myanmar agricultural and livestock products and their export to China. In the future, more Myanmar high-quality agricultural products will enter Chinese market.

In November 2014, the Ministry of Livestock, Fisheries and Rural Development of Myanmar and the Ministry of Agriculture of China jointly signed *Memorandum of Understanding on Livestock and Fisheries Cooperation between China and Myanmar*, which promoted the further development of China-Myanmar agricultural cooperation.

② Agricultural cooperation with Thailand

In March 2017, the Joint Working Committee on the Myanmar-Thailand Border Trade reached a resolution to jointly develop trade between the two countries and focus on developing border trade. They decided to set up a Single Stop Inspection (SSI) to facilitate customs clearance of goods between the two countries. At the same time, Myanmar's representatives put forward a request to export rubber to Thailand, hoping that Thailand will give more relaxed management measures. Thai representatives promised to study and try to provide more convenient conditions under the premise of inspection in accordance with Thai quarantine standards[1]. On September 3, 2019, Thailand Prime Minister and Defense Minister Bayu met Myanmar Defense

---

[1] Business Office of the Consulate General in Chiang Mai, 2017. Strengthen Border Trade Cooperation Thailand and Myanmar Will Set Up a Single Stop Inspection [EB/OL]. http://chiangmai. mofcom. gov. cn/article/jmxw/201703/20170302541489. shtml.

Force Commander-in-Chief Min Aung Hlaing in Bangkok. The two sides agreed to work together to solve the border problem and strengthen cooperation in maritime security and fishery[①].

③ Agricultural cooperation with Vietnam

On August 25, 2017, Myanmar and Vietnam issued a joint statement in Naypyitaw, the capital of Myanmar, and decided to establish a comprehensive partnership. In the future, the two sides will focus on the cooperation in transportation infrastructure and tourism, and expand cooperation in agriculture, forestry, telecommunications and banking, and take measures to improve the investment environment and encourage mutual investment[②]. In 2018, the two countries held an enterprise meeting at Yangon Federation of Industry and Commerce, indicating that in the future the two countries' enterprises will strengthen cooperation in agriculture and rural development, rubber and other fields. According to the data of the Chamber of Commerce and Industry, Vietnam invested in 20 projects in Myanmar in 2018, with the investment amount reaching 2.106 billion USD, ranking the seventh among the countries and regions invested in Myanmar, of which agricultural investment increased significantly compared with previous years.

④ Agricultural cooperation with Cambodia

Agricultural cooperation between Mynamar and Cambodia is detailed in the Cambodian chapter of this book (10.3.1).

⑤ Agricultural cooperation with Laos

Agricultural cooperation between Mynamar and Laos is detailed in the

---

① Wang Guoan, 2019. Thailand and Myanmar Agreed to Work Together to Solve the Border Problem [EB/OL]. (09-03) [2020-12-22]. https://www.chinanews.com/gj/2019/09-03/8946459.shtml.

② Tu Bin, 2017. Myanmar and Vietnam Agreed to Establish a Comprehensive Partnership [EB/OL]. (08-26) [2020-12-22]. http://news.cri.cn/20170826/51534702-8f24-e07f-8eac-32d0344c3995.html.

Lao chapter of this book (11. 3. 1).

12. 3. 2 Results and Experience

Since the launch of Lancang-Mekong cooperation, Myanmar has been continuously expanding its cooperation with the other LMC countries and has achieved great results. The implementation of LMC Special Fund projects has greatly promoted the development of agriculture in Myanmar. For example, the Myanmar Coffee Production and Quality Improvement Project has made Myanmar's coffee industry accelerate its pace with the world. After the implementation of the Coffee Production Increase Project, the output and quality of coffee have been greatly improved, which has further increased Myanmar's coffee exports and increased the income of coffee farmers. Meanwhile, focusing on the five priority areas of Lancang-Mekong cooperation, Myanmar has gradually strengthened its ties with other Lancang Mekong countries and comprehensively promoted Myanmar's economic development.

(Written by Xu Lu and Li Lu, Translated by Xu Lu,
International Agriculture Research Institute,
Yunnan Academy of Agricultural Sciences, China)

13 | Agricultural Development and the Progress of Lancang-Mekong Agricultural Cooperation in Thailand

13. 1　Overview of Agricultural Development

13. 1. 1　Resources and Development

(1) **Resources and main agricultural products.** Thailand is located in the central Indochina Peninsula, bordering Myanmar in the northwest and west, Laos in the northeast, Cambodia in the east and Malaysia in the south. It faces the gulf of Thailand in the southeast and Andaman Sea in the southwest, with a coastline of about 2,705 kilometers and a land area of 513,100 square kilometers. Most of the whole area is low and sloping gently mountains and plateaus, which are divided into four regions: the mountainous forests in the north, the semi-arid farmlands in the northeastern plateau, the vast rice fields in the central plains, and the tropical islands in the southern peninsula. The total agricultural land area in Thailand is 221,100 square kilometers, accounting for 43.09% of the country's total land area. Among them, the arable land covers an area of 168,100 square kilometers, permanent crops land of 45,000 square kilometers, permanent pasture 8,000 square kilometers[①]. Forests cover

---

　① The ASEAN Secretariat, 2018. ASEAN Statistical Year Book 2018 [M]. The ASEAN Secretariat [2020-12-22]. www. asean. org.

144,000 square kilometers, accounting for 28% of the total land area, and the main timber resources are rubber and eucalyptus. Thailand has a tropical monsoon climate, and the seasons are clearly divided: hot season from March to June, rainy season from July to October, dry season from November to March. The average annual temperature is 24 - 30℃, and the average annual precipitation is about 1,000 mm, with abundant rainfall. In 2018, rural population accounted for 50.05% of the total population of 69,428,500, and agricultural employment accounted for 30.67% of the total[1].

Agricultural production in Thailand are based on abundant natural resources. Planting industry is the most important part of Thai agriculture, and it has been developing towards diversification, forming a comprehensive planting industry with five major crops, rice, rubber, sugarcane, cassava and maize, supplemented by oil palm, tropical fruits, vegetables and flowers. Among them, rice is the most important crop in Thailand, with paddy fields accounting for 52.0% of the country's arable land, and farmers engaged in rice production accounting for 77.5% of the total, with an output of more than 30 million tons[2]. Thai rice enjoys a high reputation in the international market, and Thailand enjoys the reputation as "Southeast Asia Granary". Natural rubber is the second largest crop in Thailand, with 52 of the country's 77 provinces planting rubber. The country's output is about 4.6 million tons, and its export volume has been the world's largest for many years. Sugarcane is one of the main cash crops in Thailand, with an annual output of more than 100 million tons, ranking among the top in the world. According to the data sources of the Food and Agriculture Organization of the United Nations (FAO), the top 10 crops harvested in Thailand in 2018 are shown in Table 13 - 1.

---

① Data source: https://data.worldbank.org.cn.
② Wang Yu, Li Zhemin, Yong Xi, et al, 2017. Current Situation and Prospects of Agricultural Development in Thailand [J]. Journal of Agriculture (11): 100-105.

Table 13 - 1   The Yield and Planting Area of Major Crops in Thailand in 2018

Serial number	Variety of crops	Area harvested (hectare)	Yield (ton)	Yield per unit area (kg/hectare)
1	Rice	10,647,941	32,348,114	3,038.0
2	Natural rubber	3,203,696	4,813,527	1,502.5
3	Sugarcane	1,790,208	135,073,799	75,451.5
4	Cassava	1,332,379	29,368,185	22,041.9
5	Corn	1,103,147	5,069,143	4,595.2
6	Oil palm fruit	856,422	15,534,984	18,139.4
7	Tropical fresh fruit	577,890	2,551,900	4,415.9
8	Mango, mangosteen, guava	207,758	1,576,419	7,587.8
9	Fresh bean	154,482	291,846	1,889.2
10	Coconut	121,248	858,235	7,078.3

Source: http://www.fao.org/faostat/en/#data.

Thailand is one of the world's major fish products suppliers and the third-largest marine fishery country in Asia after Japan and China. The gulf of Thailand and Andaman Sea has major marine fisheries areas with 342,800 square kilometers[1]. Thailand also has more than 300,000 hectares of lakes and nearly 1,100 square kilometers of freshwater aquaculture area. Bangkok, Songkhla and Phuket are important fishing centers and distribution centers for fishing products. At present, Thai fisheries have developed from small scale and coastal fishing to large-scale operation in the deep sea, and from pure fishing to commercial production that pays equal attention to fishing and breeding. Freshwater aquaculture

---

[1] Zhang Chenglin, Wang Jian, Liu Huang, et al, 2018. Development Status and Thinking of Fishery and Aquaculture Engineering in Thailand [J]. Science Fish Farming, 352 (12): 60-61.

is mainly for domestic consumption. The main species of freshwater aquaculture are: *Oreochromis niloticus*, hybrid catfish (*Clarias macrocephalus* X. C. *gariepinus*), silver *Barbodes gonionotus*, *Macrobrachium rosenbergii*, and *Trichogaster pectoralis*. Salt-water aquaculture usually produces high-quality products for export, the main types include *Peneaus monodon*, *Litopenaeus vanamei*, *Perna viridis*, *Anadara* spp., and oysters (*Crassostrea commercialis*). In 2018, according to the data sources of the Food and Agriculture Organization of the United Nations, the total aquaculture production in Thailand reached 891,900 tons, including 93,000 tons marine aquaculture production, 412,000 tons freshwater aquaculture production and 386,000 tons brackish aquaculture production.

The main livestock breeding in Thailand are chicken, duck, pig, cattle, sheep and horse, the country is divided into nine livestock area. Pigs, beef cattle and breeding cattle are mainly concentrated in the north, while layers, broilers, ducks, pigs and cows are mainly concentrated in the middle. Thai livestock husbandry has made great achievements in the past ten years. The production of major livestock varieties has increased significantly. Notably, the poultry industry has developed rapidly, making Thailand once the world's third largest exporter of processed poultry products, accounting for more than 80% of the total value of livestock and meat processing exports. In 2017, Thailand exported 2.65 billion USD of broilers, while exports of livestock and meat processing totaled 3.2 billion USD, an increase of 4.5% over the previous years[1]. The basic livestock production in Thailand in 2018 is shown in Table 13 – 2.

---

① Chen Ge, Wang Yuning, Wei Mi, et al, 2019. Analysis of Agricultural Development Status in Thailand and China-Thailand Agricultural Science and Technology Cooperation [J]. Journal of Guangxi University of Finance and Economics (3).

Table 13 - 2　Basic Situation of Thailand Animal Husbandry in 2018

Serial number	Name of the livestock and poultry	Breeding quantity（head）
1	Chicken	277,994,000
2	Duck	12,309,000
3	pig	7,847,507
4	Cow（including buffalo and cattle）	5,576,993
5	Sheep（including goats）	511,500
6	Horse	6,142

Sources：http://www. fao. org/faostat/en/♯data.

（2）**Current status of agricultural development.** Agriculture is a traditional industry in Thailand and one of Thai pillar industries. Over the past 20 years，Thai agriculture has maintained a long-term and stable growth rate，with an average annual growth rate of around 2%，and the proportion of agricultural value added in GDP has remained between 8% and 12%（Figure 13 - 1）. In 2018，Thai agricultural economy grew by 4. 6% year-on-year，crops grew by 5. 4%，poultry by 1. 9%，fisheries decreased by 1%，agricultural management increased by 4% and forestry increased by 2%[①].

The steady growth of Thai agriculture benefits from the effective policy support of the government. The Thai government has long been committed to taking advantage of its agricultural resources and developing diversified and export-oriented agriculture to support and promote the development of other industries. As early as the 1990s，the Thai government began to develop organic agriculture，and vigorously developed export trade with organic agricultural products as the leading

---

　①　Business Office of Consulate General in Songka，2018. Thai Agriculture Is Expected to Grow by 2. 5%- 3. 5% Next Year［EB/OL］. （12-27）［2020-12-22］. http://songkhla. mofcom. gov. cn/article/jmxw/201812/20181202820695. shtml.

324

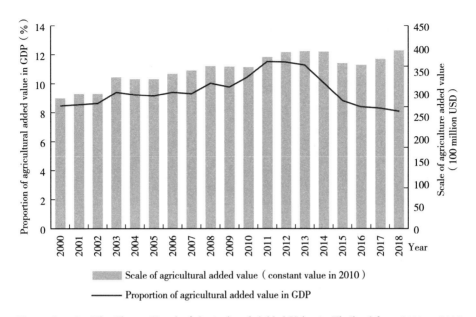

Figure 13 - 1 The Change Trend of Agricultural Added Value in Thailand from 2000 to 2018

Source: https://data. worldbank. org. cn.

role. At present, Thailand has established a relatively complete organic agricultural industrial chain, including organic agricultural technology research and development and application, organic agricultural production, organic food processing, marketing network and quality assurance system. In addition, among the Lancang-Mekong countries, Thailand has a good foundation, a high level and a strong research strength in agricultural science and technology. In terms of agricultural science and technology policy-making, scientific research fund management and scientific and technological management system construction, a complete operation system has been formed from the central government to the local government, involving diverse participants of government agencies, scientific research institutes, colleges and universities, farmers' cooperative organizations and enterprises, etc.

325

13. 1. 2 Import and Export Trade of Agricultural Products

Thailand is one of the world's five largest exporters of agricultural products, a major exporter of rice and natural rubber, the third largest marine fishery country in Asia and the world's largest producer of shrimp. Rice is the top priority in Thailand's agricultural exports, accounting for more than 25% of the global rice trade, and it has maintained the first position in the world market for a long time. Currently, the main rice export markets of Thailand include Asia, Africa, North America and the Middle East. Natural rubber is also one of the main export commodities of Thailand since the 1990s. More than 90% of the rubber produced in Thailand is used for export. The rubber products mainly include cigarette adhesive, No. 20 standard adhesive, No. 5 constant adhesive standard adhesive and concentrated latex. Thailand is also the world's second-largest exporter of cassava after Brazil, with about 80% of the crop processed and exported annually. Canned tuna, canned pineapple, frozen shrimp, chicken products, canned seafood and canned fruit are also the main products exported by Thailand.

According to the ASEAN database, the top 10 agricultural trade exporters of Thailand in 2018 are shown in Table 13 – 3. Thailand exported 17. 12 billion USD worth of agricultural products to these ten countries, accounting for 61. 33% of its total exports. In addition to the top 10 agricultural export trading countries, Thailand has established good agricultural products export trade partnerships with Laos, Cambodia, South Korea, the Netherlands, Canada, the republic of South Africa, Singapore, the Philippines and other countries, with agricultural products exported to these countries exceeding 400 million USD. In terms of the types of commodities exported, Thailand main agricultural products exported are meat and other products of aquatic invertebrates; grain; sugar and sugared food; fruit and nuts; vegetables, fruits and nuts; fish

326

and other aquatic animals.

Table 13 - 3　Top 10 Countries of Thailand Agricultural Products Exported in 2018

Serial number	Exported countries	Export value (USD)
1	China	3,819,540,639
2	Japan	3,811,995,524
3	United States	2,797,713,351
4	Indonesia	1,406,403,374
5	Vietnam	1,348,977,711
6	Malaysia	930,439,948
7	United Kingdom	856,822,195
8	Philippines	776,274,128
9	Myanmar	698,329,950
10	Australia	672,726,570

Note: Based on the 2 digits' code of HS, the data of goods trade (IMTS) was sorted out by selected data from HS (01 - 20).

Source: https://data.aseanstats.org.

Thailand's top 10 agricultural product import trading countries in 2018 were shown in Table 13 - 4. The total amount of agricultural products imported by Thailand from these ten major trading countries was 5.297 billion USD, accounting for 61.54% of its total imports. In addition to the top 10 agricultural import trading countries, Thailand also imports agricultural products from Myanmar, South Korea, Japan, Singapore and other countries. The value of agricultural products imported from these countries is more than 200 million USD. The main agricultural products imported by Thailand are fish and other aquatic animals; seeds, nuts and fruits containing oil, medicinal plants; fruit and nuts; edible vegetables, roots and stems; dairy products, eggs, natural honey, etc.

Table 13 - 4   Top 10 Countries of Thailand Agricultural Products Imported in 2018

Serial number	Imported countries	Import value（USD）
1	China	1,343,930,583
2	United States	1,026,727,429
3	Viet nam	458,582,395
4	Indonesia	426,497,695
5	India	410,430,888
6	Brazil	382,987,497
7	New Zealand	357,351,889
8	Australia	348,077,798
9	Malaysia	289,164,178
10	Japan	253,359,362

Note：Based on the 2 digits' code of HS，the data of goods trade（IMTS）was sorted out by selected data from HS（01 - 20）.

Source：https：//data. aseanstats. org.

13. 2   Agricultural Investment Policy

13. 2. 1   Macro Policies

Thailand is now a middle-income developing country with relatively liberal economic policies. As a traditional agricultural country in Southeast Asia，its agriculture has always been the key basic industry of the country，effectively supporting the overall economic development.

Thai agricultural development macro policy stated in the Twelfth National Development Plan（2017 - 2021）mentions in short term it will get rid of the traps of middle-income countries，maintain stable economic growth，reduce poverty and reduce social gap between rich and poor，meanwhile，continue to vigorously promote the foundation of national transportation and logistics system，as the present stage industrial development goals including agriculture. In the long term，its 20-year

Agricultural Development Plan (2017 – 2036) specifies its long-term development goals is farmer stability, agricultural surplus and sustainable development of agricultural resource. At the same time, the "Thailand 4.0 Strategy" focuses agricultural development on cultivating smart farmers, applying new inventions and modern technologies to agriculture, including information research, determining planting plans, and effective management of agricultural products throughout the supply chain. Therefore, the future development direction of agriculture in Thailand focuses on the upgrading of agricultural science and technology and the development of high value-added agricultural industries, making the farmers move towards the high-income group.

13. 2. 2 Legal System Related on Agriculture

Thailand has well-established agricultural laws, policies and regulations. Laws and regulations related to factors of production include: Land Law, Fishery Act, Thai Water Resources Act, Plant Variety Protection Act, Plant Quarantine Act, Animal Feed Quality Control Act, Fertilizer Act, Hazardous Substances Act, etc. Laws and regulations related to agricultural environmental protection include the Act on Improving and Preserving the Quality of the Natural Environment, the Regulations on National Environmental Promotion and Protection, etc. Laws and regulations related to the circulation and sale of agricultural products include Agricultural Product Specification Law, Agricultural Futures Trading Law, Export and Import Commodity Law, etc. Laws and regulations related to production and management include Food law, Feed Management Law, etc. Tax systems and policies related to agricultural investment include Tax Law, etc. Laws and regulations related to agriculture protect and finance support include Labor Protects Law, Labor Relations Law, Social Insurance Law, Cooperative Act, Agriculture and Agricultural Cooperative Bank Law, etc. Thailand regulates different elements of the whole agricultural cycle by various separate acts or regulations. At the same time, the supporting policies of relevant agricultural sectors should be extended to every specific agricultural producer through the agricultural cooperative system. In this way, the precise regulation of legislators on each subdivision of agriculture can be realized.

13. 2. 3　Market Access and Agricultural Products Trade Systems

(1) **Legal and policy system of foreign investment management in agriculture.** The regulatory approach of Thailand in the field of foreign agricultural investment includes two aspects restriction and promotion: on the one hand, it has set up a negative list for foreign investment in the Foreign Business Act B. E. 2542 (1999), which is a creed law governing Foreign investment. The list includes three categories of businesses in which foreign investment is prohibited or restricted. They are respectively "restricted investment business for special reasons"; "restricted investment business for adverse impact on natural resources and ecological environment"; and "restricted investment business because Thailand is not ready for equal competition" (in case of exemption, approval is required from the relevant department of the central government of Thailand). The agricultural sector on the negative list mainly covers most upstream industries in agricultural production, including planting and fishing. On the other hand, the Thai government through the Board of Investment (BOI) and other foreign investment management and promotion departments carry out its consistent preferential policies in the field of foreign investment in agriculture, in order to match Thailand's short-, and medium-and long-term agricultural development plans. This type of regulation means that the Thai government hopes to use foreign capital to invest in the downstream industry of agriculture on the base of protecting the interests of domestic farmers, establishing a high value-added industrial chain, thereby stimulating the growth of domestic agricultural economy, improving the degree of agricultural development, increasing farmers'

income, and alleviating the social contradictions caused by uneven social development and large gap between rich and poor in Thailand.

- Access system for foreign investors   A company established in Thailand above 50% of its shares held by foreigners or foreign companies will be regarded as foreign company under the Foreign Business Act and subjected to restrictions on industry access. In Thailand, it is strictly forbidden for foreign capital to enter the agricultural investment field and the forestry investment field, and foreign capital is not allowed to acquire ownership and contractual management rights of agricultural arable land and forestry farmland.

  The minimum investment for foreigners to start commercial operation in Thailand shall not be less than 2 million THB (approximately 380,000 CNY), and the minimum investment shall not be less than 3 million THB (about 580,000 CNY) when it comes to the approved industries. Thailand does not have legal regulations specifically for security review of foreign capital mergers and acquisitions and foreign state-owned enterprises mergers and acquisitions.

- Tariff restrictions on agricultural products   In terms of import and export management, Thailand has a free import policy for most commodities, and any importer issuing letters of credit may engage in import business. Thailand only implements management measures such as import bans, tariff quotas and import licenses on some products. Tariff-quota products include 24 kinds of agricultural products such as longan, rice, sugar, coconut meat, garlic, corn for feed, palm oil, coconut oil, tea, soybeans and soya cakes. These products are subject to low tariffs within the quota and high tariffs outside the quota. But the tariff quota measure does not apply to imports from ASEAN members countries. In terms of export management, most of the product can be exported freely in Thailand, except through export registration, licenses, quotas, export tax, export bans or other restrictions control products, there are 45 kinds of products subject to export controls, including export tariffs have rice, fur, leather, teak and other wood, rubber, steel slag and iron slag, animal leather, etc.

- Foreign exchange control system and policy The Ministry of Finance of Thailand has authorized the Central Bank of Thailand to take charge of Thailand's foreign exchange control. The Foreign Exchange Management Law puts forward relevant guiding principles for foreign exchange control.

Thai and multinational corporations can set up capital centers in Thailand to manage foreign currency for their group companies. Thailand levies a 15% withholding tax on interest income earned by non-residents in Thailand. Commercial Banks can handle the repayment of foreign exchange loans without any restrictions. However, if the amount of loans remitted exceeds 50,000 USD or equivalent, they should provide the certificate of remittance. Foreign currencies can be freely remitted into Thailand, but they must be sold or deposited into foreign currency accounts within 360 days from the date of receipt of foreign currency.

- Legal system and policy of agriculture related labor Alien Employment Act is the basic law governing the work of foreigners in Thailand. It was enacted in 1978 and revised in 2008. The Employment Department of the Ministry of Labor of Thailand is the central management authority for work permits for foreigners in Thailand. In January 2017, Thai Prime Minister Prayuth Chanocha signed a prime minister's amnesty during his inspection of the Ministry of Labor, which will comprehensively lift restrictions on the types of work for foreign workers in Thailand. Foreign workers in Thailand will enjoy the same employment opportunities as Thais in the future, but the mobility of foreign workers has not been fully liberalized, and they must choose employment nearby.

(2) **Trade System of Agricultural Materials and Products.** The government department in charge of trade in Thailand is the Ministry of Commerce. Its main responsibilities are divided into two parts: internally, it is responsible for promoting the development of enterprises, domestic commodity trade and service trade, supervising commodity prices, safeguarding consumers' rights and interests, and protecting intellectual property rights; externally, it is responsible for participating in WTO and various multilateral and bilateral trade negotiations, and promoting the sound development of international trade.

The market system of agricultural products and food is divided into several levels: farmers' market, wholesale market, retail market, terminal market and futures market. The main trade-related laws and regulations of Thailand include the Export Commodity Promotion Act (1960), the Export and Import Commodities Act (1979), the Export Management Regulations of Certain Commodities (1973), the Export Commodity Standards Act (1979), and the Anti-dumping and the Anti-Subsidy Act (1999), the Customs Law (2000), and the Import Surge Safeguard Measures Law (2007), etc.

13. 3　Progress and Results of Lancang-Mekong Agricultural Cooperation

13. 3. 1　Main Progress

Under the Lancang-Mekong Cooperation, Thailand has taken an active part in LMC agricultural cooperation, vigorously promoted export-oriented agricultural development, expanded cooperation areas and achieved remarkable results in many areas.

(1) **Participating in exchange activities of the Lancang-Mekong mechanism.** Under the mechanism of Lancang-Mekong Cooperation, China, Laos, Thailand and other countries are more active in water trade through the

Lancang-Mekong River. Fresh fruits from China come down the river by means of a transport ship and disembark at Chiang Saen Port of in Thailand. Thailand took this opportunity to establish Chiang Saen Port as an interconnected international port and logistics center, and set up a large number of warehouses to undertake the goods transported by various countries, and promote the commodity trade between countries in the Lancang Mekong basin. In April 2018, China and Thailand jointly signed the agreement for the first batch of Thailand's cooperation project supported by Lancang-Mekong Cooperation Special Fund. According to the agreement signed between the two sides, China will finance four projects including joint development of cross-border special economic zones, upgrading of trade and logistics border facilities, the Lancang-Mekong business forum and rural e-commerce development in the subregion. In March 2019, the signing ceremony of the memorandum of understanding for the cooperation project of "Capacity Building of LMC National Coordinators" supported by Lancang-Mekong Cooperation Special Fund held in Bangkok. This project will effectively improve the ability of officials of LMC six countries to participate in LMC in various fields, so as to provide human resources guarantee for promoting LMC growth, upgrading quality[①]. In July 2019, the Mekong Institute of Thailand and the Chinese Academy of Tropical Agricultural Sciences signed a memorandum of understanding on cooperation. The two sides will carry out cooperative researches on big data in the agricultural science and technology policy and agricultural policy of the Lancang Mekong countries, jointly apply for international agricultural cooperation projects, share regional agricultural data and information resources, and jointly build the agricultural development research base of the Lancang Mekong countries.

---

① Yang Zhou, 2019. China and Thailand Sign the Cooperation Agreement on the Special Fund Project of Lancang Mekong Cooperation [EB/OL]. (03-20) [2020-12-22]. https://www.xinhuanet.com/2019-03/19/c_1124255694.htm.

In October 2019, Thai Deputy Prime Minister and Minister of Commerce Jurin Laksanawisit met with Han Changfu, Minister of Agriculture and Rural Affairs of China, and his delegation in Bangkok. The two sides exchanged views on China-Thailand relations, bilateral and multilateral agricultural cooperation, mutual visits of agricultural experts, personnel exchanges and training, etc①. The meeting will further promote practical cooperation in agriculture between China and Thailand.

（2） **Implementation status of agricultural projects supported by Lancang-Mekong Cooperation Special Fund （LMCSF）②.** In 2018, Thailand began to plan to implement five LMC SF projects as below.

- Development of Rice Pest and Natural Disasters Monitoring, Forecasting and Warning Center for Sustainable Rice Production under Climate Change in Lancang-Mekong Subregion. Implemented from 2019 to 2021, the project will target rice farmers, rice-related managers and departments in LMC countries as beneficiaries, and carry out personnel training, meetings and seminars, joint research and other activities.

- Development and Implementation of Common Rice Products Standard in LMC countries. Implemented during 2019 – 2021, the project will target rice farmers, rice managers and traders in the rice industry in LMC countries as beneficiaries, carrying out personnel training, meetings and seminars.

- Promoting Integrated and Sustainable Agricultural System in LMC countries. Implemented from 2018 to 2021, the project will target the agricultural sectors of LMC countries as beneficiaries, carrying

---

① Li Min, 2019. Jurin, Deputy Prime Minister of Thailand, Meets with Changfu Han, Minister of Agriculture and Rural Affairs of China to Deepen Agricultural Cooperation [EB/OL]. （10-20） [2020-12-22]. http://news.cri.cn/uc-eco/20191020/3f0cce69-b4d9-837b-62a3-317b25797236.html.

② According to the reports of participants from Thailand on the Second Meeting of the Lancang-Mekong Cooperation (LMC) Joint Working Group on Agriculture in 2019.

out activities such as technical exchanges, personnel training and platform construction.

- Expansion and Development of Forage Seed Trade Cooperation. Implemented from 2018 to 2021, the project will target the agricultural production sectors in Thailand, Myanmar and Cambodia, and the consumer sectors in China, Myanmar and Vietnam as the beneficiaries, with personnel training, field trips and trade matching activities.

- Climate Change Adaptation and Food Security for Small Farmers. The project will be implemented from 2019 to 2021, and the LMC countries will be the target beneficiaries of the project, carrying out personnel training, meetings and seminars, platform construction and other activities.

(3) Agricultural cooperation with other LMC countries

① Agricultural cooperation with China

China and Thailand are both big agricultural countries with a long history of cooperation. In August 2009, China and Thailand signed a free trade agreement to promote bilateral investment and trade cooperation. Since China-ASEAN Free Trade Area (CAFTA) was officially launched in 2010, China-Thailand agricultural cooperation has accelerated, deepened and expanded. Since 2013, China has become Thailand's largest trading partner, with types of agricultural products imported and exported between the two countries' increasingly rich resources. Thai products such as rice, rubber and tropical fruits are popular with Chinese consumers. Relevant data show that agricultural trade has always been at the top of bilateral trade between the two countries, and the close cooperation between China and Thailand in the field of agriculture has reached a new height[①]. Currently, China-Thailand agricultural cooperation mainly involves five areas: food,

---

① Wu Yong, 2006. China-Thai Agricultural Cooperation Research [D]. Wuhan: Huazhong Agricultural University.

fishery and aquaculture, animal disease prevention and control, cash crops and rural energy. In November 2019, Chinese Premier Li Keqiang of the State Council of China went to Thailand to attend a series of leaders' meetings of East Asia Cooperation and pay an official visit to Thailand. The two sides reached broad consensus on synergizing their development strategies and expanding cooperation in trade, investment, production capacity and other areas, which will promote innovation cooperation between enterprises of the two countries in agriculture, science and technology and other fields.

② Agricultural cooperation with Vietnam

Thailand and Vietnam have long-term exchanges and cooperation in agricultural production. In April 2003, Thailand proposed the "Irrawaddy River-Chao Phraya River-Mekong River (three river basins) Economic Cooperation Strategy" (ACMECS) involving Cambodia, Laos, Myanmar and Thailand at the ASEAN special leaders' meeting. In February 2004, the governments of Vietnam and Thailand held a meeting in Da Nang, where they exchanged extensive views on expanding bilateral cooperation in various fields such as agriculture, economy, education and society, and reached an agreement on Vietnam's accession to ACMECS. In addition to inter-governmental agricultural cooperation, Thailand and Vietnam also frequently carry out mutual investment among agricultural enterprises.

③ Agricultural cooperation with Cambodia, Laos and Myanmar

Agricultural cooperation with Cambodia, Laos and Myanmar are detailed in the corresponding chapters of each country (Cambodia 10.3.1, Laos 11.3.1, Myanmar 12.3.1).

13.3.2 Results and Experience

(1) **Promoting agricultural development through science and technology and strengthening cooperation with other LMC countries.** Thailand has made some achievements in promoting agricultural science and technology innovation, strengthening personnel exchanges, and promoting sustainable

agricultural development among LMC countries. There are similar agricultural development situation in Lancang Mekong basin. Cooperation in agricultural science and technology between Thailand and LMC countries should be strengthened and common agricultural development in the Lancang-Mekong subregion should be promoted. At present, the Thai government and the Ministry of Science and Technology of China have made remarkable achievements in the research on the prevention and control of rice planthopper in the subregion.

（2）**Expanding cooperation fields and deepening Lancang-Mekong cooperation.** With the continuous development and enrichment of the LMC, innovative fields of agricultural cooperation should be explored. Thailand has always been a major rice exporter in the world. In recent years, with the increase of the world population and the development of social economy, the demand for rice yield and quality has become higher and higher. Thailand has helped reduce rice diseases and insect pests and improve rice quality through the application of the Lancang Mekong Cooperation Special Fund (LMCSF). In the future, Thailand will join hands with other LMC countries who have the same needs or complementary advantages to carry out multilateral cooperation, continuously deepen the level of agricultural science and technology cooperation, and enhance the development and application of organic agriculture, ecological agriculture, agricultural biotechnology, and agricultural new energy, deepen exchanges and cooperation in frontier scientific research, such as agricultural biodiversity and agro-ecosystem protection.

（3）**Taking win-win cooperation as the goal and integrating multiple strategies for development.** At present, Thailand is committed to building the "Eastern Economic Corridor", which is open to the outside world and the "Thailand 4.0 Strategy" oriented by digital smart agriculture. These development policies are highly compatible with the Belt and Road Initiative and fully comply with the priority development direction of LMC in

agriculture and other fields. Thailand has promoted the cooperation and coordinated development between Thailand and LMC countries by integrating domestic and foreign strategies to form synergy in policies.

(Written by Li Xinwei, Xu Lu and Li Lu,

Translated by Li Xinwei,

International Agriculture Research Institute,

Yunnan Academy of Agricultural Sciences, China)

14 | Agricultural Development and the Progress of Lancang-Mekong Agricultural Cooperation in Vietnam

14.1 Overview of Agricultural Development

14.1.1 Resources and Development

(1) **Resources and main agricultural products.** Vietnam is located in the east of Indochina Peninsula, with a total land area of 331,230 square kilometers. It borders Guangxi and Yunnan in the north and Laos and Cambodia in the west, and is administratively divided into 64 provinces. More than three-quarters of Vietnam is mountainous and hilly, with a hot, humid and rainy climate. The north has four distinct seasons, while the south is divided into rainy and dry seasons. It is rich in water resources and has a dense water network of 2,360 rivers, the average annual rainfall is about 1,820 mm, and the rainy season lasts from April or May to October or November. Vietnam has an agricultural area of 121,780 square kilometers, including 115,360 square kilometers of arable land. In 2018, the total population was 95.540,4 million, of which the rural population was 61.233,2 million, accounting for about 64% of the total population[1].

According to the statistics from the World Food and Agriculture Organization in 2018, the main crops planted in Vietnam are shown in

---

[1] Data source: http://www.fao.org/faostat/en/#data.

Table 14 - 1.

Table 14 - 1   The Yield and Planting Area of Major Crops in Vietnam in 2018

Serial number	Variety of crops	Area harvested (hectare)	Yield (ton)	Yield per unit area (kg/hectare)
1	Rice, paddy	7,570,741	44,046,250	5,818.0
2	Maize	1,032,598	4,874,054	4,720.2
3	Vegetables	865,681	14,879,631	17,188.4
4	Rubber, natural	689,486	1,137,725	1,650.1
5	Coffee, green	618,879	1,616,307	2,611.7
6	Cassava	513,021	9,847,074	19,194.3
7	Cashew nuts, with shell	283,986	266,388	938.0
8	Sugarcane	269,434	1,7945,204	66,603.3
9	Fruit, fresh	245,374	2,801,751	11,418.3
10	Groundnuts, with shell	185,899	456,762	2,457.0

Source: http://www.fao.org/faostat/en/#data.

In recent years, with the rapid development of Vietnam's economy, animal husbandry and fishery have also been valued and developed rapidly. Aquaculture and intensive pork breeding have taken shape[①]. Aquaculture is dominated by shrimp, and the breeding area is mainly concentrated in the southern Mekong River basin, mostly extensive measures. In 2014, the government of Vietnam put forward the plan of animal husbandry reorganization, and adopted measures to centrally develop the husbandry in Mekong Delta Plain, providing financial support for farmers, and improving the technological level of animal husbandry. The main husbandry situation in Vietnam in 2018 is shown in Table 14 - 2.

---

① Wei Jinyi, Lai Zhiqiang, Pan Zhongtuan, 2010. Investigation Report on Animal Husbandry in Vietnam [J]. Guangxi Animal Husbandry and Veterinary, 26 (3): 140-142.

Table 14 - 2　Basic Situation of Vietnam Animal Husbandry in 2018

Serial number	Name of the livestock and poultry	Breeding quantity (head)
1	Pig	28,151,948
2	Cow (including buffalo and cattle)	8,228,012
3	Goat	2,683,942
4	Horse	53,473
5	Chicken	316,916,000
6	Duck	76,911,000

Source: http://www. fao. org/faostat/en/♯data.

(2) Current situation of agricultural development. In 2018, the added value of agriculture in Vietnam was 35. 697 billion USD (current price), accounting for 14. 6% of GDP. The change of agricultural added value in Vietnam from 2000 to 2018 (according to the statistics of constant price in 2010) are shown in Figure 14 - 1. In general, the added value of agriculture in Vietnam has been rising gradually from 2000 to 2018, with an average annual growth rate of 3. 22%. However, the proportion of agricultural added value in GDP showed a trend of fluctuation and decline, with an average annual decline rate of 2. 85%.

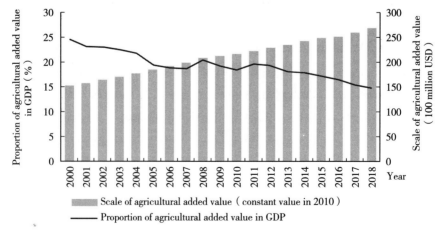

Figure 14 - 1　The Change Trend of Agricultural Added Value in Vietnam from 2000 to 2018
Source: https://data. worldbank. org. cn.

14. 1. 2　Import and Export Trade of Agricultural Products

Vietnam is the fastest developing country among the 10 ASEAN countries, and its agricultural trade has continued to increase after joining the WTO[1]. Agriculture has become one of Vietnam's largest export sectors, a third of its rice, 90% of its natural rubber, 90% of its coffee and more than 50% of its aquatic products produced in Vietnam are used for export every year[2]. Vietnam is one of the 15 major export countries of agricultural products in the world. According to FAO statistics, the total export of cashew nuts and black pepper in Vietnam ranked the first globally, coffee and cassava ranked the second, rice ranked the third, rubber ranked the Fourth, and tea ranks the fifth in 2017.

In 2017, agriculture accounted for 8.0% of Vietnam's import share, up 0.7 percentage points compared with 2016, and 12.1% of its export share, up 0.9 percentage points compared with 2016[3]. According to the statistical analysis of data from the ASEAN database, Vietnam's total imports of agricultural products were about 14.238 billion USD in 2018, and its exports were about 24.967 billion USD, with a trade surplus of 10.729 billion USD.

The top 10 exporters of Vietnam's agricultural products in 2018 and the export value (ranked by export trade value) are shown in Table 14 - 3. The major agricultural exporters of Vietnam are China, the United States, Japan, South Korea, Netherlands, Germany, Philippines,

---

① Huy N T, Xia Yun, Tan Yanwen, et al, 2015. Use Foreign Direct Investment in Agriculture in Vietnam and Its Implications for China [J]. The World's Agriculture, 440 (12): 177-180.

② Feng Huaiyu, 2015. To Explore the Application of Agricultural Standardization Model in Vietnam [R]. Chengdu: Market Practice Standardization: The 11th China Standardization Forum: 758-762.

③ The ASEAN Secretariat, 2018. ASEAN Statistical Year Book [M]. The ASEAN Secretariat [2020-12-22]. www. asean. org.

United Kingdom Thailand and Indonesia. Vietnam exports 68.9% of its total agricultural export products to the ten countries. Among them, nearly 40% of export agricultural products go to China and the United States. China is the largest exporter of agricultural products in Vietnam, accounting for 24.9% of Vietnam's total export of agricultural products. The largest agricultural exports by category were "fish and crustaceans, other aquatic invertebrates", worth 6.41 billion USD, followed by "fruit and nuts, edible; peel of citrus fruit or melons" at 5.99 billion. The third was "coffee, tea and spices", worth 4.07 billion USD. In addition, the export value of "cereals" and "meat" were also large.

Table 14 - 3   Top 10 Countries of Vietnam Agricultural Products Exported in 2018

Serial number	Exported countries	Export value (USD)
1	China	6,210,352,288
2	United States	3,663,892,842
3	Japan	1,818,305,598
4	South Korea	1,310,815,387
5	Netherlands	871,315,302
6	Germany	828,098,034
7	Philippines	791,333,244
8	United Kingdom	600,071,109
9	Thailand	587,245,666
10	Indonesia	527,607,820

Note: Based on the 2 digits' code of HS, the data of goods trade (IMTS) was sorted out by selected data from HS (01-20).

Source: https://data.aseanstats.org.

The top 10 importers of Vietnam's agricultural products in 2018 and the import value (ranked by import trade value) are shown in Table 14 - 4. The major import countries are United States, China, Argentina, Thailand, Australia, Russian Federation, Brazil, Côte d'Ivoire, Indonesia and Cambodia. Vietnam imported 66.2% of its total import agricultural products from the ten countries. The largest importer is United States, which accounts for about 11. 9% of Vietnam's total agricultural imports. In terms of the types of imports, the largest agricultural products were "cereals", with an import value of 3. 38 billion USD, followed by "fruit and nuts, edible; peel of citrus fruit or melons", with an import value of 3. 15 billion USD, and the third were "fish and crustaceans, mollusk and other aquatic invertebrates", with an import value of 1. 52 billion USD. The import value of "animal or vegetable fats and oils and their cleavage products" "oil seeds and oleaginous fruits; miscellaneous grains, seeds and fruit, industrial or medicinal plants; straw and fodder", "vegetables and certain roots and tubers; edible", "preparations of cereals, flour, starch or milk; pastrycooks' products" and "dairy produce; birds' eggs; natural honey; edible products of animal origin" were also high.

Table 14 - 4　Top 10 Countries of Vietnam Agricultural Products Imported in 2018

Serial number	Imported countries	Import value (USD)
1	United States	1,687,732,273
2	China	1,113,096,037
3	Argentina	1,094,528,280
4	Thailand	1,050,671,063
5	Australia	934,020,787
6	Russia	789,400,473
7	Brazil	731,555,581
8	Côte d'Ivoire	726,949,157
9	Indonesia	687,822,473
10	Cambodia	607,052,432

Note: Based on the 2 digits' code of HS, the data of goods trade (IMTS) was sorted out by selected data from HS (01-20).

Source: https://data. aseanstats. org.

14. 2   Agricultural Investment Policy

14. 2. 1   Macro Policy

Vietnam began to reform and open in 1986. The Ninth National Congress of the Communist Party of Vietnam decided to establish a socialist market economic system in 2001. The 12th Ninth National Congress of the Communist Party of Vietnam made it clear in January 2016 that the overall goal of Vietnam's economic and social development from 2016 to 2020 is to continue to consolidate the foundation and turn Vietnam into a modern industrial country at an early date.

Agriculture is the pillar industry of Vietnam's national economy, and its output value accounts for about 30% of GDP. On July 17, 2019, Vietnamese government issued the resolution of 53 "Encouraging and Promoting Effective, Safe and Sustainable Investment in Agriculture by Enterprises", which put forward a vision that by 2030, agriculture will develop in the direction of modernization, sustainability, large-scale production, application of science and technology, and innovation, and strive to improve agricultural productivity, quality, efficiency and competitiveness, improve people's lives and build a modern and civilized countryside. By 2030, Vietnam's agriculture will rank among 15 most developed countries in the world, and its agricultural processing industry will rank among the top 10 countries in the world.

14. 2. 2   Legal System Related on Agriculture

Agriculture is an industry area where investment preferences can be obtained in Vietnam. In 2018, the government promulgated the "Mechanisms and Policies on Promoting Enterprises to Invest in Agriculture and Rural Areas", through exempting and reducing land use fees, waiving and reducing government land leases and water surface rents, investing in agriculture and rural infrastructure, supporting land concentration, human resources training and market development, public services, etc.; by giving priority directly to support enterprises to carry out agricultural scientific research, purchase and transfer advanced technologies for directly into production, develop high-tech agricultural parks, and participate in the construction of production-processing-product-sale-supply chain, the investment procedures are regulated in the directive.

Investment in agriculture involves many basic laws and regulations, such as Investment Law, Land law, Commercial Law, Forestry Protection and Exploitation Law, Irrigation Law, Small and Medium-sized Enterprises Support Law, Science and Technology Law, Trade Law, Customs Law, Import and Export Tax Law, Intellectual Property Law, Enterprise Law, Foreign Trade Administration Law, Environmental Protection Law, Labor Law, Social Insurance Law of Vietnam.

14.2.3 Market Access and Agricultural Products Trad System

(1) **Legal and policy system of foreign investment management in agriculture**

- Foreign investors access system   The government has devolved approval authority for almost all foreign projects to provincial authorities, maintaining approvals for only a few industry sectors. For national monumental projects, the Congress shall decide on the investment approval and project standards, and the government shall be responsible for formulating project approval procedures and issuing investment licenses. There are 35 items of the amendments to Article 6 and Annex 4 of the Investment Law that restrict investment, including the export of rice. Incentives for investment include industry and region. The agricultural industry mainly focuses on planting, raising, and processing agriculture, forestry, and aquatic products; salt production; and cultivation of new plants and livestock and seeds. According to the administrative divisions, regional encouragement can be divided into two types: the areas with particularly difficult social and economic conditions and the areas with difficult conditions.

- Agricultural land, housing sales, leasing policies   Vietnam promulgated the fourth Land Law on November 29, 2013. According to the current land law, land ownership belongs to the state and does not recognize private ownership. Collectives and individuals can enjoy the right to use state-owned land. The term of land use can be divided into two cases: long-term stable use and time-limited use. The transfer of land use rights must go through relevant formalities with the competent national authority. Foreign investors cannot purchase land, but can lease land and obtain the right to use. The term of use is usually 50 years. In special circumstances, an extension can be applied for, but the maximum is not more than 70 years.

- Agricultural investment system and policy   According to the Investment Law of Vietnam, both foreign-invested enterprises and domestic enterprises adopt uniform tax standards, and implement different tax rates and tax reduction and exemption periods for projects in different fields. Starting from January 1, 2016, the basic corporate income tax rate in Vietnam is 20%. To encourage foreign-funded enterprises, the government has issued relevant preferential policies, and granted preferential tax and other preferential policies to projects in some special regions and of special industries, such as in particularly poor areas, high-tech agricultural areas, "large farmland", concentrated raw material producing areas and industries of agricultural machinery, salt, water irrigation, animal husbandry and food processing. In addition, personal income tax, value-added tax, non-agricultural land use tax, agricultural land use tax, etc., have been reduced or exempted in agricultural production.

- Foreign exchange control system and policy   The Vietnamese currency is the Vietnamese Dong and is not freely convertible. In early 2016, Vietnam introduced a new exchange rate management mechanism to replace the long-term fixed exchange rate mechanism with the daily announcement of the central reference exchange rate price. Commercial banks floated up and down the central reference exchange rate benchmark by 3% to set their own exchange rate prices. Foreign investors can open Vietnamese Dong or foreign exchange accounts in Vietnamese financial institutions. If it is necessary to open an account in a foreign bank, it shall be approved by the National Bank of Vietnam. Foreign investors may purchase of foreign exchange from financial institutions engaged in foreign exchange operations to meet the needs of project transactions, capital transactions and other transactions. If the foreign exchange financial institutions cannot meet the needs of investors, the government will solve the problem of foreign exchange balance according to the project situation. In terms of capital and profit repatriation, after the completion of the investment project, the foreign investor can remit out of Vietnam the shares enjoyed in the foreign investment institution or the capital shares in the business cooperation contract.

- Legal system and policy of agriculture related labor   Foreigners are not allowed to work in Vietnam with tourist visas. Foreign laborers who have worked in Vietnam for more than 3 months must apply for a labor license.

From January 1, 2018, foreign workers who have worked in Vietnam for more than one month will be required to participate in compulsory social insurance. Foreign workers shall pay 8% of their retirement and death benefits at monthly wages. Employers pay a maximum of 18% of compulsory social insurance at monthly wages, including 3% of illness and maternity insurance, 1% of work injury insurance and occupational disease insurance, 14% of retirement and death benefits. Workers in countries that have reached an intergovernmental agreement with the Vietnamese government are excluded to avoid double collection of social insurance.

(2) **Trade system of agricultural materials and product.** The major trade laws and regulations in Vietnam include: Trade Law, Foreign Trade Law, Civil Law, Investment Law, Electronic Transaction Law, Customs Law, Import and Export Tax Law, Intellectual Property Law, Information Technology Law, Anti-dumping Law, Anti-Subsidy Law, Enterprise Law, Accounting Law, Statistics Law, etc. In accordance with its WTO accession commitments, Vietnam has gradually lifted import quota restrictions and basically managed by market principles. Regarding exports, Vietnam mainly adopts export bans, export tariffs, quantity restrictions and other measures for management. The inspection and quarantine of import and export commodities in Vietnam shall be carried out by different departments, the inspection of food and drugs shall be carried out by the Ministry of Health, and the inspection of animals, plants and other agricultural products shall be carried out by the Ministry of Agriculture and Rural Development.

14.3 Progress and Results of Lancang-Mekong Agricultural Cooperation

14.3.1 Main Progress

(1) **Participating in exchange activities of the Lancang-Mekong cooperation mechanism.** On March 18, 2019, a seminar on LMC and regional cooperation opportunities was held in Hanoi. Vietnam attaches great importance to

LMC, and various departments have actively participated in relevant cooperation under this framework. At present, Vietnam is studying some new concepts proposed by the LMC to identify specific cooperation projects supported by the LMC special fund.

（2）**Implementation status of agricultural projects supported by Lancang-Mekong Cooperation Special Fund （LMCSF）**[①]. Vietnam has not yet implemented the agricultural projects supported by LMCSF. In terms of fund application, Vietnam has submitted some proposals to the LMCSF such agricultural projects as "Challenges and opportunities of agriculture sector in Vietnam, China, Laos, Cambodia, and Myanmar in the context of next industrial revolution" "Improving the effectiveness of border agricultural trade among Vietnam, China, Laos, Cambodia, and Myanmar" "Strengthening and promoting management capacity of water resources and drought risk in the Sesan-Srepok-Sekong river basin" "Community based tourism for poverty reduction in Sop Cop District, Son La Province, Vietnam" "Gender Responsive Equitable Agriculture and Tourism for Poverty Reduction in Hai ha District, Quangninh Province, Vietnam".

（3）**Agricultural cooperation with other LMC countries**

① Agricultural cooperation with China

At present, Vietnam and China have reached consensus on strategic synergy and cooperation between the Two Corridors and One Circle Concept and the Belt and Road Initiative. Differences in natural conditions and development levels have resulted in complementarity in agricultural products, agricultural science and technology and agricultural production factors. In recent years, the central and local governments, agricultural institutions of the two countries have continuously strengthened cooperation in crop production and variety extension, agricultural machinery production,

---

① According to the reports of participants from Vietnam on the Second Meeting of the Lancang-Mekong Cooperation (LMC) Joint Working Group on Agriculture in 2019.

agricultural product processing, human resources development, animal and plant disease prevention and control, fishery and other fields. Signing *Memorandum of Understanding on Agricultural Cooperation between China and Vietnam*, *Cooperation Agreement on Animal and Plant Inspection and Quarantine* and *Memorandum of Understanding on the Cooperation on the Proliferation, Release and Conservation of Fishery Resources in the Beibu Gulf*, the two countries built a good foundation for cooperation. In January 2018, Vice Minister of Agriculture of the two countries co-chaired the first meeting of the China-Vietnam Agricultural Cooperation Joint Committee, which determined the cooperation in such fields and projects as fishery proliferation, release and conservation, the China-Vietnam rice hybrid research and development center, livestock and poultry waste treatment and biogas, plant protection and pesticide and cross-border animal epidemics prevention control, and discussed and approved the organization structure of the joint committee, which means that the formation of a new agricultural cooperation mechanism between China and Vietnam.

In terms of agricultural trade, China and Vietnam have signed several bilateral economic and trade agreements since the 1990s. In 2000, the two countries signed *Joint Statement on Comprehensive Cooperation in the New Century*, which made it clear that the two countries should actively promote mutually beneficial cooperation in agriculture, forestry and fishery, and encourage and support relevant enterprises and departments of the two countries to strengthen exchanges and cooperation in crop, livestock and poultry breeding, agricultural and forestry products processing, agricultural machinery manufacturing, marine fishing and aquaculture, etc. In 2015, the two countries signed *Memorandum of Agricultural Cooperation*, expanded the cooperation to include agricultural research, technology, trade, breeding of animal and plant varieties, tracking and disease prevention and control, production of agricultural machinery and equipment, processing of agricultural products, experts and information exchange. In June 2019, Vietnam's Ministry of Agriculture and Rural Development held a joint meeting with China's General Administration of Customs to seek measures to promote better and faster development of agricultural trade between the two countries.

② Agricultural cooperation with other LMC countries

Vietnam's agricultural cooperation with Cambodia, Laos, Myanmar and Thailand is detailed in the corresponding chapters of each country (Cambodia 10. 3. 1, Laos 11. 3. 1, Myanmar 12. 3. 1, Thailand 13. 3. 1).

14.3.2　Results and Experience

(1) **Expanding foreign trade of agricultural products and promoting common growth of agricultural economy.** Vietnam plays an important role in the agricultural foreign trade of other LMC countries. For example, Vietnam is one of the major agricultural trade countries of Cambodia, ranking the top among the top ten importers and exporters of Cambodia agricultural products and the largest agricultural exporter of Laos. In recent years, through the signing of agricultural trade-related cooperation agreements with China, Cambodia, etc. , Vietnam's agricultural trade cooperation with other Lancang Mekong countries has been strengthened, and its cooperation in the field of agriculture has been further strengthened.

(2) **Extensiving international agricultural investment cooperation to promote agricultural and rural development.** Vietnam has extensively carried out agricultural investment activities with other LMC countries. For example, through signing a number of memorandums of agricultural cooperation with China, Chinese funds have been invested in Vietnam's agricultural and rural development[①]. More than 400 Vietnamese

---

① VAN, 2019. Vietnam and China Promote Trade in Agricultural Products [EB/OL]. (06-19) [2020-12-22]. https://zh. vietnamplus. vn/%E8%B6%8A%E4%B8%AD%E4%BF%83%E8%BF% 9B%E5%86%9C%E4%BA%A7%E5%93%81%E8%B4%B8%E6%98%93/98386. vnp.

investment projects in Laos are in agriculture[①]. Vietnam jointly held trade and investment promotion forum With Cambodia to exchange investment preferences of enterprises[②], increased agricultural investment in Myanmar compared with the previous years, and frequently carried out mutual investment among agricultural enterprises with Thailand. In recent years, Vietnam has stepped up foreign capital introduction in the agricultural sector. In order to encourage more international agricultural investment, Vietnam has formulated a series of preferential policies to provide preferential tax support for foreign-funded enterprises directly investing in agricultural product processing, forestry cultivation, animal husbandry, aquaculture and processing. In addition, relevant laws and regulations have been revised to reduce the land rent for foreign investment by up to 50% for agricultural and rural investment, facilitating agricultural investment in Vietnam for enterprises from other LMC countries[③].

(Written by Rui Yanlan and Guo Wen,

Translated by Rui Yanlan,

International Agriculture Research Institute,

Yunnan Academy of Agricultural Sciences, China)

---

① Anonymity, 2019. Vietnam and Laos have Upgraded Their Investment and Trade Substance of the Partnership [EB/OL]. (09-11) [2020-12-22]. https://yuenan.zhaoshang.net/2019-09-11/724741.html.

② VAN, 2019. The Vietnam-Cambodia Trade and Investment Promotion Forum Was Held in Phnom Penh, the Cambodian Capital in 2019 [EB/OL]. (07-10) [2020-12-22]. https://zh.vietnamplus.vn.

③ Gong Yutao, 2014. The New Measures of Agricultural Reform in Vietnam in Recent Years [J]. Agricultural Economy (5): 14-16.